From the Land of Enchantment

Gifted Treasury Series

Jerry D. Flack, Series Editor

Creative Thinking and Problem Solving for Young Learners. By Karen S. Meador.

From the Land of Enchantment: Creative Teaching with Fairy Tales. By Jerry D. Flack.

Integrating Aerospace Science into the Curriculum: K-12. By Robert D. Ray and Joan Klingel Ray.

Inventing, Inventions, and Inventors: A Teaching Resource Book. By Jerry D. Flack.

Lives of Promise: Studies in Biography and Family History. By Jerry D. Flack.

Mystery and Detection: Thinking and Problem Solving with the Sleuths. By Jerry D. Flack.

TalentEd: Strategies for Developing the Talent in Every Learner. By Jerry D. Flack.

Teaching Teenagers and Living to Tell About It: Gifted Students and Other Creatures in the Regular Classroom. By Pamela Everly.

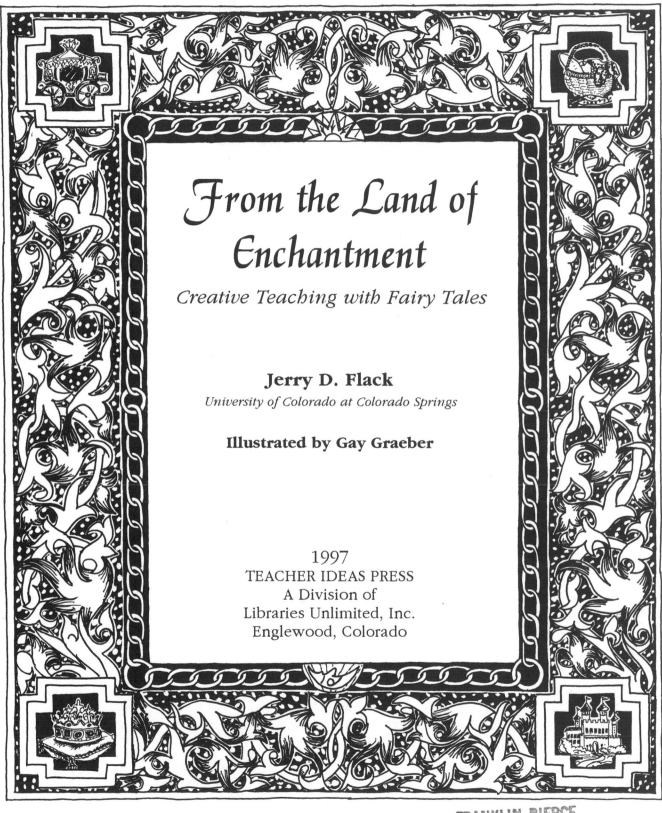

From the Land of Enchantment

Creative Teaching with Fairy Tales

Jerry D. Flack

University of Colorado at Colorado Springs

Illustrated by Gay Graeber

1997
TEACHER IDEAS PRESS
A Division of
Libraries Unlimited, Inc.
Englewood, Colorado

This book is dedicated to Gay Graeber. She is the best collaborator and friend anyone could ever hope to have. Her wonderful illustrations always enhance the meaning of my words many times over. She is an unfailing inspiration to me. She always offers not only wisdom but love. No one could ask for more.

Jerry Flack

TEACHER IDEAS PRESS
A Division of
Libraries Unlimited, Inc.
P.O. Box 6633
Englewood, CO 80155-6633
1-800-237-6124/www.lu.com

Production Editor: Kay Mariea
Copy Editor: Thea de Hart
Proofreader: Beth Partin
Design and Layout: Pamela J. Getchell

Library of Congress Cataloging-in-Publication Data

Flack, Jerry D.
    From the land of enchantment : creative teaching with fairy tales
/ Jerry D. Flack ; illustrated by Gay Graeber.
    xx, 241 p. 22x28 cm. -- (Gifted treasury series)
    Includes bibliographical references and index.
    ISBN 1-56308-540-2
    1. Creative thinking--Study and teaching. 2. Cognitive styles in
children. 3. Fairy tales--Study and teaching. 4. Gifted children--
Education. I. Title. II. Series.
LB1590.5.F52   1997
370.15'7--dc21   97-26027
                                                    CIP

Contents

4 Creative Problem Solving with the Three Bears

5 In the Kingdom of Ideas

5 In the Kingdom of Ideas (Continued)

6 "The Emperor's New Clothes" and Student Productions 135

7 The Frog Prince: Thinking and Problem Solving with Art 155

Preface

From the Land of Enchantment is the seventh volume in Teacher Ideas Press's Gifted Treasury series. In the same manner as previous volumes, this work focuses upon sharing important ideas, substantive curricula, valuable resources, and practical, easily implemented teaching strategies with teachers, administrators, library media specialists, parents, and other mentors of talented youth.

Previous volumes have found their center in topics such as mysteries, inventions, and aerospace science and in specific, successful teaching tactics and strategies. This volume places special emphasis on learning processes. Because fairy tales are so well-known to students they are used in this book as the common content base for the teaching and practicing of these processes. Some of the processes and skills described in these pages are associated with the scholarship of particular individuals or groups, such as the multiple-intelligences theory of Howard Gardner and the cognitive-performance objectives authored by Benjamin Bloom and his colleagues. Other methods and procedures, such as making books and creating newspapers, are generic processes not identified with particular individuals. All are shared with the intent of helping educators who work with young people make that precious task enjoyable and successful.

The processes, ideas, activities, and projects suggested in *From the Land of Enchantment* are similar to those found in other volumes in the Gifted Treasury series. They are practical, and they yield success. Enthusiastic educators and parents have tested and used all the ideas and strategies and have found that the learning approaches are not bound by age. These ideas work as well with 25-year-old learners as they do with 5-year-olds. Versatility is a key to the lessons in this book. The fundamental strategies may be used with home-schooled children, with high school science classes, in college writing courses, or in a fourth-grade elementary classroom.

The important role of the library media specialists in schools and in public libraries is paramount in the talent-development process of youth. That role is accentuated in every book in the Gifted Treasury series. Library media specialists are outstanding observers and facilitators of talent discovery and development, and they should always be seen as indispensable allies of parents and teachers in the talent-development process. Their role becomes even more critical as electronic media increasingly play a pivotal role in world-class educational offerings. Many suggestions for great collaborations between teachers and library media specialists are noted in these pages.

Finally, every attempt has been made to integrate and align the contents of this book with current developments in American education. Literacy is paramount in all the ideas and strategies suggested, and integrated learning across many disciplines is promoted throughout. Thinking skills and problem solving are described, and implementation strategies are emphasized in a multitude of activities. The rich literary selections cited in every chapter underscore diversity. Academic excellence and high standards are the foundation of everything found in this book and in the entire Gifted Treasury series. Of course, the whole reason for the series is for it to serve as an aid in promoting the maximum development of human potential. The gifts and talents of students must be recognized, developed, and celebrated.

Acknowledgments

The author wishes to thank the many people who have shared endless ideas with him over the years as well as those who contributed specific tactics, words, pictures, a great deal of inspiration, and much support for this book.

Priscilla Barsotti

Susan Valleroli Brock

Pat Broderick

Kathy Dutke

Jan Fall

Gay Graeber

Chris Hickerson

Holly Hudson

Phyllis Johnson

Joyce Juntune

Rick Kartas

Kristine Kuen

Caren Kutch

Leslie Sniff

John Stansfield

George Summers

Donald J. Treffinger

The author wishes to thank all of the fine editors and staff members at Libraries Unlimited and Teacher Ideas Press, especially Susan Zernial, Kay Mariea, and JoAnne Ricca, for their unfailing support of this book and the entire Gifted Treasury Series.

The author also wishes to thank Trina Schart Hyman for the generous sharing of her words and her art concerning Little Red Riding Hood. The text (p. 64) is from *Self-Portrait: Trina Schart Hyman* (New York: Harper & Row, 1981) and the art (p. 67) is from *Little Red Riding Hood*. Copyright © 1983 by Trina Schart Hyman. All rights reserved. Reprinted by permission of Holiday House, Inc.

The poems "Story Hour" (p. 42) and "The Grandmother" (p. 76) by Sara Henderson Hay are from *Story Hour*, published by the University of Arkansas Press, copyright by the author 1961, 1963, 1982.

The CPS vertical graphic depiction found in the creative problem solving chapter (p. 91) is used with the generous permission of Donald J. Treffinger and the Center for Creative Learning. It is from D. J. Treffinger, S. G. Isaksen, and K. B. Dorval. *Creative Problem Solving: An Introduction*. [Rev. ed.]. Sarasota, FL: Center for Creative Learning, © 1994. Reproduced with permission.

Introduction

The Magic of Fairy Tales

Fantasy is the most valuable attribute of the human mind and should be diligently nurtured from the earliest childhood.
—Kornei Chukovsky

Fairy tales are magical. It is said that a wise person once asked Albert Einstein what kind of reading fare should be given to young people who hoped to have careers in science. Einstein purportedly responded, "Why, fairy tales, of course."

Using the vast array of fairy tales found in world literature, teachers can teach virtually any content or process. Fairy tales can be used to enrich the lives of all students and to differentiate curriculum for gifted and talented and highly creative students. But to teach well, the teacher must first engage the learner, and few motivators are as powerful as the allure of the classic fairy tales.

Fairy tales are stories that have been passed from one generation to the next for centuries. With such magical elements as a fairy godmother who can turn a pumpkin into a regal coach or a beautiful princess whose kiss breaks an evil spell and transforms a frog back into a prince, they take readers and listeners to make-believe times and places. But the magic is also to be found in the telling, hearing, and reading of fairy tales. Although children and adults know the outcome of classic tales even before they are read or told, they still—as if by magic—anxiously wait for the wicked to be punished, the vulnerable to be rescued, and the good and kind to live "happily ever after."

Fairy tales are tales filled with wonder, but not all contain fairies, and some—such as "The Three Little Pigs"—do not have human characters. Many have both human and animal characters ("Little Red Riding Hood" and "Goldilocks and the Three Bears"). Some fairy tales, notably "Beauty and the Beast," are romances. While numerous fairy tales have characters of royal birth ("The Frog Prince" and "Sleeping Beauty"), there are also many fairy tales in which the protagonists are common people ("Jack and the Beanstalk" and "Hansel and Gretel") who must endure great hardships and dire poverty before being elevated to a better life in the resolution of the story. With rare exceptions, such as Hans Christian Andersen's "The Little Match Girl," fairy tales have happy endings.

Other characteristics common to the stories that students know broadly as fairy tales are familiar phrases such as "once upon a time" and "lived happily ever after"; settings that are often in woods or castles or both; and archetypal characters who are not well-defined but who represent such polarities as good and evil, beauty and ugliness. The number three is a also a motif common to many fairy tales.

> *Everything you need to know about life you can learn from a fairy tale.*
> —Michael Hague

Fairy tales speak to us of eternal truths and verities that still have relevance. There's many a home owner, for example, who wishes he had taken the time and care to build his house of bricks, and there are innumerable young ladies, even in the absence of red capes, who wish too late that they had listened to their mothers' words and had never strayed from the path.

In the past century, many of the most horrific and gruesome episodes found in fairy tales have been purged. It is rare today, for example, to find the Brothers Grimm version of "Cinderella" wherein the stepsisters horribly mutilate their feet and birds pick out their eyes on their travels to the wedding of Cinderella and the prince. Even so, modern versions of classic fairy tales retain enough malevolent characters and scary events to continue to provide thrills and goose bumps for young children. The wolf still eats Grandmother, the queen in "Snow White" continues to be venomous, and the ogre or giant still chases Jack down the beanstalk.

Often, folklorists separate or make divisions among various kinds of fairy tales. Folk fairy tales evolved from oral traditions and were told for hundreds of years before finally being written down and published in book collections in the eighteenth and nineteenth centuries. Typically, they follow set patterns of action and characterization. The tales of the Brothers Grimm are usually so classified. Literary fairy tales may have antecedents in oral tradition, but authors pay less attention to the fairy tale formulas found in older storytelling traditions and put greater emphasis on the literary qualities of the stories. Where folk fairy tales are primarily oral stories set to paper, literary fairy tales evidence much greater attention to the artistry involved in the telling of the tale. The most famous author of the literary fairy tales is Hans Christian Andersen.

It is not the purpose of this book to provide a particular set of definitions of fairy tales, theories of their origins and diffusion around the world, or an examination of the various kinds of folktales and classifications. Readers who want to explore further the history, national origins, and classifications of fairy tales, folktales, myths, and legends will find several good commentaries about folk literature in classic children's literature textbooks such as:

Bernice E. Cullinan, and Lee Galda. 1994. *Literature and the Child*. Third Edition. New York: Harcourt Brace.

Charlotte S. Huck, Susan Hepler, and Janet Hickman. 1993. *Children's Literature in the Elementary School*. New York: Harcourt Brace.

Donna E. Norton. 1995. *Through the Eyes of a Child: An Introduction to Children's Literature*. Englewood Cliffs, NJ: Prentice-Hall.

Zena Sutherland and May Hill Arbuthnot. 1991. *Children and Books*. New York: HarperCollins.

The primary mission of *From the Land of Enchantment* is to point out to teachers and parents how rewarding it can be for students to explore the world's great fairy tales. Fairy tales activate the imagination. They are wonderfully rich literature for developing the creativity and imagination of youth. There are no limits to the kinds and numbers of imaginative products students may create in response to their interactions with fairy tales.

Fairy tales may be read over and over and serve as the springboard for completely different teaching aims related to the ages and maturity of students. "Jack and the Beanstalk" may be read to young children as a pure adventure story. But students in the middle and secondary grades can approach the tale thematically, examining it as a metaphorical tale of the individual's struggle to achieve maturity. Jack must show initiative and demonstrate personal courage if he is to leave behind the bonds of childhood and grow toward manhood. "The Three Little Pigs" is a simple, charming story of repetition for young children, but it may also be interpreted as a morality tale that carries the societal message for older youth that pleasure should never be purchased at the expense of security. Life rewards those who avoid the easy solutions and who plan, work hard, and put their houses in order.

From the Land of Enchantment highlights and suggests ways that familiar fairy tales can be revisited and employed both in the home and in schools as a means to introduce and teach important, new skills such as creative and productive thinking, critical thinking, and creative problem solving to students of all ages. Similarly, models for curriculum construction such as Howard Gardner's multiple-intelligences theory and Bloom's Taxonomy can be explored using fairy tales as a content base. Creative teachers can introduce to students virtually any content or process through fairy tales. Classic fairy tales in the learning equation represent a way of *using the familiar to teach the unfamiliar.*

One observation this educator has made is that teaching is less effective when students are inundated with too much "stuff." This is most likely to occur when the teacher attempts to teach new content and new processes simultaneously. When learners fail to achieve the instructional goals that have been set, it cannot be determined with any certainty whether it was the process, the content, or both that were not mastered. To remedy this problem, use familiar content in the initial phases of teaching new processes. Fairy tales are especially well suited to this end.

Reading fairy tales to children is a pervasive American custom. Moreover, motion-picture versions, especially animated full-length cinema treatments by Walt Disney and his successors, have exposed millions of children and adolescents to fairy tales such as "Beauty and the Beast" and "Cinderella." Fairy tales provide a shared cultural background. There exists an almost universal knowledge of fairy tales. Students do not have to engage in in-depth research in a new content area to participate in class activities. They are free to focus on the process skills to be learned. Most students are reasonably equal in their knowledge of fairy tales; thus, no one student or group of students is particularly advantaged because of prior knowledge. Fairy tales are wonderful in and of themselves, but they also serve as a gold mine as the content base for teaching all kinds of new reading, writing, and thinking skills and processes.

Fairy tales also provide a "safe" content focus. Teachers and students tend to associate fairy tales with merriment, and they feel freer to explore "wild ideas" when dealing with fairy tales than with, say, U.S. history or long division. Fairy tales are inventive by nature and all but beg for creative and innovative applications and manipulations. Fairy tales provide a content base that is open to countless, new, additional ideas and applications for creative teaching and learning. Scarcely a week passes without the appearance in the media of a new cartoon, satirical newspaper column, or advertisement that alludes to fairy tale characters, plots, and motifs. New interpretations suggest the universal appeal of fairy tales and offer unlimited future resources and project ideas.

In this book, the story "Cinderella" is used as the content base for exploring the multiple intelligences of children and for designing creative curriculum experiences to develop their multiple talents. The story "Jack and the Beanstalk" is used to promote and explore ways to engage students in critical thinking. The great versatility of fairy tales can be seen in the chapter devoted to reading and writing with "Little Red Riding Hood." "Goldilocks and the Three Bears" is the medium used to teach creative problem solving. The "In the Kingdom of Ideas" chapter contains a collection of sterling ideas to further promote creative thinking. As the emperor tries on new "clothes" in Hans Christian Andersen's famed fairy tale,

students endeavor to use new and fresh media products. Art is given its due with a celebration of "The Frog Prince," and two exemplary teachers share their imaginative teaching strategies in a chapter celebrating "The Three Little Pigs." Finally, students bring to bear all they have learned from the many pursuits advocated in the book by building their own "Beauty and the Beast" classroom museum exhibitions.

The ideas presented here are not meant to be all-inclusive. Because fairy tales offer so many tantalizing possibilities for the development and enhancement of creative thinking, innovative teachers and students will undoubtedly think of countless novel adaptations and additional superb ideas for meaningful learning. Fairy tales are certainly magical for all students and can be used with particular creativity to extend and differentiate instruction for gifted, talented, and creative students. To that end, many challenges and extensions, especially those features titled Happily Ever Afters, are shared in each chapter. The contents of this book should stimulate the use of fairy tales and other folk literature and the practice of innovative teaching techniques, and it should promote differentiated instruction for gifted students as well as creative instruction that leads to the discovery and celebration of gifts and talents in all students.

Many of the strategies are highly effective when used at the beginning of a course or school year. The aim is to teach basic process skills such as critical text reading and creative problem solving to students who can then transfer these skills to new situations and content as they progress through the school year. The strategies may, however, be equally well employed anytime new skills are introduced. All the ideas found herein may also be used as talent-development tactics in a language-arts unit devoted to the exploration of fairy tales, in a creative problem-solving course, or in Saturday or summer enrichment classes.

Classroom environment, of course, plays a critical role in fostering creative thinking among students. The emotional climate of the classroom is crucial. Laughter is heard frequently in classrooms where creative minds are at work. It is the music of joyous, shared experiences. Words of praise, encouragement, and acceptance also echo throughout classrooms where creativity flourishes. The physical environment is equally important. Creativity thrives in a visually stimulating atmosphere. Imaginative posters, bulletin boards, and interest centers serve not only to remind students to employ, on a daily basis, the process skills being taught but also contribute significantly to a stimulating atmosphere conducive to creative thinking. Even the classroom seating arrangement plays an important role in the creative classroom: Students sitting rigidly in symmetrical rows may be similarly rigid in their thinking. Teacher behavior as seemingly simple as physically altering seating arrangements can trigger a powerful, positive psychological change in students' thinking behaviors. Creativity is contagious. Enthusiasm for an original idea may be communicated as often nonverbally as it is verbally. Students should see more than the backs of other students' heads. Allow students to sit in a circle, facing one another, so that the shared joy of creative moments may be fully communicated.

A final note. Even though the use of fairy tales with older students has already been cited, there may yet remain the assumption that fairy tales—hence, the strategies in this book—are for children only. The frequent and skillful use creative writers, cartoonists, and advertisers make of fairy tales belies that notion. Try any activity in this text—say, helping the Three Bears with creative problem solving—and witness the sheer delight and enthusiasm with which high school students and adults approach the task. The magic of fairy tales and the joy of using one's mind creatively do not exist only in the once-upon-a-time phase of life known as childhood. Sage teachers and parents will see the wisdom inherent in the words of C. S. Lewis: "Someday you will be old enough to start reading fairy tales again."

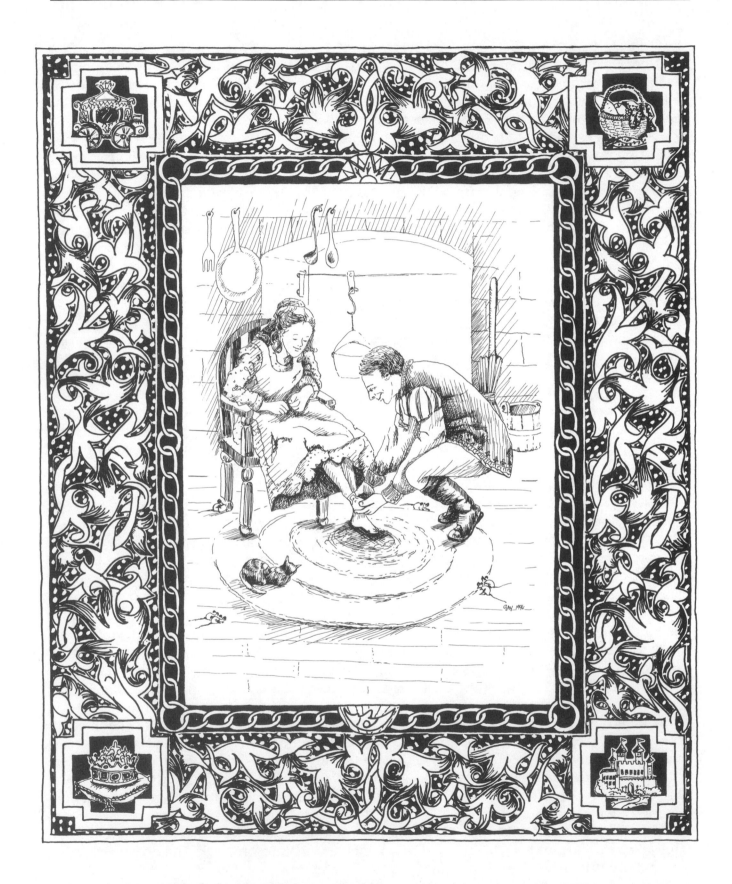

Chapter *1*

Cinderella Meets a Prince: Howard Gardner

CHAPTER PREVIEW

In this chapter Cinderella meets a princely fellow, Howard Gardner. A primer on the origin and operations of multiple-intelligences (MI) theory is presented, and then the theory is applied to a study of "Cinderella," the most famous fairy tale in the world. In addition to highlighting many activities accentuating all the seven intelligences, a brief biographical sketch of Charles Perrault and a list of activities that go beyond multiple-intelligences activities are provided in Happily Ever Afters.

THE THEORY OF MULTIPLE INTELLIGENCES

Fairy tales such as "Cinderella" illumine human experience and give lessons about life. Just so, an examination of multiple-intelligences theory may also reveal to teachers and students truths about human potential and the diversity of talent and experience. One of the most fortunate educational developments of the past decade has been the growing awareness and popularity of Howard Gardner's princely MI theory. Educators' acceptance of Gardner's pluralized concept of intellect coupled with their growing recognition of students' diverse background experiences and many equally valid learning styles bode well for the all-important talent-development process in education. Our nation and world can afford nothing less than the full realization of the gifts, talents, and creative productivity of every citizen. Howard Gardner underscores this importance:

> It is of the utmost importance that we recognize and nurture all of the varied human intelligences, and all of the combinations of intelligences. We are all so different largely because we all have different combinations of intelligences. If we recognize this, I think we will have at least a better chance of dealing appropriately with the many problems that we face in the world (Gardner 1993c, 12).

A beginning point in the talent-development process is an exploration of the meaning of multiple intelligences. It is not the intention of this author to provide an exhaustive discussion of multiple-intelligences theory here. Readers can turn to a growing body of literature by Howard Gardner and other scholars noted at the end of this chapter to find in-depth explanations of multiple intelligences. Nevertheless, a brief introduction to some of the salient definitions and tenets of MI theory is appropriate before proceeding directly to MI-theory-based activities related to explorations of the classic fairy tale "Cinderella."

Multiple Intelligences Defined

Frames of Mind (Gardner 1983) establishes and explains the theory of multiple intelligences. In this seminal work, Gardner postulates that traditional definitions of *intelligence* are too narrow. Further, subsequent assessments or measurements based on limiting definitions have been far too dependent upon linguistic and logical-mathematical intelligences. The most significant tenet of MI theory is Gardner's pluralization of the concept of *intelligence*. Intelligence is not a single entity. Individuals do not have just one general intelligence that can be determined through such psychometric means as IQ tests. Individuals possess multiple intelligences. Gardner identified seven discrete intelligences in *Frames of Mind*:

- ♦ Linguistic Intelligence
- ♦ Bodily-Kinesthetic Intelligence
- ♦ Musical Intelligence
- ♦ Interpersonal Intelligence
- ♦ Logical-Mathematical Intelligence
- ♦ Intrapersonal Intelligence
- ♦ Spatial Intelligence

Closely related to the pluralized concept of intelligences is the second critical tenet of MI theory. Intelligences are not fixed. Cultural conditions, experiences, and history affect each individual's intelligences profile. Gardner also rejects the "inherited versus learned" dichotomy found in many traditional discussions of intelligence. Instead, he emphasizes the interaction between genetic and environmental factors (Gardner 1995b, 203). One of the underpinnings of MI theory is the belief that people have the potential to develop all their intelligences. Whether an intelligence develops fully is dependent upon biological endowment, personal history, and cultural and historical conditions. An example of the interaction of these various determinants may be seen in the life of the nineteenth-century verbal prodigy Hilda Conkling.

Conkling began writing poetry at age four. By the time she was eight years old, her verse had been published in *Poetry*, one of the most distinguished literary magazines in the world. When Conkling was nine, a major New York publisher produced a volume of her poems entitled *Poems by a Little Girl*, which was praised by poet Amy Lowell as a work of genius. Clearly, Conkling possessed remarkable *linguistic intelligence*. However, the precocious flowering of her linguistic intelligence illustrates the cultural context associated with talent development. Her mother was a professor of poetry at Smith College, and Conkling grew up in a home environment in which poetry was valued, practiced, and experienced daily. Young Conkling was as much immersed in verse in her time as today's children are absorbed in television and computer games. Finally, Conkling also was fortunate to live at a time in the history of American literature when poetry was very much in fashion.[1]

　　Gardner defines an intelligence as ". . . a biological and psychological potential; that potential is capable of being realized to a greater or lesser extent as a consequence of the experiential, cultural, and motivational factors that affect a person" (Gardner 1995a, 202).

　　Gardner makes distinctions between three highly important yet separate entities related to talent development: *intelligence*, *domains*, and *fields*. It is appropriate to refer to one or more intelligences when speaking of individuals. An individual may have as a birthright a highly sensitive musical intelligence, for example. But individuals are born into cultures that exhibit many recognized and prized *domains* of human activity, such as navigation, hunting, and musical performance. Domains are impersonal and are not bound to particular individuals. That is, a culture can develop a hierarchy of skills in a domain and make assessments about performances in that domain irrespective of special persons. Moreover, an individual may need to bring several intelligences to bear on a given domain-focused activity. For example, a successful music performance requires not only musical intelligence but also relies upon bodily-kinesthetic and personal intelligences as well. The third definition Gardner cites is a *field* of endeavor. A field is a sociological construct. People who operate within domains create structures that regulate activities within them. Individuals and groups organize meetings, share ideas, award prizes, and determine

1.　For a discussion of Hilda Conkling and other remarkable young people whose gifts exemplify multiple intelligences, see Jerry Flack, October 1993. "Putting Faces with Multiple Intelligences." *THINK* 4 (1): 12-15. For additional information about Conkling, see Dennis Brindell Fradin, *Remarkable Children* (Boston: Little, Brown, 1987).

standards and the future directions of any given field. Fields include the medical profession, interscholastic athletics, and children's literature. Gardner has used this trio of definitions to describe the talent-development pathways taken by remarkably gifted adults such as Albert Einstein, Pablo Picasso, and Martha Graham (Gardner 1993a). Each of these people was a creative individual who possessed unique intelligences as demonstrated by their consistently remarkable problem solving and creation of products in specific domains such as physics, art, and dance. Further, their accomplishments and contributions were acknowledged and recognized by experts and professionals within their respective fields (Gardner 1993b, xvi-xvii).

Some psychologists selectively distinguish between the words *intelligence* and *talent* and their applications. Gardner eschews the practice of using, for example, the word *talent* to describe musical and bodily-kinesthethic behaviors while reserving *intelligence* to describe linguistic or mathematical performances. He believes that to do so connotes a lesser status upon the former. "In my view it is fine to call music or spatial ability a talent so long as one calls language or logic a talent as well" (Gardner 1993b, xx).

Gardner has not prescribed new intelligences beyond the seven he first articulated in 1983 in *Frames of Mind*. He does suggest that future research should examine the kind of intelligence most often associated with naturalists—people who appear predisposed to interest in the flora and fauna of the world or who evidence great understanding and success with farming, hunting, biology, and other nature-related endeavors. Still another proposed line of research would investigate "spirituality" as a separate intelligence (Gardner 1995a, 206).

Educational Implications of MI Theory

Gardner admits great surprise that educators have seized upon MI theory and translated it into so many diverse educational practices. He attempts to stay neutral and avoids endorsements of particular MI-theory-based projects: "I have become convinced that there is no 'right way' to conduct a multiple intelligences education" (Gardner 1995a, 206). Even so, he is critical of purported applications of MI theory, such as using background music in the teaching of mathematics or dancing while reciting spelling words and then claiming that musical and bodily-kinesthetic intelligences have truly been addressed in the classroom. He does believe there are positive ways to translate MI theory into practice in classrooms and schools. Specific intelligences can be cultivated so that capabilities such as leadership and musical knowledge—judged worthy by society—are given the capacity to grow and develop (Gardner 1995a, 207-08). Educators can also approach topics and disciplines in a variety of ways. Using multiple approaches to examine a topic of study helps students find their own strengths as well as perceive the breadth of possibilities any inquiry can have. In Gardner's view, MI theory properly used also personalizes education:

> When I visit an MI school, I look for signs of personalization. Humans are not all the same; students are not identical. The best education is that which takes human differences into account and celebrates and honors diversity. Any uniform educational approach is likely to serve only a minority of children (Gardner 1995a, 208).

Although Gardner sees great value in using MI theory to guide curriculum planning, he does not advocate that all intelligences be addressed continuously. "There is no point in assuming that every topic can be effectively approached in at least seven ways, and it is a waste of effort and time to attempt to do this" (Gardner 1995a, 206).

Values and Practices of MI Theory

If educators accept the worth of MI theory, the next step is to put the theory into practice. First, educators need to recognize and respect talent diversity. The MI theory points to *at least* seven different and largely independent talents or intelligences that are vitally needed and prized by society. Second, they must also appreciate that every individual's particular combination of intelligences and talents is unique. Third, educators need to help students recognize the diversity of talents and intelligences that are found in themselves and in humanity. Students need to believe in themselves and appreciate their own unique constellations of talents or intelligences. Further, they must be challenged to believe that they can accomplish things of significance. It is not enough to possess many intelligences. All people, regardless of age, must use their intelligences positively and constructively.

A vital first step is to define, describe, and discuss the seven intelligences that make up MI theory. Share the basic definitions found in figure 1.1 with students. Also, share the contents of figure 1.2, which highlights the activities in which people participate when they are using each of the seven intelligences.

These definitions and lists of activities originated from the author's dozen-plus years of working with teachers and students in translating MI theory into practice. The terms are intended to be helpful, not restrictive. Obviously, there will be some blurring of categories, but even first-grade children are capable of differentiating between definitions of musical and mathematical intelligences, for example, and the activities characteristic of each. The generic activities cited in figure 1.2 may be seen as highly flexible in their usage. Activities are shaped by the age and maturity of participants as well as by the context in which they are utilized. Hence, journal keeping is listed in figure 1.2 as an activity associated with linguistic intelligence, but it might also be found in other domains. Keeping a personal journal is surely an artifact of activating one's intrapersonal intelligence; a gifted mathematician may also keep a log or journal articulating steps she takes in solving an equation. A musician or composer may also make musical notations in his journal just as an artist will carry a personal sketchbook.

Note that even young children can learn to appreciate MI theory and practice when concrete examples are presented. At Pine Valley Elementary School on the United States Air Force Academy in Colorado Springs, Colorado, the curriculum model for instruction is based upon MI theory. There, kindergarten and first-grade teachers routinely inform children which intelligences they are chiefly using when they participate in classroom and playground activities. Bulletin boards in the school hallways not only identify great heroes and remarkable people, but they also indicate which intelligences particular heroes used in achieving their greatness. Hence, in February during Black History Month, bulletin boards celebrate great African Americans such as Duke Ellington and Toni Morrison. Beside pictures of Ellington and Morrison, their respective musical and linguistic intelligences are noted.

Fig. 1.1. Multiple-Intelligences-Theory Definitions*

Linguistic Intelligence refers to the knowledge, skills, and use of language in oral and written communications. Facility with language or linguistic intelligence involves phonology, syntax, and semantics; understanding and using the sound, order, and the meaning of words.

Musical Intelligence refers to the ability to compose, perform, and appreciate music. The principal components of musical intelligence are pitch, rhythm, and timbre.

Logical-Mathematical Intelligence is the ability to solve problems and to "figure things out." Activities include mathematical operations using numbers in problem solving but can just as readily include scientific problem solving or invention wherein a person makes a startling analogy or intuitive leap and suddenly solves a problem or offers an explanation of natural phenomena previously unknown. The core intelligence is not necessarily verbal. History is replete with examples of mathematicians and other problem solvers who discovered or understood solutions to problems before they were eventually able to articulate their conclusions.

Spatial Intelligence involves the capacity to orient one's self to spaces and to inhabit and navigate those spaces whether they be small spaces such as a classroom or the oceans of the world. But spatial intelligence involves more than just visual perception as evidenced by the fact that blind persons can learn to expertly navigate within their world, excelling in what may seem unlikely areas and becoming, for example, first-rate sculptors. Artists and navigators are among people who use space, distance, and perception with particular skill.

Bodily-Kinesthetic Intelligence allows people to use bodily movement to physically solve problems, create new products, and perform with or without the use of tools. A fine surgeon exhibits bodily-kinesthetic skill as do a mime and a baseball pitcher. Tailors and construction workers also rely heavily on their bodily-kinesthetic intelligence.

Interpersonal Intelligence is the first of two personal intelligences Gardner cites. Interpersonal intelligence involves the ability of people to interact successfully with other human beings. Some individuals exhibit remarkable skill in their ability to read other person's needs, wishes, and intentions. Teachers, religious leaders, and politicians are among the professionals who widely use interpersonal intelligence.

Intrapersonal Intelligence refers to the internal knowledge people possess about themselves. This intelligence involves introspection and an understanding of one's feelings, behavior patterns, and reactions to the world and being able to use such self-knowledge to positive effect. People who recognize their tendency to procrastinate and thus create action plans to make sure they fulfill responsibilities are persons who effectively employ intrapersonal intelligence.

*As this book entered final production, Howard Gardner proposed to extend his MI Theory to include another intelligence, Naturalist Intelligence. Persons exhibiting high levels of this intelligence demonstrate expertise in recognizing and classifying the flora and fauna of their environment. Exemplars of naturalist intelligence would include Rachel Carson, John James Audubon, and Charles Darwin. Source: Howard Gardner, "Are There Additional Intelligences?" *Gifted Education Press Quarterly* Vol. 11 (2): 2-5. (Spring, 1997)

Fig. 1.2 Multiple-Intelligences Activities

Activities and performances commonly associated with each of the seven intelligences follow.

Linguistic Intelligence Activities
reading
writing poetry and prose
editing
formal speaking
journal keeping
storytelling
giving directions
learning foreign languages
appreciating verbal humor such as puns

Musical Intelligence Activities
singing
playing an instrument
improvising
composing
keeping time
humming
using percussion instruments
making rhythmic patterns
responding to music

Logical-Mathematical Intelligence Activities
outlining and conducting science experiments
predicting outcomes
estimating
mathematical calculations and problem solving
reasoning and debating
understanding analogies and abstractions
detecting and solving mysteries
deciphering or creating codes
solving brain teasers
playing chess

Spatial Intelligence Activities
painting
drawing
imaging
composing photographs
orienteering
building models
inventing
designing and building
mapping
creating diagrams
working with mazes and jigsaw puzzles

Bodily-Kinesthetic Intelligence Activities
dancing
acting
skating
sculpting
sewing
crafting
playing sports
physically illustrating
pantomiming
practicing martial arts
tinkering with machines

Interpersonal Intelligence Activities
leading people
cooperating
mediating and solving disputes
teaching others
organizing
negotiating
empathizing
counseling
sharing
interviewing
collaborating
understanding others
brainstorming
volunteering
peer coaching and tutoring

Intrapersonal Intelligence Activities
silently reflecting
keeping a diary or journal
daydreaming
understanding one's self
imagining future roles and opportunities
analyzing one's own behaviors, motives, and performances
goal setting
clarifying values
making personal choices
designing, implementing, and evaluating daily, weekly, monthly, and life plans

Indeed, one of the most effective ways to help students understand the MI theory is through examinations of the kinds of intelligences utilized by remarkably accomplished people. Gardner uses this case-study approach in virtually all his writing. He uses figures such as Yehudi Menuhin (musical intelligence), Babe Ruth (bodily-kinesthetic intelligence), Nobel Prize-winner Barbara McClintock (logical-mathematical intelligence), and Anne Sullivan (interpersonal intelligence) to exemplify the various intelligences (Gardner 1983, 1993b). Similarly, in *Leading Minds: An Anatomy of Leadership*, he makes use of profiles of Martin Luther King Jr., Eleanor Roosevelt, and Mahatma Gandhi to illustrate the finest examples of leadership in action (Gardner 1995b). In an article for *THINK* magazine, this author (Flack 1993) examined the extraordinary youthful accomplishments of such historical figures as Claude Debussy, Anne Frank, Thomas Edison, and Sacagawea to note how each person called upon one or more of the multiple intelligences to achieve goals or solve problems.

Examining the events in the lives of people, both remarkable children and adults, allows students to note how different intelligences surface and flower in individual lives. A second point that can be made is that everyone has a different multiple-intelligences profile. The classic bar graph is one way to visualize this phenomenon. Students can create a bar-graph profile to demonstrate the particular strengths of famous youth such as Sacagawea, who used her spatial intelligence to help find the pathway to the West for Lewis and Clark and her exceptional linguistic skill as an interpreter, speaking English and Shoshone languages. Obviously, she had to be able to get along with a diverse group of people—mostly men—so she no doubt also had strong interpersonal skills. Hence, the bar graph for Sacagawea would show dominance in at least three areas: spatial, linguistic, and interpersonal intelligences. Any famous person's life can be examined in a similar fashion. What intelligences does the person have in abundance? What intelligences has the same person perhaps not fully explored or utilized?

Next, encourage students to create their own multiple-intelligences profiles. Ask students to review the definitions and the kinds of activities associated with each of the different intelligences. Can they imagine their own MI profiles? Which intelligences have they had the opportunity to develop most fully? Do they possess particularly strong combinations of intelligences? Do they have intelligences in which they do not exhibit strengths? Are there any cultural or societal barriers that have impeded their talent development? Are boys given more opportunities to develop spatial intelligence than girls in contemporary American society? If so, how might young women overcome the disadvantage? This activity should help students understand themselves better as well as make the important point that there is not just *one* way to succeed but *many* equally valid paths to excellence.

Cinderella's MI Profile

It is not much of a jump to examine Cinderella's MI profile. Ask students to consider a multiple-intelligences profile of Cinderella such as in figure 1.3.

Fig. 1.3. Gardner's Multiple Intelligences

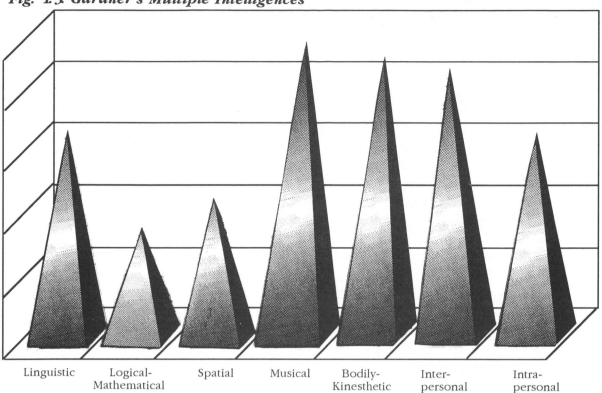

Howard Gardner's Multiple Intelligences as Applied to Cinderella

Of course, in creating the profile students are pretending that Cinderella is not a fictional character—and a largely two-dimensional one at that. Nevertheless, certain qualities and characteristics come forth through a consideration of several different Cinderella portrayals. Most children are familiar with the heroine of the Disney animated film *Cinderella*. That particular Cinderella has great musical talent as evidenced by her lovely singing voice. She also is graceful and moves with elegance on the ballroom dance floor. Hence, another strong plus for Cinderella is bodily-kinesthetic intelligence. She is kind, loyal, and generous in most portrayals, so her endowment of interpersonal intelligence is also high. Interesting and fun debates or discussions may arise as students finish their own multiple-intelligences bar graphs for Cinderella (or, alternatively, Rough-Face Girl, Yeh-Shen, or even Cinderlad). Some may believe she has not had any real opportunities to develop her mathematical talent and will thus score her "low" in that area while giving her high marks for verbal intelligence. After all, she should receive credit for telling her story and helping it become such a famous part of world folk literature.

In addition to examining figure 1.3 and creating their own Cinderella MI profiles, students might review definitions and characteristic activities associated with the seven intelligences and attempt to identify at least one famous fairy tale or nursery-rhyme character who excels in each of the intelligences. Jack of "Jack and the Beanstalk" demonstrates remarkable bodily-kinesthetic intelligence when

he nimbly climbs the beanstalk at least three times. Both Hansel and Gretel are savvy and display fine logical problem-solving skills in outwitting and eventually destroying the wicked witch who would have eaten them except for their cunning. Puss in Boots is still another fairy tale character who is a first-rate problem solver.

Why Cinderella and MI Theory?

What does MI theory have to do with fairy tales, and why are we taking valuable school time to apply MI theory to the fairy tale "Cinderella"? These are valid questions. One of the most important lessons this educator has learned in more than 30 years of teaching is to separate process (the *how* of learning) from content (the *what* of learning) when teaching new skills. When students fail to "make meaning," it is typically because too much "stuff" has been thrown at them to absorb at one time. Predictably, this occurs when teachers try to teach new content and new processes simultaneously. The prescription for better teaching is to use familiar content when teaching new processes, strategies, or operations. Because of their reasonably universal familiarity, fairy tales work especially well as the content base for introducing new processes or operations to students of nearly any age or maturity level. Elsewhere in this book, for example, "Goldilocks and the Three Bears" is used to explore how one particular creative problem-solving model works. For many years, the author has found the classic story "Cinderella" to be an extremely useful vehicle for applying newly learned information and newly acquired practices related to MI theory. Fairy tales—particularly "Cinderella" stories—provide safe and fertile ground for helping students come to understand the theory of multiple intelligences and how it may be generally understood for use with their schoolwork and practically used elsewhere in their lives.

Without pushing a point too far, there are some interesting parallels between the two entities. Both multiple intelligences and fairy tales are universal. Each is found in cultures all over the world. "Cinderella" is almost surely the most famous fairy tale in the world. The story of the child of ashes who rises to greatness because of her basic goodness and sweetness is found in cultures on almost every continent (even Antarctica, if one considers Janet Perlman's *Cinderella Penguin*). Most teachers and children are familiar with at least one "Cinderella" story, most likely the French version first published in 1697 by Charles Perrault. Many variants of the story exist, as is demonstrated in the lengthy annotated listing of "Cinderella" stories found at the end of the chapter. This variety makes it possible for teachers to select several "Cinderella" stories to use with different groups of students dependent upon such factors as age and culture. For example, when the author explains MI theory to high school students and uses "Cinderella" stories to illustrate the seven intelligences in action, he often uses Babette Cole's tongue-in-cheek version, *Prince Cinders*. "Sophisticated" high school students who might otherwise view the introduction of a fairy tale into their midst as a put-down of their maturity enjoy the humor and the fresh look at an old tale that Cole provides. The marvelous diversity of "Cinderella" stories also underscores one of the basic tenets of MI theory. Differences are to be celebrated, not evaluated as to which entity is better or worse. "Cinderella" and "Yeh-Shen" (the Chinese Cinderella) are equally wonderful fairy tales. One is not superior. They simply exist as two equally valid stories of wonder from different cultures.

Most fairy tales, and especially "Cinderella," contain archetypal characters. Cinderella is a totally good character, and the stepsisters and stepmother are completely evil characters. These archetypes are products of interpersonal intelligence in action over time; they are stories handed down from one generation to another to preserve the culture and to make the point with children that goodness and selflessness are rewarded and that envy, jealousy, and abuse of children is met with severe punishment—frequently a horrible death or mutilation.

One of the fun and instructive ways to use fairy tales as a content base is to ask students to "play" being teachers. The classroom is a familiar milieu for students. They have little trouble imagining how they would do things if they were in charge of the classroom. This author's experience is that students enjoy the exploration of curriculum planning. Students, individually or in cooperative learning groups, should explore how they would ask their students to respond creatively to "Cinderella" stories to put the MI theory into practice. Create seven cooperative learning groups, one for each of the seven intelligences articulated in the MI theory. Invite each group to assume the responsibility for determining how "their" students could best demonstrate learning achieved through one of the seven intelligences applied to an exploration of the "Cinderella" story. What exciting projects and activities can they devise? Of course, a logical next step is to then complete one or more of the creative activities they have conceived.

Teachers can use the activities highlighted in figure 1.4 as models to share with students, or they can hold them in reserve to use as prompts from which students can choose favorite activities to complete. Of course, these prompts are only the beginning of investigations students can pursue relative to multiple intelligences and "Cinderella" stories.

The multiple-intelligences theory is not a miracle drug that will instantly cure student apathy or overcome severe learning deficits. Those drugs have not been invented. Nevertheless, Howard Gardner has made teachers more conscious of the fact that all children have gifts and talents and that traditional approaches to assessing intelligence may be seriously flawed. The MI theory excites teaching staffs like no other theory or program this author has seen in 30 years of teaching, and there is no substitute for enthusiasm. This chapter serves as an introduction to MI theory and suggests ways that teachers of students of various ages can make their learners appreciate their own intelligences, especially in the class examination of "Cinderella," a fairy tale that is known the world over and appreciated. It is time for all the Cinderellas and Cinderlads who are not succeeding in America's classrooms to get up from the ashes, dust themselves off, and walk (or ride in a magic coach) forward to the ball and to school success now and happily ever after.

Included in this chapter is an extensive, annotated bibliography of "Cinderella" stories. A brief biographical sketch of Charles Perrault follows, along with a list of suggested reading resources about multiple intelligences. Happily Ever Afters included in the chapter are suggestions for creative "Cinderella" extensions for individuals, small groups, and whole classes.

Fig. 1.4 "Cinderella" Activities Related to Multiple Intelligences

---

Linguistic Intelligence

Read different versions of "Cinderella," choose a favorite, and provide reasons for the choice. Conduct an imaginary interview with Cinderella before or after the ball. Keep a journal or diary that Cinderella, Rhodopis, or Vasilisa (or one of the Cinderella story characters such as Prince Charming) might have kept. Create a unique version of "Cinderella" (e.g., a futuristic, Mars-based Cinderella who cannot attend an intergalactic ball). Practice telling a version of "Cinderella," and share it with younger students. Write a new "magic spell" for Cinderella's fairy godmother to recite. Summarize in one or two sentences the moral of Charles Perrault's "Cinderella." Transpose a prose passage describing any scene from a "Cinderella" story to verse form.

Musical Intelligence

Create a Cinderella rap, perhaps voicing Cinderella's view of her stepsisters. Choose background music, and use rhythm instruments to accompany a telling of any "Cinderella" story. Compose a musical theme for "Cinderella." Listen to music from the countries of origin for various "Cinderella" stories, such as Egypt's "Rhodopis" and Vietnam's "Tam." (Note: Public libraries often have extensive international music collections as well as opera and ballet collections for the next activity.) Listen to music from Sergey Prokofiev's ballet *Cinderella* or Gioacchino Rossini's opera *La Cenerentola* (Cinderella). With crayons and markers, draw the pictures that the selected music passages suggest.

Logical-Mathematical Intelligence

Create a Venn diagram illustrating two versions of the "Cinderella" story such as Shirley Climo's *The Egyptian Cinderella* and Rafe Martin's *The Rough-Face Girl*, an Algonquian Indian folktale. Describe a logical plan for how Cinderella might go to the ball without using the magic of a fairy godmother. Create a board game, complete with rules, based upon story characters and elements found in "Cinderella." Add some measurements (e.g., miles to the castle, shoe sizes), then write a mathematical story problem based upon some aspect of "Cinderella."

Spatial Intelligence

Draw a scene from any "Cinderella" story. Create a map that notes the central characters in "Cinderella" and reveals connections and relationships among the characters. Use LEGO, K'NEX, Robotix, or other modular building materials to build a castle, carriage, or other artifacts from various "Cinderella" stories. Draw a sketch of one stage setting for a theatrical version of "Cinderella." Blindfolded, use molding clay to sculpt a magic slipper or a statue of any character from any "Cinderella" story. Create blueprints for a new castle for Cinderella and Prince Charming.

Bodily-Kinesthetic Intelligence

In small groups, choreograph a dance Cinderella and Prince Charming might perform. Teach the dance to the class. Demonstrate how to perform a dance such as a square dance, two-step dance, and so on. Pantomime scenes from any "Cinderella" story. Improvise a humorous scene from any of the many parodies of "Cinderella," such as Babette Cole's *Prince Cinders* or Bernice Myers's *Sidney Rella and the Glass Sneaker*.

Interpersonal Intelligence

Create a list of personality improvement tips for Cinderella's stepsisters. Negotiate a truce between Cinderella and her tormentors. Exchange notes and positive critiques of student performances in re-creating scenes from "Cinderella" stories with other classmates. Analyze and discuss the lessons that can be learned from reading or listening to "Cinderella" stories (e.g., envy and cruelty are punished; selflessness and goodness are rewarded). Be sure to read *The Good Stepmother* by Marguerita Rudolph. Write an advice column for a newspaper about ballroom-dancing etiquette or stepsibling rivalry.

Intrapersonal Intelligence

Students should ask themselves, If I could be a fairy godperson, how would I help people improve their lives? Imagine portraying Yeh-Shen, Rhodopis, Prince Charming, Cinderlad, or Cinderella. Ask them, "What do you like or dislike about your role?" Have they ever felt like Cinderella or Sydney Rella? In the absence of a fairy godmother (or godfather), how would they overcome the feeling of being mistreated or not appreciated?

Charles Perrault

The oldest and most famous European version of the "Cinderella" story was penned by Charles Perrault (1628-1703), a Paris intellectual with connections to the French royal court. Perrault can truly be acclaimed as the father of fairy tales. Born the fifth son of a distinguished French family, he learned to read early and was expected to do his lessons in French and Latin. One of his many intellectual pursuits was the study of law. A lawyer by training, Perrault was an influential member of the French Academy, serving as its director for a time. He wrote poetry and was at the center of an intellectual debate over the relative merits of classical literature and the growing French writing of his time. Perrault truly found his greatness in life, however, in setting to paper the tales he had long told his four children. He first published a collection of folktales, *Stories or Tales of Times Past, with Morals*, in 1697. The book, which is perhaps better known by its subtitle, *Tales of Mother Goose*, included eight stories, among them "Cinderella: or, The Little Glass Slipper," "Sleeping Beauty," "The Master Cat, or Puss in Boots" and "Little Red Riding Hood." Although most of the tales had been told since at least the Middle Ages, Perrault did much more than just preserve them. He transformed these simple stories into tales of wonder and magic for children. The basic "Cinderella" story can be traced to the folklore of antiquity, but he embellished the story with three significant details: the fairy godmother, the pumpkin coach, and the glass slipper.

One of the marked differences between Perrault's 1697 "Cinderella: or, The Little Glass Slipper" and the Brothers Grimm version of "Cinderella," published in *Children's and Household Tales* more than a century later, is the treatment of the stepsisters at the end of the tale. In Perrault's version of the story, the stepsisters are forgiven for their previous cruel treatment of Cinderella, while in the German telling the sisters' eyes are pecked out by pigeons—but only after they have already mutilated themselves by carving up their feet. One explanation of the differences is that Perrault was connected to the royal court of Louis XIV of France, and a tale about the wrongdoings and dire punishment of the royalty and the upper classes would hardly have been met with favor in court circles.

"CINDERELLA" RESOURCES

"Cinderella" is thought to be the most popular fairy tale in the world (Sierra 1992), and authors of the following "Cinderella" stories have found elements of the story in the writings of the first century B.C. historian, Strabo, as well as in Chinese manuscripts dating to the T'ang dynasty (618-907 A.D.) (Climo 1989; Louie 1982). Hence, it should not be surprising that myriad titles of "Cinderella" can be found in bookstores and libraries.

The following annotated bibliography cites some especially fine visual interpretations and translations of Charles Perrault's French "Cinderella" story, first told in 1697; retellings of "Cinderella" stories and folktales tales from around the world; and some popular, updated "Cinderella" stories and parodies. The annotations begin with traditional stories, either Perrault's "Cinderella" or multicultural variations of the timeless tale of a persecuted child whose true spirit of goodness allows her (or him) to triumph over adversity. Invariably, those who have persecuted her are punished. A number of parodies, reversals (boy heroes), and other treatments are also cited. Among these are two-in-one books that feature traditional stories paired with a retelling from the point of view of another character. Because stepmothers and stepsisters take such a beating in many "Cinderella" stories—especially in those variants from Europe and Asia—a number of "antidote" books featuring positive stepmothers are also suggested. Finally, four videocassettes of note are recommended.

Traditional Stories

Brown, Marcia. 1954. *Cinderella, or, the Little Glass Slipper*. New York: Charles Scribner's Sons.
Brown's illustrations are faithful to the styles and manners of French royalty of Perrault's day. Despite the book's receiving the Caldecott Medal, contemporary children may find the illustrations pale in comparison to the bold colors and designs found in today's picture books.

Climo, Shirley. 1989. *The Egyptian Cinderella*. Illus. by Ruth Heller. New York: HarperCollins.
Rhodopis is a Greek slave in ancient Egypt who is sought by the Pharaoh Amasis after one of her red-gold slippers is brought to him by a majestic falcon through the intervention of the Egyptian sky god Horus. Climo provides background notes citing the origin of the story from the first century B.C. historian, Strabo.

———. 1993. *The Korean Cinderella*. Illus. by Ruth Heller. New York: HarperCollins.
A virtuous, young woman, Pear Blossom, is mistreated by her jealous stepmother, Omoni. Magical animals help Pear Blossom triumph. Heller's bold color illustrations make the tale magical. A real plus of this book is the substantial end notes provided by the author and illustrator to explain the authenticity of their work.

———. 1996. *The Irish Cinderlad*. Illus. by Loretta Krupinski. New York: HarperCollins.
Climo continues her around-the-world telling of "Cinderella" stories—but with a new twist: The protagonist of the universal story is a boy. Krupinski's colorful illustrations have a captivating folk-art appeal.

Compton, Joanne. 1994. *Ashpet: An Appalachian Tale*. Illus. by Kenn Compton. New York: Holiday House.
A spunky, fresh mountain girl is the heroine of this "Cinderella" story, and the doctor's handsome son is Prince Charming. The drawings are as witty as the text. Please note the *Ashpet* videocassette reference at the end of the chapter.

Delamare, David. 1993. *Cinderella*. New York: Green Tiger Press.
Delamare's magnificent paintings set the story in the splendor of Venice in centuries past, and the heroine's conveyance to the masked ball is by gondola. Ella, the heroine of this retelling, achieves womanhood when her mother and father die and her world begins to fall apart.

Galdone, Paul. 1978. *Cinderella*. New York: McGraw-Hill.
Galdone's fine illustrations boldly overflow the pages with their portrayals of treachery, cruelty, suspense, and even good humor—what a joy to see a master at work. Note his subtle touches, such as the natural affinity the house cat has for the kind Cinderella, not the cruel and artificial stepsisters. The period flavor of the costumes and ornaments is equally splendid.

Hooks, William H. 1987. *Moss Gown*. Illus. by Donald Carrick. New York: Clarion Books.
From the oral traditions of North Carolina's eastern tidewater region, Hooks relates the folktale, "Moss Gown," an intriguing combination or synthesis of both the characters and situations of the European Cinderella and Shakespeare's *King Lear*. In the story, a vain old man asks his three daughters to tell him how much they love him. His calculating older two daughters, Retha and Grenadine, play to his vanity. Misunderstanding his youngest and most loving daughter Candace's response, "I love you as much as meat loves salt," the foolish man gives his plantation to Retha and Grenadine, who promptly banish Candace from her home. In the heart of the swamp, Candace meets a black witch woman who uses magic to fashion a gown for her from Spanish moss. The story lines converge: Candace, or "Moss Gown," who has been reduced to serving as the lowest of the kitchen maids, wins the love of a handsome plantation master. In the denouement, the old father—chased off the land he formerly owned by his two ungrateful daughters and reduced to begging—is reunited with his beloved Candace and finally understands her long-ago response about her love for him. Hooks provides notes explaining the origins of the tale and the spell-casting powers of the mysterious witch woman, and Carrick's illustrations are as wonderful as Hooks's retelling. But the book may best serve as a reference or curiosity. Teachers and librarians need to recognize the potential controversy surrounding the racial stereotypes reinforced in the story as well as the narrative's heavy dependence upon powerful magic spells. The same basic story line is found as the English folktale "Cap o' Rushes" in Judy Sierra's *The Oryx Multicultural Folktale Series: Cinderella*.

Huck, Charlotte. 1989. *Princess Furball*. Illus. by Anita Lobel. New York: Greenwillow Books.
This delightful variant of the "Cinderella" story features a young princess who relies upon her own ingenuity rather than upon magic or a fairy godmother. Lobel's full-color illustrations will charm readers of all ages.

Karlin, Barbara. 1989. *Cinderella*. Illus. by James Marshall. Boston: Little, Brown.
The ace here is Marshall's delightful and humorous approach to illustrating the classic tale. Marshall's characters leap off the pages to provoke smiles on the faces of readers young or old.

Kha, Dang Manh. 1979. *In the Land of Small Dragon*. Told by Ann Nolan Clark. Illus. by Tony Chen. New York: Viking Press.

Tam, the heroine of this Vietnamese folktale, is maltreated by the selfish stepsister Cam but triumphs in the end as in all "Cinderella" tales. This Vietnamese tale, especially as told by Clark (Newbery Medal winner for *The Secret of the Andes* and Caldecott Medalist for *In My Mother's House*), is a more richly textured story than most northern European versions of this nearly universal folktale. Clark's narration is interspersed with Vietnamese proverbs such as "A man's worth is what he does, not what he says he can do." Chen alternates lush watercolors with black-and-white pen-and-ink illustrations. Unfortunately, the book is currently out of print. For additional versions of the Tam and Cam "Cinderella" fairy tales from Vietnam, see Darrell Lum's *The Golden Slipper: A Vietnamese Legend*; Judy Sierra's *The Oryx Multicultural Folktale Series: Cinderella*; and Lynette Dyer Vuong's *The Brocaded Slipper and Other Vietnamese Tales*.

Kroll, Steven. 1993. *Queen of the May*. Illus. by Patience Brewster. New York: Holiday House.

Sylvie lives in a Scandinavian village and longs to be chosen Queen of the May, but her stepmother and stepsister keep her so weighted down with difficult tasks that she has no time to pick a bouquet of flowers for May Day. Gudrun, her bitter stepsister, refuses to stop and help a chipmunk, beaver, and a large crow, all of whom have had misfortunes. Sylvie helps all three, and her reward is to be crowned the May Queen while her stepmother and stepsister are chased away by attacking crows. Brewster's lovely paintings are as fresh as springtime.

Louie, Ai-Ling. 1982. *Yeh-Shen: A Cinderella Story from China*. Illus. by Ed Young. New York: Philomel.

This Chinese version of the familiar tale of a kind and lovely girl who is mistreated by a stepmother and stepsister predates Perrault's "Cinderella" fairy tale by at least a thousand years. Caldecott Medalist Young made two trips to China to research the costumes, traditions, and locales where Yeh-Shen's story originated for his elegant watercolors.

Lum, Darrell. 1994. *The Golden Slipper: A Vietnamese Legend*. Illus. by Makiko Nagano. New York: Toll Associates.

A simple, yet effective retelling of the story of the sweet, kind, and selfless Tam, who is tricked and mistreated by her stepmother and stepsister Cam. Animal characters figure strongly into this Vietnamese "Cinderella" fairy tale. Colorful illustrations featuring Asian motifs enhance the story's presentation.

Martin, Rafe. 1992. *The Rough-Face Girl*. Illus. by David Shannon. New York: G. P. Putnam's Sons.

Martin eloquently retells an Algonquian version of the "Cinderella" story. Shannon's rich paintings evoke the ethereal quality of this story. Critical thinking can be enhanced when children compare the Martin and Shannon work with Robert D. and Daniel San Souci's *Sootface: An Ojibwa Cinderella Story*.

Mayer, Marianna. 1994. *Baba Yaga and Vasilisa the Brave.* Illus. by K. Y. Craft. New York: Morrow Books.
Mayer's storytelling and Craft's luminous paintings beautifully reveal a Russian tale with many "Cinderella" parallels. Vasilisa's story is a more complex tale filled with a greater diversity of characters. Moreover, the story features a witch, Baba Yaga, whom Vasilisa must confront rather than a fairy godmother.

Onyefulu, Obi. 1994. *Chinye: A West African Folk Tale.* Illus. by Evie Safarewicz. New York: Viking.
Guided by an antelope, a hyena, and a mysterious old woman, Chinye's bravery and respectfulness are honored, just as her jealous stepmother, Nkechi, and stepsister, Adanma, are punished and driven off by the same forces. The story remarkably parallels the African American tale of the South, *The Talking Eggs,* by Robert D. San Souci.

Perrault, Charles. 1983. *Cinderella.* Illus. by Roberto Innocenti. Mankato, MN: Creative Education.
Innocenti's luminous paintings accompany Perrault's tale. The fairy tale is given an Edwardian setting in this interesting version.

———. 1985. *Cinderella.* Retold by Amy Erlich. Illus. by Susan Jeffers. New York: Dial Books.
The true magic of fairy tales is captured in Erlich's retelling of the classic French folktale and Jeffers's magnificent colored drawings. The tale is abridged considerably for this picture-book retelling.

———. 1994. *Cinderella.* Retold by Christine San Jose. Illus. by Debrah Santini. Honesdale, PA: Boyds Mill Press.
An outstanding contemporary storyteller weaves magic with Perrault's classic tale of envy and maltreatment. She sets the retelling in Manhattan, circa 1900. The atmosphere of splendor and opulence in New York society nearly a century past is captured in Santini's lustrous watercolor illustrations.

Pollock, Penny. 1996. *The Turkey Girl: A Zuni Cinderella Story.* Illus. by Ed Young. Boston: Little, Brown.
A Native American version of "Cinderella". The story concludes sadly when Turkey Girl takes for granted the great gift that has been given to her. The Zuni moral is clear: Do not abuse the gifts and resources of the Earth.

San Souci, Robert D. 1989. *The Talking Eggs.* Illus. by Jerry Pinkney. New York: Dial Books.
The Talking Eggs has its American origins as a Creole folktale. Although there are no princelike character, ball, or slipper elements in the tale, the story of Blanche's maltreatment and eventual triumph is similar to many "Cinderella" stories. It is remarkably like Obi Onyefulu's *Chinye: A West African Folk Tale.*

———. 1994. *Sootface: An Ojibwa Cinderella Story.* Illus. by Daniel San Souci. New York: Doubleday.
Exquisite illustrations capture the spirit of an Ojibwa community in the eighteenth century, which is the dramatic background for this Native American

"Cinderella" story of a mistreated young woman. See Rafe Martin's *The Rough-Face Girl* for comparison.

Sierra, Judy. 1992. *The Oryx Multicultural Folktale Series: Cinderella*. Illus. by Joanne Caroselli. Phoenix, AZ: Oryx Press.
This is a wonderful resource for examining many variants of the basic "Cinderella" fairy tale. Sierra retells 24 versions of the tale from such diverse parts of the world as Egypt, France, Ireland, Russia, India, Africa, Iraq, the Philippines, and the American Southwest. The retellings are brief enough to be easily read aloud to classes. Excellent source materials and suggested activities are also included.

Steel, Flora Annie. 1976. *Tattercoats: An Old English Tale*. Illus. by Diane Goode. Scarsdale, NY: Bradbury Press.
There is no evil stepmother or jealous stepsisters in this old English tale beautifully rendered with Goode's exquisite watercolor-on-parchment illustrations. In this fairy tale the negative character is the natural-born grandfather, who blames the loss of his beloved daughter in childbirth on the daughter's infant. He refuses to name the infant and vows never to set eyes upon the child. The girl child grows up with no love and is reduced to wearing clothes fashioned of tatters of cloth even the poor have discarded—hence, her name. The magic is provided by a gooseherd who helps the prince of the kingdom by the sea fall in love with Tattercoats and turns her tatters into a beautiful gown at the king's ball.

Steptoe, John. 1987. *Mufaro's Beautiful Daughters: An African Tale*. New York: Lothrop, Lee & Shepard.
This magnificently illustrated African story with its many parallels to the hundreds of "Cinderella" stories worldwide richly deserved being selected as a Caldecott Honor Book. One delightful sidelight recently reported at a teachers' conference: A third-grade teacher smiled when one of her students asked if she could borrow the book the teacher had read to the class about "Mia Farrow's daughter."

Vuong, Lynette Dyer. 1982. *The Brocaded Slipper and Other Vietnamese Tales*. Illustrated by Vo-Dinh Mai. New York: J. B. Lippincott.
The author retells a Vietnamese story of a mistreated stepdaughter, Tam, whose slipper is found by a prince, an event that ultimately leads to a great love. The Vietnamese tale of Tam contains many more pivotal animal characters and a more complicated plot than most European "Cinderella" stories. Other tales in the collection introduce characters who are similar to such European characters as Thumbelina and the Frog Prince.

Wegman, William. 1993. *Fay's Fairy Tales: Cinderella*. New York: Hyperion.
Wegman skillfully and quite incredibly uses his three weimaraners in a dazzling and creative photographic re-creation of the classic fairy tale. Readers of all ages will wonder what magic Wegman used to requisition the three dogs to pose in such realistic stances. Since the telling is faithful to the original Perrault tale and is clearly not intended to be a parody, it is included here with other straightforward retellings.

Winthrop, Elizabeth. 1991. *Vasilissa the Beautiful*. Illus. by Alexander Koshkin. New York: HarperCollins.

An American writer and a Russian artist collaborate to bring forth a rich re-creation of a "Cinderella" story from Russia. A poor girl, left behind by a loving father, is subsequently abused by a cruel stepmother and jealous stepsisters. Instead of being rescued by a benevolent fairy godmother, Vasilissa must outwit a fierce witch to be triumphant.

Variations and Other Treatments

Because "Cinderella" is so well known around the world, it is not especially surprising that a large number of parodies, variations, and other treatments exist in children's literature. Several comic versions substitute a male hero in the Cinderella role. Some writers update the tale to the present time, substitute male heroes, or use unlikely animals as characters, such as Janet Perlman does in *Cinderella Penguin*. Other writers, such as Caralyn Buehner, muse about what happens when Perrault's fairy godmother does not magically appear before Cinderella on the night of the prince's ball. Yet other writers look beyond the classic story and tell it from the point of view of other characters, especially the stepsisters. The following titles are recommended.

Baehr, Patricia. 1995. *The Search for Happily-Ever-After*. Illus. by Randel J. Chavez. BridgeWater Books.

In this highly original chapter book treatment for intermediate readers, Ketti, a middle child, feels mistreated and unappreciated in her family. In this fantasy, she meets a talking rat who was the coachman in Perrault's "Cinderella." He promises her a "happily ever after" existence if she will accompany him on his quest to become a man rather than a rat. On their journey, Ketti and the rat meet Hansel and Gretel, Briar Rose, and Cinderella. From each of them, Ketti learns new lessons about life. She comes to understand that everyone is special in his or her own right. The chapters make good read-aloud passages for upper-elementary and middle-school language-arts classes. Gifted children who often appear to have a special liking for fantasy will enjoy the book and may be motivated to use its literary conceit in their own fashion.

Buehner, Caralyn. 1996. *Fanny's Dream*. Illus. by Mark Buehner. New York: Dial Books.

This picture-book variation on the "Cinderella" theme is one of the sweetest stories to come along is a long time. It was a 1996 *Boston Globe*-Horn Book honor book in the picture-book category. Fanny is a frumpy, overweight farm girl on the Western frontier. She dreams of marrying a prince, particularly the son of the mayor of her wild Wyoming town. Girlfriends and her brother scoff at her dreams, yet she persists. She summons her fairy godmother, but only Heber Jensen, who is terribly short, answers her call. Fanny reluctantly accepts Heber's proposal and moves on with her life, building a home and family with Heber. Several years later, Fanny's fairy godmother appears—ridiculously late. Fanny now has three children. The charming ending of this tale is as

sweet as its telling. Buehner's inspired and clever illustrations are reminiscent of Chris Van Allsburg's wonderful picture book, *The Polar Express*.

Cole, Babette. 1987. *Prince Cinders*. New York: G. P. Putnam.
Cole combines wit and charm to retell the "Cinderella" story with a young man, Prince Cinders, as the hero. The prince is at the mercy of his three big, hairy brothers who party all night long, leaving him home to clean up after them. Children will love the hapless fairy princess's many miscues while attempting to turn Prince Cinders into a winner. Cole's book is designed to produce giggles, and it succeeds. See also the video version.

Graham, Amanda. 1992. *Cinderella/Alex and the Glass Slipper*. Mission Hills, CA: Australian Press.
Graham tells the traditional story, which reaches its happy ending at the halfway point of the book. Then children turn the book over, and, presto, they start reading the book from the opposite direction and discover a new story, "Alex and the Glass Slipper." Alex is a kitchen hand at the Flinders' Cellar restaurant, where he is at the mercy of two lazy chefs who claim all of Alex's great recipes as their own. Alex's story produces unpredictable twists and turns that make it fresh and witty to read. The bold color illustrations are delightful. Note: This title is produced in Australia; it is available in the United States from Australian Press, 15235 Brand Blvd. #A107, Mission Hills, CA 91345.

Granowsky, Alvin. 1993. *Cinderella/That Awful Cinderella*. Illus. by Barbara Kiwak and Rhonda Childress. Austin, TX: Steck-Vaughn.
The classic story of "Cinderella" *and* the stepsisters' side of the story are told in these two versions—both packed in the same volume.

Jackson, Ellen. 1994. *Cinder Edna*. Illus. by Kevin O'Malley. New York: Lothrop, Lee & Shepard.
In Jackson's deft hands, the traditional telling of "Cinderella" takes on a fun, contemporary twist. Here is the story of Cinder Edna, Cinderella's neighbor, who also had to do lots of dirty housework. Cinder Edna, however, uses her own imagination and grit to solve her problems. She takes the city bus—not a magic carriage—to the royal ball. There she meets the prince's hip, younger brother, Rupert. O'Malley's humorous paintings perfectly complement Jackson's playful text.

Minters, Frances. 1994. *Cinder-Elly*. Illus. by G. Brian Karas. New York: Viking.
In this funny and contemporary retelling of Cinderella's story, the setting is New York City, Prince Charming is a basketball player, and Cinder-Elly's fairy godmother is a bag lady who provides the heroine with a new bike and glass sneakers. Karas cites MTV as one of the sources of inspiration for his brilliantly colored contemporary illustrations. The narration is in raplike verse. The collaborators have followed up this effort with *Sleepless Beauty* (Viking, 1996) also set in present-day New York City.

Morris, Ann. 1989. *The Cinderella Rebus Book*. Illus. by Ljiljana Rylands. New York: Orchard.
Here is an interesting twist. Rebus word-picture pages are used to tell "Cinderella" in a fresh way that will delight children who love solving puzzles. A rebus dictionary is included at the end of the book. The author-illustrator team have also collaborated on *The Little Red Riding Hood Rebus Book* (Orchard, 1987).

Myers, Bernice. 1985. *Sidney Rella and the Glass Sneaker*. New York: Macmillan.
Boys and girls will love this retelling, which finds a young boy left home to clean the family garage while his big brothers go off to achieve football glory for their town. Surprise! The town finds a new hero, one who appears mysteriously wearing glass sneakers.

Perlman, Janet. 1992. *Cinderella Penguin, or, The Little Glass Flipper*. New York: Viking.
"Cinderella" is given a delightful anthropomorphic turn in Perlman's version, which features penguins. If children enjoy this retelling, they may want to check out the author-illustrator's joyful interpretation of the *Emperor Penguin's New Clothes* (Viking, 1994), which also utilizes penguin characters.

Shorto, Russell. 1990. *Cinderella/Cinderella: The Untold Story*. Illus. by T. Lewis. New York: Birch Lane.
Shorto writes a colorful and humorous double telling of "Cinderella." The latter of the two stories presents the point of view of the much-maligned stepsisters and stepmother. Lewis's illustrations are appropriately eye-popping.

Yorinks, Arthur. 1990. *Ugh*. Illus. by Richard Egielski. New York: Farrar, Straus & Giroux.
In this hilarious send-up of "Cinderella," Ugh, the hero, is a cave boy much put upon by his loutish brothers and sisters. While they have fun watching dinosaurs eat trees, Ugh is left behind to wash clothes, find food, and clean the cave. An ingenious lad, Ugh invents the bicycle. When the leaders of the tribe decide that the inventor of this miraculous object should be the next king, Ugh's brothers and sisters claim ownership. But Ugh is the only one capable of riding the bicycle, and he becomes the new boy king. Young children may well miss the parody, but upper-elementary and middle-grade students will delight in both the language construction and Egielski's clever pictures in this Stone Age "Cinderella" story.

Stepmothers and Stepsisters

First and foremost, "Cinderella" is not a fairy tale about all stepmothers being evil. It is a story of envy and deceitfulness. Many of the "Cinderella" variants from cultures around the world such as Rafe Martin's *The Rough-Face Girl* feature no stepmother character. Hence, it is a mistake to paint "Cinderella" as a tract against stepparents simply because the version most American children recognize—Charles Perrault's French "Cinderella"—features a particularly dreadful stepmother. Readers also need to take into account changes in language and the subtleties of language

translations. Marina Warner (1994) explains in her fine work, *From the Beast to the Blonde: On Fairy Tales and Their Tellers*, that until at least the middle of the nineteenth century the terms *mother-in-law* and *stepmother* were used interchangeably in England. Hence, a daughter-in-law would have been referred to as a stepdaughter. At least one English translation of Perrault's fairy tale refers to Cinderella's stepmother as her mother-in-law. Teachers and parents should also note such books as Alvin Granowsky's *That Awful Cinderella*, which provides the "other side of the story"; that is, the stepsisters' voices are heard. Wise educators will want to share many versions of the "Cinderella" story, including those devoid of stereotypes. Equally well, they can share with impressionable youngsters some wonderful books about good stepmothers. The following are noteworthy in their portrayals of exemplary stepmothers.

Day, Nancy Raines. 1995. *The Lion's Whiskers: An Ethiopian Folktale*. Illus. by Ann Grifalconi. New York: Scholastic.
  Stunning collage art and rich text combine magically in this book to tell the story of a brave, courageous, and loving stepmother.

Hoffman, Mary. 1995. *Boundless Grace*. Illus. by Caroline Binch. New York: Dial Books for Young Readers.
  In this wonderful sequel to the awarding-winning *Amazing Grace*, the heroine visits her father in Gambia in Africa. She is wary of her new stepmother, stepbrother, and stepsister. The fairy tales she has loved as a child have portrayed stepmothers and stepsisters negatively. In this beautiful book, Grace comes to love and value her larger family and realizes the errors of stereotypes and their perpetuation.

Leach, Norman. 1993. *My Wicked Stepmother*. Illus. by Jane Browne. New York: Macmillan.
  Tom is happy with his life with his father until his "wicked stepmother" comes to live with them. The problem is that it becomes increasingly difficult for him to dislike his stepmother as she extends one act of love after another. The last line perfectly captures the charm of this wonderful picture storybook: "I used to have a wicked stepmother but I kissed her, and now she's turned into a fairy godmother." Leach's wonderful story is complemented by Browne's simple, charming illustrations.

Rudolph, Marguerita. 1992. *The Good Stepmother*. Illus. by Darcy Day. New York: Simon & Schuster.
  This is a must book to share with young children to accompany many readings of "Cinderella." It beautifully breaks down stereotypes about stepmothers. The special relationship and bond between father and child is also a plus, as are Day's beautiful, magical paintings.

Videocassettes

Cinderella's story has been told in many formats and media. Rossini created the opera *La Cenerentola*, and Prokofiev composed music for the ballet *Cinderella*. It is not surprising that the fairy tale has been filmed many times. The following five video treatments are worth viewing and sharing with various ages of students.

Ashpet. Tom Davenport, director. Delaplane, VA: Davenport Films. 1989. 45 minutes. Videocassette.

Ashpet is a clever and witty cinema treatment of Perrault's "Cinderella." This time the story is set in the American South in the early years of the Second World War. Lily is the real name of Ashpet, who is bedeviled by two stepsisters who are deliciously dreadful characters. Only the foolish and vain believe in real magic in this retelling. A wizened African American woman, Dark Sally, who had been Lily's mother's caregiver, is thought by the villainous sisters to have supernatural powers—especially in the making of love sachets designed to snag a husband—but she is really just a caring woman who deeply loves the kind and unjustly treated Lily. Filmed in rural Virginia, this live-action version has a wonderful 1940s feel to it, especially its period costumes, music, and house decor. Prince Charming is a handsome, young soldier who meets Lily on the eve of his departure for war. Through the film's final voice-over, supplied by the sagacious Dark Sally, the audience knows this particular prince will come home from the war safely and that he and Lily will live happily ever after. Eminently suitable for middle-school and secondary student audiences, though probably inappropriate for younger children. All will delight in both the film's humor and their own sly recognition of the similarities between the film counterparts and Perrault's more famous characters.

Cinderella. Walt Disney, producer; Wilfred Jackson, director. Burbank, CA: Walt Disney Home Video. 1995. 76 minutes. Videocassette.

Walt Disney's 1950 feature-length animation classic is without doubt the version of "Cinderella" with which most American children are familiar. Disney and his associates based the film animation upon Perrault's French fairy tale. Although this version is popularly criticized by children's literature specialists, it is purely magical for children, young and old. The drama, joy, and sense of wonder found in fairy tales is evident in every frame of the film. The Disney addition of the animal characters—especially Lucifer, the odious cat, and the delightful mice, valiantly led by Jaq and Gus—is wonderful. The animal characters add comic relief to the story line and serve as a sort of anthropomorphic Greek chorus in moving the story forward. Cinderella is spared the task of promoting herself; through lovely song, the mice and the birds reveal to the audience her basic goodness and kindness. The musical score does not have the blockbuster titles found in Disney's *Snow White and the Seven Dwarfs*. Still, it is music fit for a princess.

Cinderella. Shelley Duvall, producer; Derek Hayes, director. Faerie Tale Theatre Series. Livonia, MI: Playhouse Video. 1987. 53 minutes. Videocassette.

Jennifer Beals, Matthew Broderick, Jean Stapleton, and Eve Arden star in this Shelley Duvall-produced Faerie Tale Theatre presentation of Perrault's French "Cinderella." Humor laces a good deal of the fun in this lavishly costumed version. A special feature is the bonding relationship portrayed between Cinderella (Beals) and her fairy godmother (Stapleton). The role of the fairy godmother, deliciously played by Stapleton, adds a new dimension to this retelling. The fairy godmother becomes as much a friend and surrogate mother to Cinderella as the manufacturer of such miracles as transforming pumpkins into royal coaches and mice into great white horses.

Cinderella. Richard Rodgers, producer; Charles Dubin, director. Los Angeles, CA: Fox Video. 1991. 84 minutes. Videocassette.

The talents of Richard Rodgers and Oscar Hammerstein II are brought to bear on this live-action version of "Cinderella" created for television in 1964. Lesley Ann Warren stars and is ably supported by Celeste Holm, Ginger Rogers, and Stuart Damon. Songs by Rodgers and Hammerstein include "In My Own Little Corner of the World" and "Do I Love You Because You're Beautiful?"

Prince Cinders. Derek Hayes, director. New York: First Fun Features. 1995. 26 minutes. Videocassette.

Stuck at home and burdened with the work of his three big, hairy older brothers, Prince Cinders despairs that he cannot go to Princess Lovelypenny's big party. A fairy in training sends all awry when she turns the young hero into—literally—a big, hairy ape. The British accented voices may be difficult for some children to understand and the humor is most suited to middle schoolers, but all should enjoy this clever, animated version of Babette Cole's wacky *Prince Cinders.* The combination of pop music, lively animation, and British accents in the narration make this an instance of a multimedia package surpassing the original picture book in quality.

Happily Ever Afters

In addition to the activities already outlined in the chapter as extensions of sharing multiple-intelligences theory and practice with students through the lens of "Cinderella," the following explorations based upon the fairy tale may also whet the appetites of students for creative engagement.

Cinderella City Mall

Kids love shopping malls and fairy tales, so why not combine the two to produce creative group work for young learners? Ask cooperative learning groups to work together as problem-solving teams to conceive, design (draw a blueprint-type map), and build a scale model of the nation's first all-children's mall, Cinderella City. All the stores and activities and food venues should focus on the needs and likes of children, and the mall's theme should be based upon fairy tale titles, characters, and events. Teachers may suggest some possible stores to serve as catalysts for student thinking. Sample businesses may include Rapunzel's Hair Care, Prince Charming's Formal Wear, Little Red Riding Hood's Candy Basket, and Cinderella's Glass Slipper (a children's shoe store). Once students have brainstormed about all the stores they want to have in their children's mall, they can proceed to build a scale model of the mall and even plan a grand-opening celebration. For example, might there be a Midnight Madness sale at Cinderella's Glass Slipper as part of a grand opening?

If the Shoe Fits

One of the most common motifs found in "Cinderella" variants around the world is a slipper or shoe. Both the Egyptian "Rhodopis" story and the Chinese "Yeh-Shen" story involve slippers, and the dominant symbol found in Perrault's French "Cinderella" is the glass slipper. Also well-known is the proverb "If the shoe fits. . . ." Indeed, it is so well-known and understood that the last part of the sentence, ". . . wear it," is often left unspoken. Help students see the connection to "Cinderella." Find a variety of pictures of shoes, sandals, boots, and other footwear from a broad sampling of catalogs. Cut out the pictures and affix them to sturdy pieces of construction paper or bristol board. Draw a large question mark beside each example of footwear and place one or two blank lines beside or underneath each picture. Share the pictures with students, asking them to determine which personality from the vast pantheon of fairy tale characters belongs to each shoe. For example, what footwear might Jack have used for his three trips up the beanstalk? Does a Frog Prince need waders? Encourage students to further create a full-page advertisement for the shoe store Cinderella's Glass Slipper in the mall Cinderella City. The advertisement should display a minimum of three examples of footwear matched to three famous fairy tale characters.

A question to provoke creative thinking is: What might the prince do if the stepsisters shared the same shoe size as Cinderella?

Inventing a Solution

Imagine that Cinderella's fairy godmother is at home, sick with the flu. She just cannot get out of bed and come to the Cinderella's rescue. How might Cinderella combine the following items into an invention that will transport her to the ball? Students can add other items that might reasonably be at Cinderella's disposal.

1 large dog	1 blue satin pillow
1 yellow cat	1 rusty wheelbarrow
6 feet of clothesline	1 red scarf
5 gerbils	1 magazine (*Seventeen*)

Electronic Cinderella

Yes, Cinderella has come of age. Students and teachers with access to the Internet can surf the Net in search of variant "Cinderella" stories, locate copies of "Cinderella" books that are 200 years old, and find information about "Cinderella" themes published by online bookstore catalogs. Two cautions: The author's attempt to search the Internet resulted in learning about a Cinderella's Bridal Shop in Rhode Island; discovering the biographical details of members of a rock group that goes by the name Cinderella; and finding out about an educational foundation called the Cinderella Manifesto, which is a public charity to support educational efforts in Cameroon, West Africa. Also, an attempt to use the World Wide Web address for the Cinderella Project listed in a brand-new book about children's resources on the Internet was unsuccessful because the site was no longer active at the given address. However, persistence pays off. By using the World Wide Web browser Netscape Navigator 2.0 combined with the search tool Yahoo! and by doing a word search for *Cinderella*, a number of worthwhile options surfaced. The online text of a Scottish "Cinderella" story, "The Princess and the Golden Shoes," was accessible as was a lengthy and highly useful annotated bibliography of "Cinderella" stories from a children's multicultural bookstore in California. Some persistence and creative searching on the Internet may yield great discoveries.

Other Netscape Navigator search tools include Infoseek, Excite, and Magellan. As of the writing of this text, the following World Wide Web addresses were useful.

The Children's Literature Web Guide: http://www.ucalgary.ca/~dkbrown/

The Cinderella Project: http://www-dept.usm.edu/~engdept/cinderella/cinderella.html

A Cinderella Joke

Here is an end-of-chapter funny to share with students. What did Cinderella say to the clerk at the photo-processing store when he told her that the pictures she had expected on Monday still were not ready for pickup on Friday? Answer: "Someday my prints will come."

SUGGESTED READINGS

Multiple-Intelligences Resources

Many fine books about the application of MI theory in education have been published in the past several years. The following works have special merit. Two outstanding publishers of multiple-intelligences books and curriculum materials are IRI/Skylight Training and

Publishing, Inc. (200 East Wood Street, Suite 274, Palantine, IL 60067. Phone: 1-800-348-4474) and Zephyr Press (3316 North Chapel Avenue, P.O. Box 66006-C2, Tucson, AZ 85728-6006. Phone: 1-520-322-5090; Fax: 1-520-323-9402).

Armstrong, Thomas. 1993. *Multiple Intelligences in the Classroom.* Alexandria, VA: Association for Supervision and Curriculum Development.

Gardner, Howard. 1991. *Unschooled Mind: How Children Think and How Schools Should Teach.* New York: Basic Books.

———. 1995. *Leading Minds: An Anatomy of Leadership.* New York: Basic Books.

Lazear, David. 1991. *Seven Ways of Knowing: Understanding Multiple Intelligences.* Palantine, IL: Skylight Publishing.

———. 1991. *Seven Ways of Teaching: The Artistry of Teaching with Multiple Intelligences.* Palantine, IL: Skylight Publishing.

Marks-Tarlow, Terry. 1996. *Creativity Inside Out: Learning Through Multiple Intelligences.* Menlo Park, CA: Addison-Wesley.

REFERENCES

Climo, Shirley. 1989. *The Egyptian Cinderella.* New York: HarperCollins.

Flack, Jerry D. 1993. Putting Faces with Multiple Intelligences. *THINK 4* (1): 12-15.

Gardner, H. 1983. *Frames of Mind: The Theory of Multiple Intelligences.* New York: Basic Books.

———. 1993a. *Creating Minds: An Anatomy of Creativity Seen Through the Lives of Freud, Einstein, Picasso, Stravinsky, Eliot, Graham, and Gandhi.* New York: Basic Books.

———. 1993b. *Frames of Mind: The Theory of Multiple Intelligences.* 10th anniversary ed. New York: Basic Books.

———. 1993c. *Multiple Intelligences: The Theory in Practice.* New York: Basic Books.

———. 1995a. Reflecting on Multiple Intelligences: Myths and Messages. *Phi Delta Kappan.* 77 (3): 200-209.

———. 1995b. *Leading Minds: An Anatomy of Leadership.* New York: Basic Books.

Louie, Ai-Ling. 1982. *Yeh-Shen: A Cinderella Story from China.* New York: Philomel.

Sierra, Judy. 1992. *The Oryx Multicultural Folktale Series: Cinderella.* Phoenix, AZ: Oryx.

Warner, Marina. 1994. *From the Beast to the Blonde: On Fairy Tales and Their Tellers.* New York: Farrar, Straus & Giroux.

Chapter *2*

Jack Meets Messieurs Bloom, Maslow, and Kohlberg

CHAPTER PREVIEW

In this chapter an old friend from England, Jack of "Jack and the Beanstalk," meets a dynamic model for curriculum construction, Bloom's Taxonomy. Questioning strategies, especially those emphasizing critical thinking, are also accented. The basic values found in such fairy tales as "Jack and the Beanstalk" receive attention, especially as viewed through the lenses of motivation, needs, and moral development theories. Finally, Happily Ever After activities and several worthy versions of "Jack and the Beanstalk" are recommended.

BLOOM'S TAXONOMY

The taxonomy of cognitive objectives commonly referred to as Bloom's Taxonomy may been seen as "old hat" by some educators, but it remains in this writer's view the single most effective and easily used strategy at the disposal of educators to help students of all ages build strong knowledge structures and develop process skills that enable them to continuously access, add to, and evaluate information bases. One of the best avenues for developing critical-thinking skills is the path of questioning, and Bloom's Taxonomy is especially effectual when used in conjunction with inquiry teaching and problem-based learning. Students who become effective in answering questions and asking questions have greater opportunities to construct meaningful learning and to transfer learning from existing situations to new circumstances.

One of the greatest virtues of Bloom's Taxonomy is its simplicity. The model is uncomplicated and easily comprehended. Even primary-age students can understand the hows and whys of learning and can apply the taxonomy's basic principles to their own constructive learning. To be sure, there are models of curriculum design and construction that are far more complicated than Bloom's Taxonomy. But, a legitimate question is, Why bother? Educators should not be so dazzled by curriculum models that they lose sight of the reality that models are only a means to an end. The end is student learning of content and processes. Teachers want students to learn history, effectively conduct research, and be able to perform mathematical operations. Curriculum models can be helpful to these ends, but they are useful only to the degree that they facilitate the learning of the core curriculum. As with other process strategies explored in this book, Bloom's Taxonomy can be easily and effectively taught to children and adolescents through the vehicle of fairy tales. In this chapter, the fairy tale used is the classic English story of "Jack and the Beanstalk."

The taxonomic hierarchy that has come to be known as Bloom's Taxonomy is the result of a meeting of college examiners attending an American Psychological Association convention in Boston in 1948. Initially, the college examiners never intended that their work should become widely used in instructional planning. Rather, they were concerned about developing a uniform set of standards and terminology that would allow for more effective communication of learning goals and objectives of professionals across virtually all fields. They sought a means of exchanging ideas and materials without succumbing to the use of nebulous terminology that made clarity of meaning among experts like themselves difficult to achieve. What, for example, did teachers and scholars mean when they said they wanted their students to "comprehend," to "really understand," or to "grasp the meaning of" core knowledge and processes in their respective disciplines?

The college examiners, lead by Benjamin Bloom of the University of Chicago as editor, elected to design a taxonomy that was in many ways analogous to the taxonomies of the biological world that allow biologists, for example, to classify all living matter into the categories of kingdom, phylum, class, order, family, genus, and species. The creators of the taxonomy did intend the six levels to be viewed as a hierarchy. That is, application builds upon and presumes student knowledge and comprehension of relevant content and skills. Evaluation is a cognitive process that evolves from all that has gone before in the way of synthesis, analysis, application, comprehension, and acquisition of knowledge. Eventually, the taxonomy designers and others who followed them perceived that such taxonomies could be beneficial in helping educators and students build curricula with a variety of intended cognitive, affective, and psychomotor outcomes. *Cognitive* is understood to include such mental activities as remembering knowledge, thinking critically, solving problems, and creating information. After many informal meetings, the hierarchical taxonomy of educational objectives for the cognitive domain was published as a handbook by Longman, Green and Company in the early 1950s (Bloom 1977). Subsequent handbooks for the Affective and Psychomotor domains were also published (Krathwohl 1964; Harrow 1972).

Figure 2.1 lists the six hierarchical levels of Bloom's Taxonomy with representative action verbs. These action verbs prove extremely handy to teachers who want to stretch and develop the thinking skills and behaviors of their students. The action verbs can be used in at least two ways. They may be used in the stems of questions teachers ask and teach their students to ask. The terms may also be used in prompts teachers give to students to provoke both higher levels of thinking and greater sophistication in the products and projects they create.

Fig. 2.1 Bloom's Taxonomy of Educational Objectives: Cognitive Domain

Knowledge	**Comprehension**	**Application**
Cite	Discuss	Apply
Define	Estimate	Complete
Describe	Explain	Demonstrate
Identify	Generalize	Dramatize
Label	Infer	Draw
List	Locate	Illustrate
Match	Predict	Operate
Memorize	Report	Practice
Name	Review	Relate
Recall	Summarize	Show
Repeat	Translate	Solve
Analysis	**Synthesis**	**Evaluation**
Analyze	Compose	Appraise
Categorize	Construct	Assess
Classify	Create	Compare
Contrast	Design	Conclude
Diagram	Fashion	Decide
Differentiate	Hypothesize	Determine
Dissect	Imagine	Evaluate
Experiment	Plan	Judge
Inspect	Propose	Rate
Interpret	Redesign	Select
Solve	Translate	Verify

Many teachers have discovered that Bloom's Taxonomy is a good "trade secret" to share with students. It is not unusual to walk into an elementary classroom and see a colorful wall chart or poster that lists the six steps to powerful thinking and sample process verbs from each step. Students familiar with Bloom's Taxonomy recognize that they can structure their own learning to acquire, apply, and analyze information and ultimately create new information.

One especially effective way to introduce Bloom's Taxonomy and its operations to students is through the use of fairy tales. Again, something new—in this case a set of cognitive objectives and processes—is explained to students using familiar fairy tale content. "Jack and the Beanstalk" is highlighted in figure 2.2 to illustrate to students how Bloom's Taxonomy can contribute to their greater understanding. These prompts are written directly for immediate student use. To prepare these lessons for students, copy activities onto individual task cards to be handed out for student use. Figure 2.3a shows task cards using examples from figure 2.2. Figure 2.3b is blank task cards that can be copied for classroom use.

Fig. 2.2 Bloom's Taxonomy Applied to "Jack and the Beanstalk"

Knowledge

Name three important characters in "Jack and the Beanstalk."

List these four objects in the sequence in which they appear in the story, first to last.

      bags of gold   golden harp   magic hen   magic beans

Recall the number of times Jack climbs the magic beanstalk.

Repeat the ogre's (or giant's) famous four-line speech indicating that he senses Jack's presence in his castle. It begins "Fee-Fi- . . ."

Name the cow that Jack is to sell in the story. (Traditionally, the name is Milky-White.)

Describe the physical attributes of the giant.

Comprehension

Explain how Jack returns home from market with five magic beans.

Summarize the story in no more than five statements.

Discuss Jack's reasons for climbing the beanstalk more than once.

Application

Draw a picture of what you think Jack's cottage looked liked from the top of the beanstalk.

Illustrate in cartoon fashion the sequence of events that occur on Jack's first trip up the beanstalk.

Paint a scene of a room in the giant's castle (especially one not shown in a book).

Dramatize a scene between any two characters who are found in "Jack and the Beanstalk."

Practice a puppet-show version of "Jack and the Beanstalk."

Complete a poster the ogre might make to warn English boys to stay off his property.

Analysis

Analyze the enduring popularity of "Jack and the Beanstalk." What characteristics or elements contribute to its appeal?

Differentiate between "Jack and the Beanstalk" and another popular English fairy tale, such as "Goldilocks and the Three Bears." In what ways are they similar? In what ways do they differ?

Contrast the opinions Jack's mother has of her son before and after he climbs the beanstalk.

Synthesis

Translate the essential characters and plot ingredients in "Jack and the Beanstalk" into a board game.

Imagine a sequel to the traditional story of "Jack and the Beanstalk" in which listeners or readers learn what became of Milky-White and the old man who traded Jack five beans for her.

Propose a solution for Jack and his mother. What are they to do with the giant's remains in their backyard?

Hypothesize what life in the future will be like for Jack and his mother now that they have not just sustenance but wealth.

Evaluation

Rate "Jack and the Beanstalk" against several other classic fairy tales, such as "Little Red Riding Hood" and "Sleeping Beauty." How does it stack up? What criteria may be used to compare various fairy tales?

Judge the effectiveness of the ending of "Jack and the Beanstalk." Is the ogre's (or giant's) demise the best way to conclude the tale? What are some other alternative endings?

Decide if the portrayal of Jack's mother is fair. What reasoning is there to support the conclusion?

Produce a mock television news program in which a variety of professional experts, including a sociologist and a public prosecutor, *evaluate* the ethics and morality of Jack's behavior in "Jack and the Beanstalk."

Fig. 23a. Sample Task Cards

Recall the number of times Jack climbs the magic beanstalk.

Complete a poster the ogre might make to warn English boys to stay off his property.

Fig. 23b. Blank Task Cards

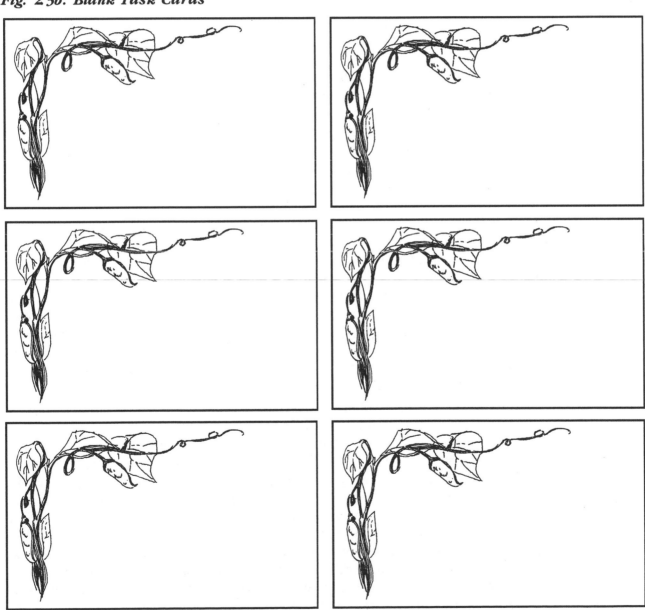

BLOOM'S TAXONOMY AND CRITICAL-THINKING SKILLS

Questioning Strategies

Good teaching involves the skillful use of questions. But teachers' questions should be designed to help move students to ever more powerful levels of cognition—in short, to become good critical thinkers. It should be evident that Bloom's Taxonomy is an especially effective tool teachers can use to accomplish that result. Questions that use Bloom's Taxonomy as a guide move from basic knowledge and comprehension queries about the content of "Jack and the Beanstalk" to investigations concerned with the structure and meaning of fairy tales. Knowledge and comprehension questions are excellent for checking basic student learning, but analysis and evaluation questions provide students with opportunities to use what they have learned to further extend their knowledge and understanding of the world.

Wise teachers may have already noted that they may actually save time when they use questions across the spectrum of Bloom's Taxonomy. Analytical, synthetic, and evaluative questions require more critical thinking on the part of students, require greater answering time, and provoke more discussions. Consequently, teachers can reduce the number of questions they need to create for any given lesson or unit. From a literacy standpoint, the use of Bloom's Taxonomy allows reading teachers to pose literal, inferential, and application questions to best gauge students' comprehension of text.

Consider "Jack and the Beanstalk" again. Teachers can begin with a literal text question, such as How many times does Jack climb the beanstalk? Skilled teachers, however, will approach a discussion of the tale from a more inferentially based question: Why do you suppose storytellers have Jack climb the beanstalk three times? This question asks for a much more sophisticated level of thinking and responding. Questions of application and synthesis, which vault beyond the text, may also be used in reading discussions. An application question might query students with regard to alternative actions that Jack might have taken. For example, Can you imagine another way that Jack might have kept the giant from climbing down the beanstalk?

Incidentally, teachers need to realize that when they move from knowledge levels of questions to more inferential and sophisticated levels of inquiry, they need to allow students adequate time to respond. Mary Budd Rowe's research relative to this point should be familiar to every educator. She found that the average "wait time" that guides teacher behavior is one second or less. That is, teachers allow one second or less to pass after they have posed a question before they rephrase the question, provide an answer, go to another student for a response, or take some other mediating action. Rowe's subsequent research has demonstrated that when teachers increase the average length of wait time to as few as three seconds, dramatic shifts in student behavior and achievement occur. The length of student responses improves between 300 percent and 700 percent. The incidence of speculative reasoning increases. Students' responses reflect more inferential thinking, and more inferences are supported by evidence. The number of student questions and student-proposed experiments increases. Failures to respond decrease. Disciplinary moves decrease, and student self-confidence improves. Student-to-student exchanges also increase. Rather impressive results considering the small investment of time—three seconds—required! (Rowe 1986, 43-44)

Perhaps the best strategy educators can learn is how to teach their students to become good questioners themselves and how to encourage all students to ask questions often. Train children how to ask questions that help them focus on what they want to learn, what they need to know, and how they can access information to fulfill their learning needs. Many basic questioning strategies can be easily implemented. Place one or more items found in or associated with fairy tales in a box, close the box, and wrap it in colorful wrapping paper. Show the box to students, and encourage them to shake it, feel its weight, and attempt to discern what the box contains by asking questions. Tell students that you will only answer yes or no, so their questions must be phrased accordingly. On the first try, place five dry beans in the box. Students ask questions until such time as they discover the box's contents.

The old parlor game of "20 Questions" can also be given a fairy tale twist. The teacher tells students she is thinking of something or someone from a fairy tale. They have up to 20 questions or chances to discover the subject matter. Again, questions must be phrased for yes and no answers. In this instance, the students have only 20 questions to use in the inquiry, so they cannot simply ask questions randomly. They have to develop questioning strategies that limit the possibilities. They might begin with this question: Is it a living thing such as a plant or animal? One technique that works well with "20 Questions" is to place the numbers 1 through 20 on the chalkboard, and log a keyword from each question that is asked. Later, when students have guessed correctly, they use the keywords as memory joggers to analyze which questions or kinds of questions provided useful answers. The game is a great time filler at the end of a class period while students are putting away materials, and its frequent use develops in students enhanced skills of questioning. A Colorado Springs, Colorado, middle-school teacher uses yet another strategy with all her classes. She challenges her students to develop an effective question-asking attitude by telling them often, "I will always answer your questions truthfully, but I will not tell you what you do not ask." Once students realize the import of her inquiry model approach, they quickly learn to hone their questioning strategies.

Creative Questions

Teachers who want to develop the creativity of their students also infuse some creative-questioning strategies into their teaching practices. While convergent-thinking questions require one correct answer, creative questions accentuate divergent thinking. A sample convergent question is, What does Jack's mother do with the magic beans when he first brings them home from market? Divergent-thinking questions anticipate a variety of answers, all of which are correct. What-if questions represent one type of creative questioning. They provoke myriad responses, all of which

are correct. Sample divergent questions from "Jack and the Beanstalk" are: What if Jack's mother had cooked the beans? What might the result(s) have been? What if Jack had told the giant of his and his mother's sad plight on his first trip up the beanstalk? What if Jack had traded Milky-White for carrot seeds instead of beans? What if the ax had not been handy?

Of course, good what-if inquiries do not have to stop with Jack's story. Here are additional sample probes that can awaken the creative thinking of students.

What if Cinderella's stepsisters happen to have the same shoe size that she does?

What if Goldilocks had a twin brother who went with her into the forest?

Creative questions are great for roll taking. Teachers may take roll by asking students questions such as Which would you rather be: Jack and the Beanstalk or Prince Charming; Cinderella or Little Red Riding Hood? Which would you rather have: a singing harp or a sack of gold? Which fairy tale character would you most like to meet: Cinderella, Rapunzel, or Sleeping Beauty? Whom would you most like to attend your birthday party: Goldilocks, Rapunzel, the Three Little Pigs, or the Frog Prince?

Creative questions can also be used to provoke thinking about the very essence of fairy tales. What do Hansel and Gretel and Puss in Boots have in common? How is a glass slipper like a golden ball? Which is deeper: Beast's loneliness or Rapunzel's isolation?

As with critical-thinking questions, creative-thinking questions do not always have to originate with the teacher. Once classroom teachers have used several creative questions with their students, the students will quickly perceive how to make up their own imaginative questions to ask peers. In creative classrooms there is always a Royal Questioner of the Realm. The Royal Questioner of the Realm is responsible for creating super what-if and other creative questions for the week. Be sure the royal office changes hands often so that all students have the opportunity to activate their creative and inventive thinking skills.

Both critical-thinking and creative-thinking questions can stimulate the imaginations of students. Questions cost nothing but yield wonderful and powerful returns in the development of talent and thinking skills.

FURTHER EXPLORATIONS OF CRITICAL THINKING

Maslow: Motivation and Needs

As stated earlier in the chapter, questioning strategies used with fairy tale literature can move well beyond the text to a consideration of profound issues, an examination of values, and considerations of morality. While the great fairy tales entertain, many communicate messages that have rich textures and many levels of meaning. They may be interpreted as simple stories to entertain or as cautionary tales, such as "Little Red Riding Hood," which carry a clear message: Do what your parents tell you to do, or you will get into big trouble. Perhaps the foremost interpreter of fairy tales in the twentieth century has been Bruno Bettelheim. In *The Uses of Enchantment: The Meaning and Importance of Fairy Tales*, Bettelheim (1975) explores the symbolism and psychological implications found in such tales as "Little Red Riding Hood," "Cinderella," "Sleeping Beauty," and "Jack and the Beanstalk." Because of the sexual discussions and interpretations found in much of Bettelheim's work, many teachers understandably shy away from pursuing the lines of inquiry he raises. His interpretations of fairy tales are probably most appropriate for adult-level discussions. Even so, teachers may find a reading of his work stimulating and his interpretations thought provoking.

Teachers with kindergarten through 12th-grade students are on far safer ground in critical-thinking explorations of fairy tales through the investigation and application of the work of other observers of human behavior. One of the foremost psychologists of the twentieth century is Abraham Maslow, whose work on motivation is particularly well known. In *Motivation and Personality* (Maslow 1970), he postulates that humans have a hierarchy of needs that range from basic survival needs to the need for personal fulfillment, or what he terms self-actualization. Maslow specifies seven levels of needs that humans have: physiological needs, safety needs, belonging and love needs, self-esteem needs, intellectual needs, aesthetic needs, and the need for self-actualization. He represents this hierarchy of needs in the form of a pyramid, with the base of the pyramid being the most basic and fundamental physiological needs, such as the necessity for food, water, and shelter. The apex of Maslow's pyramid of needs is the need for self-actualization or personal fulfillment.[1]

Maslow categorizes the seven needs he articulates into two broad groups: deficiency needs and being (or growth) needs. Moreover, he postulates that motivation is highly correlated with the fulfillment of deficiency and being needs. People are first motivated to fulfill needs for physical survival, safety, feelings of belonging, and self-esteem. Only when those needs are met are people motivated to fulfill intellectual and aesthetic needs and the desire for self-actualization. It is not difficult for students to comprehend Maslow's theory in operation. Homeless, hungry people, the children of war, and others who are deprived of the requisites of physical survival and safety are not likely to be highly motivated to study philosophy or devote much time to a consideration of long-term life goals.

Maslow's hierarchy of needs is a theory and not fact. Obviously, any theory has detractors and nonbelievers. Maslow represents the humanistic school of psychology, which in itself is a red flag for some parents and groups. It is certainly not the purpose of this text to suggest that teachers engage in indoctrination or preach "secular humanism" to impressionable students. Quite the contrary. Rather, the description of Maslow's theories about motivation and needs is shared here because the subject appears tailor-made for the incisive reading of and critical thinking about the plot and characters found in "Jack and the Beanstalk."

---

1. Abraham Maslow, *Motivation and Personality*. 2d edition (New York: Harper & Row, 1970). A discussion of Maslow's hierarchy of needs and motivation can be found in virtually any textbook survey of psychology or educational psychology. One fine example, complete with needs represented in pyramidal graphic format, may be found in Anita Woolfolk, *Educational Psychology*. 6th ed. (Needham Heights, MA: Allyn and Bacon, 1995): 340-42.

Teachers can directly share Maslow's list of needs by using figure 2.4 with students, or they can approach the subject more generally and more inductively by asking students to recall the physical and emotional needs all people must fulfill to survive and grow. Once students have generated a list of needs that is likely to include such essentials as food, shelter, security or safety, friendship, and love, a possible next step is to invite them to prioritize human needs and rank everything from absolute physical survival needs to growth needs.

Once students have a sense of what needs are and how and why people are motivated to fulfill their needs, questioning moves to a consideration of these basic needs as applied to the circumstances Jack and his mother face. For example, when the story opens, their cow, Milky-White, no longer gives milk for their sustenance. She must be sold, or they will starve. The questions on page 41 are useful critical examinations of needs and motivation as found in "Jack and the Beanstalk."

One of the things readers may note in a discussion of the events found in the telling of "Jack and the Beanstalk" is the general parallel to Maslow's posited hierarchy of needs. Jack's theft of the gold as the culminating event of his first trip up the beanstalk may be morally wrong, but he takes the gold because he and his mother are starving. With their only tangible resource, a cow, traded for the magic beans, Jack is motivated to climb the beanstalk and take something that is not his or face starvation. (It is true that the giant's wife feeds Jack, but he still has had just one meal, and his mother is back at home without any food or goods to trade or sell for food.) After living comfortably for a time on the spoils of Jack's first trip, Jack and his mother are once more poor, their wealth exhausted. Presumably to maintain the style of living to which he and his mother have become accustomed, Jack makes a second trek up the beanstalk. Of course, this action is not without risk. Motivation is a requisite. It does take courage and boldness to climb

Fig. 2 4 Maslow's Hierarchy of Needs

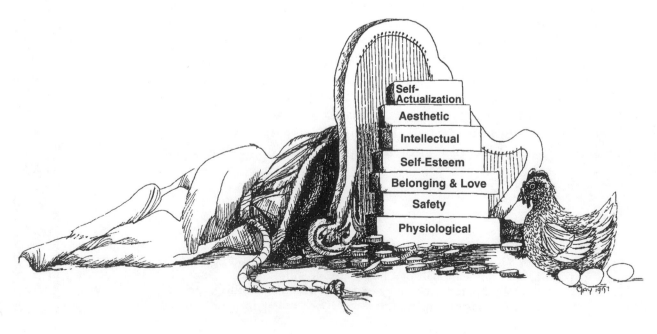

Needs and Motivations in "Jack and the Beanstalk"

What is most likely to happen to Jack and his mother when Milky-White, their cow, ceases to give milk?

What is Jack's motivation to climb the beanstalk the first time?

What are Jack's needs when he first arrives at the giant's castle in the sky?

How does the giant's wife help fill Jack's most immediate need?

Why does Jack take the giant's bag of gold?

What does Jack intend to do with the bag of gold?

How much time passes before Jack ascends the beanstalk for the second time?

Why does Jack climb the stalk a second time?

What happens when the giant's wife comments about the missing bag of gold?

What does she do for Jack on his second visit?

What does Jack take from the giant on his second visit?

How much time passes before Jack ascends the beanstalk for the third time?

Why does he climb the stalk a third time?

What does Jack take on his third visit to the giant's castle?

Why does the giant follow Jack down the beanstalk?

What becomes of the giant?

What becomes of Jack and his mother?

From *From the Land of Enchantment.* © 1997 Jerry D. Flack. Teacher Ideas Press. (800) 237-6124.

back up to the giant's castle, knowing full well that the giant is powerful and has a taste for English boys. Nevertheless, honest doubt arises here among readers. Since Jack and his mother had a bag of gold for the purchase of food for what must have been a reasonable amount of time, could not Jack (or his mother, for that matter) have learned a trade or secured some honest work in the interim so as not to become dependent upon the theft of the giant's belongings? Jack's first theft of the sack of gold is motivated by life-and-death (starvation) circumstances, but he appears to climb the beanstalk (and, of course, Maslow's pyramid) the second time to maintain a standard of comfort—perhaps even community status or self-esteem. After all, it is surely not pleasant to be chronically poor or destitute. Hence, Jack steals the hen that lays golden eggs, and he and his mother continue to live in comfort for a further period of time.

Then the wondrous hen ceases to lay golden eggs, and Jack is once more motivated to climb the beanstalk to protect or even further enhance the family's status. Intriguingly, food or survival needs do not occupy or capture Jack's attention on the third and final trip up the beanstalk. He does not seek food from the giant's wife as he did the first time he met her. On this trip he actually hides from her. Clearly, he intends to steal something from the castle, and he wants neither the giant nor the giant's wife to be aware of his presence. It is music Jack desires, and he steals the magic harp that makes beautiful music. Jack, as Maslow might well have predicted, having satisfied his most basic need for food, is then motivated by growth needs. In stealing the magic harp, Jack appears to be fulfilling an aesthetic need.

The same goal of a critical examination of "Jack and the Beanstalk" through shared, thoughtful inquiry may occur with an analysis of Sara Henderson Hay's poem about Jack's adventures. Hay (1982) wrote a small and wonderful book of poems titled *Story Hour.* (See Hay's poem "Grandmother" in the "Little Red Riding Hood" chapter.) In several poems she explores the motives, reactions, and values attendant to classic fairy tale characters. The title poem of the anthology examines the behavior of Jack as well as society's acceptance of—even applause for—his behavior.

Story Hour: Sara Henderson Hay

He swung the axe, the toppling beanstalk fell.
Hurrah, hurrah for Jack, the self-reliant.
The townsfolk gathered round to wish him well.
Was no one sorry for the murdered Giant?
Did no one, as the news spread far and wide,
Protest the means Jack took to gold and glory:
Guile, trespass, robbery and homicide?
It is not mentioned in the popular story.

Dear child, leave off such queries and suggestions,
And let that gullible innocence prevail
Which, in the Brothers Grimms' and our own time,
Applauds the climber, and ignores the crime.
How requisite to every fairy tale
A round-eyed listener, with no foolish questions.[2]

Hay's poem begs for both critical reading and a thoughtful discussion of the concerns she raises. At a literal text level, with what crimes does Hay charge Jack? At an inferential level, with whom does she appear to sympathize? For whom does she declare all fairy tales, including "Jack and the Beanstalk," are written?

Kohlberg: Moral Development

Still another avenue for critical-thinking explorations is an examination of the level of moral reasoning found in fairy tales, especially "Jack and the Beanstalk." Lawrence Kohlberg's work with moral reasoning is widely known. Kohlberg postulates that there are three broad stages in a person's moral development: preconventional morality, conventional morality, and postconventional morality. Each stage contains two kinds of moral reasoning. Early in children's lives, Kohlberg argues, moral behavior is directed toward avoiding punishment and gaining rewards. At age 10, students' morality judgments are made at the level of conventional morality. Gaining approval and avoiding disapproval are highly motivating factors to the student just entering this phase of moral development. The next step is a "law and order" orientation. Students operating at this level

---

2. Sara Henderson Hay. *Story Hour* (Fayetteville: University of Arkansas Press, 1982). Used with permission.

have clear ideas of what constitutes "right" or "wrong" behavior. As students reach their teens, they may move upward within the moral-development hierarchy to the level of postconventional morality. The nature of the public good is considered as is the notion of a "social contract" in postconventional morality. The person who operates on the sixth level of Kohlberg's hierarchy determines his or her own moral code. Universal ethical codes are adhered to and are formed as the result of an examination and understanding of ethical principles. Unfortunately, there are not a lot of examples of people operating at the highest level of Kohlberg's hierarchy of moral decision making. Some exemplary lives, past and present, that may be reviewed with students include those of Dr. Martin Luther King Jr., Mother Teresa, and Elie Wiesel—all winners of the Nobel Peace Prize.

Briefly, Kohlberg's moral development hierarchy is as follows:

Stage of Moral Reasoning	Moral Behavior
Preconventional Morality Level 1 Level 2	 Avoids punishment Receives reward
Conventional Morality Level 3 Level 4	 Seeks approval and avoids disapproval Rigid codes; "law and order"
Postconventional Morality Level 5 Level 6	 Contractual-legalistic; a social contract exists for the common good Abstract and universal ethical principles determine behavior

According to Kohlberg, every person proceeds through the steps of moral development in the same order. Movement is always forward, never backward. Kohlberg has advocated the use of moral dilemmas to help students contemplate moral behavior and decision making and to assist them to move from their present step to the next higher step of moral reasoning and behavior.[3]

Educators should be aware, however, that Kohlberg's work is not universally embraced or accepted as a valid interpretation of moral behavior. Some critics attack the validity and reliability of his assessment measures. Carol Gilligan (1982), a Harvard colleague of Kohlberg, in her book, *In a Different Voice: Psychological Theory and Women's Development*, makes a strong case against the bias found in Kohlberg's research because he used only male subjects and because all his dilemmas featured male central characters. Gilligan makes many valid points about the development of women's moral reasoning and how women do not necessarily follow the same pathways used by men as they grow morally. She especially emphasizes the role and placement of nurturing in moral-development hierarchies.

3. Lawrence Kohlberg, "Moral Reasoning," in Henry Gleitman, *Psychology* (New York: W.W. Norton & Company, 1986): 545-47. See also Anita Woolfolk, *Educational Psychology.* 6th ed. (Needham Heights, MA: Allyn and Bacon, 1995): 78-85. Woolfolk provides an excellent discussion of Kohlberg's model, criticisms of it, and alternative models, plus a point-counterpoint discussion of teaching values in schools. For original source commentary, see Lawrence Kohlberg, *The Philosophy of Moral Development: Moral Stages and the Idea of Justice* (Cambridge, MA: Harper & Row, 1981).

Again, the point here is not to provide an intense review of Kohlberg's theory or even to present a thorough discussion of moral development. Rather, one particular moral-development model is shared here as a possible tool teachers can use as an overlay with fairy tales to provoke critical examinations and thoughtful responses from students.

Moral Dilemmas in "Jack and the Beanstalk"

The behaviors of all the characters in "Jack and the Beanstalk" can be examined from the fresh lens of moral decision making. What level of moral behavior, for example, is the stranger operating on when he trades Jack magic beans for the cow Milky-White? What are the levels of moral development exhibited by Jack, his mother, the giant, and the giant's wife in the various transactions that take place in the tale? At which of the six levels of moral decision making, for example, was Jack operating when he stole the giant's gold or lied to the giant's wife later, on the second trip, stating that it was another boy who must have taken the bag of gold?

There are no absolutely correct answers to these questions. What is important is that students use good critical-thinking skills in the decisions they make about the characters and their actions. They must provide logical reasons to support and explain why they think Jack or another character was operating at a given level of moral decision making. Indeed, it may be particularly important to remind students that the characters in fairy tales are by definition archetypes and are not intended to represent complicated, fully developed people with complex histories and complicated and intricate psychological makeups. Through an examination of actions, behaviors, and possible motives of fairy tale characters, however, students can examine some of the morals and values that guide and structure society.

"Jack and the Beanstalk" is not the only tale that works well to this end, of course. Both "Hansel and Gretel" and "Rumpelstiltskin" come quickly to mind. What is society to make of parents who do the unthinkable: abandon their children to die? And while duplicity may play a role in the behavior of Rumpelstiltskin, where on the hierarchy of moral development does society place a father who makes false boasts about his daughter only to impress a king? How to rate a would-be princess who does not live up to the bargains she has made? What conditions or circumstances make her behavior excusable? In "The Frog Prince," what is to be thought of the princess who does not honor her promise to the frog? At what level of Kohlberg's hierarchy is any fairy tale character acting when he or she makes a fateful decision?

The importance of the teacher's role in discussions of values such as those addressed here cannot be overemphasized. Teachers need to demonstrate genuine curiosity about these issues to provoke authentic excitement among students for discussion and debate. Debriefing at the close of moral-dilemma discussions is equally critical. Time must be budgeted for all students to express their own feelings and beliefs and to have those feelings appreciated and validated.

"Jack and the Beanstalk" is at heart a quest story. The forced selling of his beloved pet Milky-White signals the end of Jack's childhood. He must forsake his childhood friend and at the same time assume the adult role of provider in his household. At first, he fares badly in the alien world of adult responsibilities. He obtains only a handful of beans for Milky-White in what appears to be a poor exchange. But he has a second chance with the growth of the beanstalk. If he can muster the courage to go forward (and upward) and face the risks of the unknown, he can provide for his mother and himself in previously unimagined ways. As Jack climbs the beanstalk, he truly climbs toward adulthood.

The point of using either Maslow's needs hierarchy or Kohlberg's moral-development model in the consideration of "Jack and the Beanstalk" or other fairy tales is not to achieve unanimity of agreement among students but rather to have students examine the difficult and intricate decisions life's events often require. Most important life decisions are not easily made. Most do not come with automatically "right" or "wrong" answers. Life is more complicated than it is often portrayed in novels, on television, and in fairy tales. The benefit of analyzing decision making is found in the degree of honest and open-minded inquiry and critical thinking students achieve.

Teachers working with older middle-school and secondary students may want to explore the treatment of the character of Jack from "Jack and the Beanstalk" as found in the Broadway Musical *Into the Woods* by Stephen Sondheim and James Lapine. The black-and-white morality of fairy tales is tempered, especially in the critical second act of the play, when Cinderella, Rapunzel, Little Red Riding Hood, and Jack learn that life is not as simple as fairy tales had promised them it would be. They emerge stronger and wiser for having struggled with life and having wrestled with its difficult challenges.[4]

Resources for Critical Thinking with Younger Students

The preceding critical-thinking discussions will most likely relate to students of at least middle-school age. Teachers who work with younger students and who want to invoke discussions about decision making in determining right and wrong may choose not to wade into the dense and murky waters of Maslow, Kohlberg, and others. Instead the Steck-Vaughn Another Point of View and Flip Me Over series of books might prove highly useful. For example, Alvin Granowsky (1996) tells the traditional story of "Jack and the Beanstalk" but does not conclude the tale with Jack's axing of the beanstalk. At that juncture of the book, readers flip the book over and begin reading again; the new tale is entitled "Giants Have Feelings, Too." In the alternate version, the giant's wife gives her interpretation of the story's events. Jack was not the innocent lad he is made out to be. Several other classic fairy tales such as "Rumpelstiltskin" and "Snow White" receive similar treatment in the Another Point of View Series.[5]

---

4. *Into the Woods* debuted on the New York stage in 1987. New York: RCA Victor Original Cast Recording, compact disc, 1988. Music and lyrics by Stephen Sondheim. Written and directed by James Lapine. The album notes by Sheryl Flatow are insightful and illuminating. See also Hudson Talbot's book edition of the play, *Into the Woods* (New York: Crown, 1989).

5. Readers may want to examine *Rumpelstiltskin/A Deal Is a Deal* and *Snow White/The Unfairest of Them All* among the Another Point of View Series titles. For a complete list of available titles in the Another Point of View Series, contact Steck-Vaughn (P.O. Box 26015, Austin, TX 78755).

Jim and the Beanstalk is another take on this classic story. In Raymond Briggs's (1970) clever tale, Jim proves to be a helpful lad to the giant. The reason for the giant's bad humor can be found in the infirmities of old age. The giant has grown bald and has bad teeth and poor vision. Jim does not take from the giant. Rather, he gives the giant a new wig, eyeglasses, and dentures. The result is a delightful friendship between the two characters. Of course, the lesson to be learned is one of helping people and caring for their needs.

"JACK AND THE BEANSTALK" RESOURCES

Traditional Stories

Cauley, Lorinda Bryan. 1983. *Jack and the Beanstalk*. New York: G. P. Putnam.
The classic story of the poor widow, her son, Jack, and the traded cow, Milky-White, is given a traditional telling complemented by Cauley's heavily textured, richly colored paintings. Her giant is appropriately threatening, and Jack is quick and clever.

de Regniers, Beatrice Schenk. 1985. *Jack and the Beanstalk*. Illus. by Anne Wilsdorf. New York: Atheneum.
"Jack and the Beanstalk" is retold in this instance in verse form and is accompanied by delightful color drawings.

Howe, John. 1989. *Jack and the Beanstalk*. Boston: Little, Brown.
Howe's words and dramatic illustrations convey a story of Jack and the giant that is moody and atmospheric and conjures up images of the Middle Ages.

Kellogg, Steven. 1991. *Jack and the Beanstalk*. New York: Morrow Junior Books.
Kellogg uses color and line so effectively that young readers will find the ogre and his wife genuinely frightening. This may well be the Stephen King version, visually speaking, of the old English tale. Kellogg's retelling is based on Joseph Jacobs's 1889 *English Fairy Tales*.

Pearson, Susan. 1989. *Jack and the Beanstalk*. Illus. by James Warhola. New York: Simon & Schuster.
Warhola uses bold colors and dramatic perspectives to convey the giant's immensity and Jack's thrilling challenges in climbing the beanstalk.

Variations and Other Treatments

Briggs, Raymond. 1970. *Jim and the Beanstalk*. New York: Coward-McCann.
Jim climbs a beanstalk and finds a bald, grumpy giant who has grown old, has no teeth, and cannot see well. Rather than stealing his treasures, Jim brings the giant new teeth, glasses, and a wig and makes the giant a happy man. Briggs's colorful illustrations are as delightful as his narration.

Granowsky, Alvin. 1996. *Jack and the Beanstalk/Giants Have Feelings, Too.* Illus. by Linda Graves. Another Point of View Series. Austin, TX: Steck-Vaughn.
In this two-books-in-one version, the traditional "Jack and the Beanstalk" story is presented, but so, too, is the story seen through the eyes of the injured giant's wife. Jack repaid their kindness to him with nothing but treachery and theft. What Herbert (the giant) really said was: "Fe! Fi! Fo! Fum! My Wife's Cooking is Yum! Yum! Yum!" Older children will delight in the two versions. Younger students could be confused by the variant story.

Haley, Gail E. 1986. *Jack and the Bean Tree.* New York: Crown.
Haley's paintings on wood greatly heighten the enjoyment of her Appalachian version of the classic story. Her use of dialect is clever as in "Jack clomb and he clomb and clomb, till he was tired." Haley's giant Ephidophilus and his wife Matilda are magnificent creations to behold as is her bean tree.

Harris, Jim. 1997. *Jack and the Giant: A Story Full of Beans.* Flagstaff, AZ: Northland.
Harris places Jack in the American West and uses giant rustlers as the villains. The way Harris tells it, there is a singing banjo and a buffalo that produces real gold buffalo chips. Harris previously illustrated another Southwest fairy tale transformation, Susan Lowell's *The Three Little Javelinas* (Northland, 1992).

Still, James. 1996. *Jack and the Wonder Beans.* Illus. by Margot Tomes. Lexington, KY: University Press of Kentucky.
This delightful American version of "Jack and the Beanstalk" is set in Wolfpen Creek, Kentucky, in the mountain country of Appalachia as is evident from the very first words: "Way back yonder" replaces "Once upon a time." Tomes's vibrant illustrations earned a citation as a *New York Times* Best Illustrated Children's Book of the Year in 1977. The University Press of Kentucky reissued a new edition of the book (originally published by Putnam & Grosset Group) in 1996.

Wildsmith, Brian, and Rebecca Wildsmith. 1994. *Jack and the Meanstalk.* New York: Alfred A. Knopf.
When humanity, personified by Professor Jack, a scientist, fools with Mother Nature and creates an out-of-control beanstalk, it is the animals of the Earth that come to the rescue. The father-and-daughter team of many books collaborate here, using the family story line of "Jack and the Beanstalk" to create a contemporary ecological fable.

Videocassettes and Simulations

Climb High, Jack. El Cajon, CA: Interact, 1996.
The newest entry in a series of fairy tale simulations from Interact in which students from grades five through eight produce minimusicals based upon fairy tales. Jack plus his friends climb the beanstalk, and the theme of this mini-musical is peer pressure. Contact: Interact, 1825 Gillespie Way #101, El Cajon, CA 92020-1095. Phone: 1-800-359-0961.

Jack and the Beanstalk. Shelley Duvall, producer; Lamont Johnson, director. Faerie Tale Theatre Series. Livonia, MI: Playhouse Video. 1986. 55 minutes. Videocassette.
In this live-action version of "Jack and the Beanstalk" from the Faerie Tale Theatre collection, Jack is portrayed by Dennis Christopher, and Elliott Gould and Jean Stapleton portray Mr. and Mrs. Giant. Gould's giant is unbelievably stupid. Katherine Helmond also stars as Jack's mother. This is one of the least satisfying entries in the series in terms of story line and production values. This version places any discussion of Jack's moral decision making on a new plane. The magic man who trades beans to Jack for his cow later appears in the story and tells Jack that the giant killed his father and stole the fortune that belonged to Jack and his mother. The resolution shows Jack and his mother living in the castle where the giant once resided.

Jack and the Beanstalk. C. W. Rogers, director. We All Have Tales Series. Westport, CT: Rabbit Ears Video. 1991. 30 minutes. Videocassette.
Michael Palin of "Monty Python" fame narrates the story of Jack's adventure using decidedly British accents. The ogre and his wife are especially dim-witted in this humor-laced version that features the drawings of Edward Sorel and music by David A. Stewart and the Eurythmics.

Jack and the Beanstalk. Bruce W. Smith, director. New York: Random House Home Video. Home Box Office. Happily Ever After Fairy Tales for Every Child Series. 1995. 30 minutes. Videocassette.
Jack is an African child in this animated version of "Jack and the Beanstalk." Narrated by Robert Guillaume and featuring Harry Belafonte as the Magic Man and rap artist Tone Loc as the Giant. Other titles in the admirable multicultural treatment of classic fairy tales include *Beauty and the Beast*, *The Frog Prince*, *Little Red Riding Hood*, and *Cinderella*.

Happily Ever Afters

Writing Ideas

"Jack and the Beanstalk" may serve as a great catalyst for student writers. One example is to invite students to write their own poetic interpretation of the characters and events in the story as Hay does in her poem, "Story Hour," shared in this chapter. Encourage students to respond to one or more of these additional writing invitations. The prompts may be used with students individually, or small groups of students may collaborate on projects such as creating a "Jack and the Beanstalk" newspaper.

Fast-forward to the present. Jack is being sued by the widow of the giant over the theft of gold pieces, one golden musical harp, and one magic hen. In the light of either or both of the psychological theories advanced by Maslow and Kohlberg, write a defense of Jack's actions. The defense may be written in the first person by Jack himself, or it may take the form of a legal brief prepared by his attorney. Alternately, write the plea the giant's widow makes to the court, especially in light of the theories advanced by Maslow and Kohlberg.

Imagine a modern-day inner-city Jack (or Jacqueline). What might he climb? A fire escape? What might he find in a penthouse at the top of a skyscraper? Write and illustrate a contemporary "Jack and the Beanstalk" story with either a male or female protagonist. Emphasize the moral decisions and courage of convictions the protagonist must confront and exhibit.

Plan, write, edit, produce, and share a "Jack and the Beanstalk" newspaper. The headline story should report one of the critical events in the story, such as Jack's first trip up the beanstalk or the final event of Jack chopping down the beanstalk. Of course, a good reporter always provides answers to the five Ws (*who, what, when, where,* and *why*) in an informative news story. A newspaper editorial may make a strong argument for Jack's guilt or innocence in the theft of the giant's possessions. An advice column might tell parents what to do about children who go to the store and return with useless items. A feature story may describe the market to which Jack's mother sent him with the intention of selling Milky-White. Describe the colorful sights, sounds, and smells of a typical market day. A cartoon or comic strip will visually accent some aspect, theme, or conflict from the tale. Perhaps a sports-page story will report about Jack's remarkable athletic skills in climbing. An obituary may be written for the giant, and both classified ads (white cow for sale) and display advertisements (food ad for Jack's canned beans, guaranteed to prompt growth) can be fashioned. (For more examples of newspaper-writing activities, see "The Emperor's New Clothes" chapter.)

Write a sequel story to "Jack and the Beanstalk." Imagine any point in time in Jack's future. How is his life changed by the events in the tale? Does he have children of his own? Does he have an adult job? If so, what kind of work does he do? Are there particular conflicts or tensions in his life? Of course, Jack is not the only person whose story can be flashed forward. What might the future hold for Jack's mother and the giant's widow? Whatever became of the man who traded Jack the magic beans for Milky-White? For that matter, what happened to Milky-White after Jack traded her for the beans?

Write a prequel to "Jack and the Beanstalk." Imagine what life was like for Jack and his mother when Jack's father was still living with them. Create an adult male character for Jack's father, and tell his story.

Write a set of journal or diary entries Jack might have made on the night he first acquired the magic beans and after each trip he made to the giant's castle.

"Jack and the Beanstalk" would not be much of a tale if the magic beans had not germinated and grown to a remarkable degree. Practice your technical-writing skills. Consult science and gardening books in the library media center to learn more about both controlled experiments and cultivating seeds. Design a science experiment that involves growing beans. Thoroughly and accurately describe step by step the planned experiment and anticipated results of your bean-growing experiment.

Art Ideas

Many art projects can emerge from a sharing of the fairy tale of "Jack and the Beanstalk." For example, primary teachers may invite young children to create their own "giants" from shape templates that have been created in advance. The teacher can prepare a variety of shape patterns in different sizes that children can then use to trace and cut their own supply of colorful circles, squares, rectangles, ovals, triangles, and other shapes. Alternately, teachers can eliminate a step and prepare for students dozens of colorful shapes in a variety of sizes that students then select from, assemble, and use to create their own colorful images of giants. Older students may want to try one or more of these art projects. (Be sure to see "The Frog Prince" chapter for further art-related extensions of fairy tales.)

Create a poster that the giant might have made to warn boys to stay off his property.

Sketch a picture of a doormat that may have been placed at the entrance to the giant's house.

Design a mouse pad Jack or the giant might use with a personal computer.

Create a "blueprint," or a floor plan, for the giant's castle. See home building and architecture magazines for sample floor plans.

Make a collage of Jack's bedroom. Cut pictures of bedroom furnishings, clothes, and personal items Jack might have from newspaper and magazine advertising. Supplement the cut pictures with your own drawings.

Draw two large boxes of equal size on a large piece of paper. Jack's mother sends him to bed without any supper the night he returns from the market with magic beans. In the first box, create a drawing of what Jack's bedroom looked like at that period in Jack's life. In the second box, create a second drawing of how Jack's bedroom may have appeared after he and his mother accumulated the giant's treasures.

Design and create a game board and game playing cards (e.g., "Chance" cards) for a new game you invent. You may want to use existing game boards for "Monopoly" or "Clue" as examples. When your game board is complete, demonstrate for friends how the game can be played.

REFERENCES

Bettelheim, Bruno. 1975. *The Uses of Enchantment: The Meaning and Importance of Fairy Tales*. New York: Random House.

Bloom, Benjamin S., ed. 1977. *Taxonomy of Educational Objectives: Handbook I. Cognitive Domain*. New York: Longman.

Briggs, Raymond. 1970. *Jim and the Beanstalk*. New York: Coward-McCann.

Gilligan, Carol. 1982. *In a Different Voice: Psychological Theory and Women's Development*. Cambridge, MA: Harvard University Press.

Granowsky, Alvin. 1996. *Jack and the Beanstalk/Giants Have Feelings, Too*. Austin, TX: Steck-Vaughn.

Harrow, Anita J., ed. 1972. *A Taxonomy for the Psychomotor Domain: A Guide for Developing Behavioral Objectives*. New York: Longman.

Hay, Sara Henderson. 1982. *Story Hour*. Fayetteville, AR: University of Arkansas Press.

Krathwohl, David R., ed. 1964. *Taxonomy for Educational Objectives: The Classification of Educational Goals: Handbook 2: Affective Domain*. New York: Longman.

Maslow, Abraham. 1970. *Motivation and Personality*. 2d ed. New York: Harper & Row.

Rowe, Mary Budd. Jan.-Feb. 1986. "Wait Time—Slowing Down May Be a Way of Speeding Up." *The Journal of Teacher Education* 37, no. 1: 43-44.

Chapter 3
Reading and Writing with Little Red Riding Hood

CHAPTER PREVIEW

In this chapter, readers will observe the tremendous versatility of fairy tales, specifically "Little Red Riding Hood," for developing and enhancing language skills. Reading and writing processes are highlighted. Further, one of the premier illustrators of children's literature, Trina Schart Hyman, is profiled. A basketful of good "Little Red Riding Hood" resources are also shared.

"Little Red Riding Hood" is one of the world's most popular folktales. Charles Perrault published the story in *Stories or Tales of Times Past, with Morals* in 1697, and the tale has been popular ever since. The oral tradition of the tale goes much further back in history. Perrault's French version was judged to be especially severe by later audiences because Little Red Riding Hood and her grandmother perish in his telling. Nineteenth-century British retellers found ways to save at least Little Red Riding Hood, and the Brothers Grimm's German retelling even saves the grandmother—but not the wolf. Later stories softened the telling even further by allowing the wolf to escape and never be seen in the woods again. The popularity of the tale is inestimable. Charles Dickens is said to have fallen in love with Little Red Riding Hood as a child and to have declared that he wanted to grow up to marry her. For centuries the story has been told to children to make dramatic and explicit the warnings of obeying parents and not talking to strangers.[1] Even popular culture bears the imprint of the tale: A "wolf" is a man who has less than sterling intentions toward young women.

"Little Red Riding Hood" illustrates as well as any fairy tale the incredible versatility of fairy tales. There is no basic skill that cannot be taught and learned by using fairy tales as a catalyst or model. This fact is especially apparent in language learning. Fairy tales, and most especially "Little Red Riding Hood," may

---

1. For more information about the origins of "Little Red Riding Hood," see Charles Panati, *Extraordinary Origins of Everyday Things* (New York: Harper & Row, 1987), and Jack Zipes, *The Trials and Tribulations of Little Red Riding Hood* (South Hadley, MA: Bergen & Garvey, 1983).

be used to teach and practice such fundamental language-art skills as textbook reading, critical reading, and poetry and prose writing. Storytelling is still another language-arts skill that can be practiced using fairy tales.

READING AND "LITTLE RED RIDING HOOD"

Textbook Reading Skills

One example of the versatility of fairy tales in the language-arts curriculum is how the story of "Little Red Riding Hood" can be used to develop and strengthen reading skills. The following reading lesson acquaints middle-school students with expository writing patterns found in instructional writing. When readers comprehend standard organizing formats employed by writers, they are well on their way to greater success in reading in content areas that are so necessary for success in secondary and postsecondary education.

Explain to students that there are four main models or patterns of writing found in their textbooks and other expository material. Main ideas may be stated at the beginning, middle, or end of a paragraph. In some cases, the main idea is so important that it is stated twice, first at the beginning of a paragraph and then in different words at the end. The particular model an author chooses will then dictate the placement of the supporting details that anchor the main idea. The four major writing formats can be illustrated with the following schematics in figure 3.1.

In Model A, the main idea is stated first, and supporting details follow as sustaining evidence. In Model B, this order is reversed. In Model C, some of the supporting details precede the placement of the main idea. The main idea is stated halfway through the paragraph, followed by still more supporting evidence. Model D resembles Model A; the first sentence states the main idea. However, due to the importance of the main idea, it is rephrased in a summary statement in the final sentence of the reading passage.

Once students understand the four models, ask them to read the four quite different versions of "Little Red Riding Hood" found in figure 3.2. The students' task is to read the four versions and match each with the model, A, B, C, or D that it represents. The correct answers are found at the end of the chapter.

Fig. 3.1. Models of Text Writing

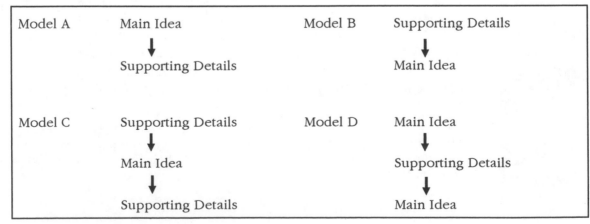

Fig. 3.2 Variations on a Theme

The writing in the following four versions of "Little Red Riding Hood" illustrates four models of expository writing. The problem for you to solve is this: Which version goes with which model?

1. Completing his investigation of the wolf slaying in nearby Woodsville yesterday, local police chief John Doe said the case once again proved that those who break the law suffer in the end. Doe was referring to the wolf slain by the local woodcutter Joe Badaxe. Police pieced together the case from assorted findings.

    a. The deceased wolf apparently discovered Miss R. Ridinghood tripping through the woods with a basket of "goodies."

    b. He allegedly tricked her into taking a slow path to her grandmother's house while he hurried to the same cottage, subdued the grandmother, and jumped into her bed, disguised in her clothing.

    c. Miss Ridinghood walked into the wolf's trap but was able to keep out of his lurching paws and simultaneously scream for help.

    d. Woodsman Badaxe was nearby, heard the screams, and rushed into the cabin in time to slay the wolf and save the girl and her grandmother.

    In summing up the case, Officer Doe proudly said, "Finally, the woods are safe; let this be a lesson to those who break our laws."

    ◆ ◆ ◆

2. Above all else, let it be said: Crime doesn't pay! A certain wolf learned this recently when he tried to outsmart a young lady in an attempt to obtain her basket of "goodies." The wolf spied the little girl while on her way to her grandmother's house to deliver food, and, upon discovering the contents of the basket she was carrying, he put into effect his plan to steal the basket. He rushed to the grandmother's cottage, overcame the grandmother, and hopped into her bed, disguised in her clothing. Shortly thereafter, the girl arrived and was puzzled to note that her grandmother looked strange. Her mother had advised her of her grandmother's illness, but this, thought the girl, was ridiculous. The young girl made several comments about the strange appearance of her grandmother (really the wolf), finally touching upon the size of her teeth. At this point the wolf leaped from the bed and threatened to eat the child and her basket of "goodies." All sorts of confusion reigned. The girl screamed and ran about. The wolf did likewise, chasing the young girl. Meanwhile, a nearby woodsman heard the strange goings-on, rushed to the scene, and saved the day by bashing the wolf's brains. The little girl and her grandmother were happily reunited.

Fig. 3.2 continued on page 56.

3. Man, like a long time back, you hear, there was a wolf that thought he was really bad. He tried to outsmart a neat-looking chick who wore red threads. He met the chick in an awesome place in the woods. Noticing that she had a basket of "goodies," he laid some jive on her about what a hip day it was for a walk. Well, the chick fell for the dude's plan and took the long road to her granny's pad while this bad wolf dude trucked on over to the old lady's place, mean and fast. There he caught the old woman off guard (she was groovin' on "General Hospital"), tied her up, and threw her in the closet. Then he put on some of the old lady's rags and hopped into her bed. The wolf thought that he was really bad. He said, "Man, I'm really cool, and I'm gonna surprise little old red cap!" But the wolf was to learn differently. He was about to find out that being bad doesn't always pay off. Meanwhile, the chick kept coming through the woods and finally arrived at her granny's cottage. She took one look at the mess in granny's bed and knew it was a bad scene. The wolf didn't look like her granny at all. She let out some really loud vibes, and a nearby woodsman rushed to her aid and wasted the wolf. Then the chick, her granny, and the woodsman had a real bash.

♦ ♦ ♦

4. Many years ago a large, carnivorous mammal frequently referred to as a wolf meanly tricked and then attacked a young female for the sole purpose of obtaining her basket filled with edibles that would satisfy his hunger. He learned of the nutritious ingredients of the basket when he happened to cross the path of the young girl as she leisurely strolled through the same fertile, wooded area. The young lady had been sent into the woods by her mother to visit her ailing grandmother. It was hoped that the combined pleasure of receiving the basket of food and seeing the pretty young girl in her smart red costume would revive the ailing woman's spirits. The mother had specifically told the young miss not to waste time in the woods, but the wolf persuaded the child to disobey and do otherwise, sending her on the prettiest but longest path to the grandmother's humble abode. In the meantime, the wolf hurriedly took a shortcut and arrived at the elderly woman's cottage ahead of the girl. He forced the grandmother into a closet, dressed himself with appropriate garments from the woman's wardrobe, and took to her bed. Soon the young lass arrived and immediately noted that something was wrong. She questioned the person in the bed about "her" strange appearance, finally touching on the enormous size of "her" dentures. On this signal, the wolf leaped from the bed and began to chase the girl. The young lass screamed loudly and thus attracted the attention of a nearby conservation officer, who, with great courage and boldness, faced the wicked wolf, slew him, and reunited the two frightened women. There are many stories of deceit and villainy known to man. Nevertheless, no story shows more clearly than this one that wickedness fails and goodness triumphs over evil.

CRITICAL READING

Critical-reading practice can also be realized with any fairy tale. Provide students with a complete or partial retelling of the basic story of Little Red Riding Hood. The following version may be used just as the four versions of the preceding activity could also be used for this activity.

"Little Red Riding Hood"

Once upon a time there was a beautiful little girl named Sasha who lived with her mother and father in a house in a small village on the edge of great forest. All the people in her village loved the sweet little girl. The little girl's grandmother who lived deep in the forest loved Sasha very much. The grandmother had made a beautiful red cape with a hood for Sasha for her birthday. Sasha loved her scarlet cape so much that she wore it every day and everywhere she went. Indeed, she wore it so often that the people of her village no longer called her Sasha. Whenever they saw her they said, "There goes Little Red Riding Hood."

Now it happened that Sasha's beloved grandmother became ill. Sasha's mother and father worried about her, but they both had so much work at home that they could not afford to take time to travel through the woods to visit her. Believing that a visit from Little Red Riding Hood would revive the grandmother's spirits and speed her recovery, the little girl's mother packed a basket of warm bread and grandmother's favorite cheeses and candies, and called the little girl to her. "Sasha, I want you to take this basket of goodies to your grandmother in the forest. Now, you must be a very good girl and not stray from the path. You must not tarry either. You must go straight to grandmother's cottage and return home before dark. Can you be a big girl and do this for Mother and Father?"

Little Red Riding Hood said that indeed she would be a helpful child, and she promised not to stray from the path through the big woods on the way to her grandmother's cottage. Thus, with a promise and the basket of goodies, Little Red Riding Hood waved good-bye to her mother and entered the big woods.

After students have read such a passage or even a complete tale, their task is to respond to a series of teacher-made statements with one of three responses: True, False, or Cannot Be Determined from Text. Sample questions and responses for the preceding passage might be:

1. The name of the little girl in the story is Sasha. (True)

2. The little girl's mother made her a beautiful red cape with a hood for Christmas. (False)

3. The mother of the child always called her Little Red Riding Hood. (False)

4. The villagers called the little girl Little Red Riding Hood. (True)

5. The little girl's grandmother had pneumonia. (Cannot be determined from text)[2]

---

2. This basic idea was first shared with the author by Anita Harnadek in a Kalamazoo Valley Intermediate School District workshop in critical thinking in Kalamazoo, Michigan, in 1978. For additional information about books and materials by Harnadek and other educators writing about critical thinking, contact Midwest Publications, P.O. Box 448, Pacific Grove, CA 93950.

The same print materials and statements may be transformed into a critical-listening activity. Record the text and the statements on audiotape cassettes, and place them in a classroom learning center where students can individually listen to the story and answer the questions. The answers may be provided for self-checks or be saved for later teacher evaluation. A helpful tip: Examine library collections for audiotape cassette versions of "Little Red Riding Hood" narrated by professional actors. These recordings can also be used for critical listening. Teachers need only then make up statements to fit particular recordings.

Comparative Literature Reading

Still another reading activity may be achieved by having students read and then compare two or more versions of "Little Red Riding Hood." The story of the little girl who invites trouble when she fails to obey her mother's instruction to be wary of strangers most likely traces its origins back to France's seventeenth-century storyteller Charles Perrault. The Brothers Grimm told a similar tale more than a century later. Even today new versions of "Little Red Riding Hood" are being told. Students will receive a fine introduction to comparative literature by examining some of the many versions of this classic cautionary tale for children. Students may examine nearly three centuries of worldwide tellings of this classic story collected by Jack Zipes in *The Trials and Tribulations of Little Red Riding Hood*. The anthology's stories range from Perrault's 1697 French tale to a humorous American version written by James Thurber.

Students may compare two diverse modern versions that represent the East and West. Trina Schart Hyman's 1983 *Little Red Riding Hood* is based on the Brothers Grimm version and was named a Caldecott Honor Book. In 1990, artist Ed Young won the Caldecott Medal for his Chinese version of the tale, *Lon Po Po*. The Venn diagram—named after British logician John Venn (1834-1923)—is a particularly useful tool for illustrating such comparisons. It is an illustration that uses circles to represent sets and their relationships. As used in children's literature, most Venn diagrams employ two intersecting circles to represent the similarities and differences between two characters, two stories, two different authors, or two books by the same author. Figure 3.3 highlights important similarities and differences between Hyman's *Little Red Riding Hood* and Young's *Lon Po Po*.

Students can complete additional Venn diagrams to compare the two wolves found in James Marshall's delightful retellings of *Red Riding Hood* (1987) and *The Three Little Pigs* (1989). Moving beyond "Little Red Riding Hood" stories, students may also compare Marshall's *The Three Little Pigs* and Jon Scieszka's *The True Story of the Three Little Pigs* (1989).

Mature students may want to engage in comparative-literature studies with a definite historical eye and examine texts and illustrations from the outstanding collection made available on the Internet by the "Little Red Riding Hood Project." Eighteenth-, nineteenth-, and early-twentieth-century versions reside in the deGrummond Children's Literature Research Collection at the University of Southern Mississippi (USM). As part of a graduate class in bibliography and methods of research taught by Michael N. Salda of the USM English Department, students sought, located, and converted to electronic text the words and images from "Little Red Riding Hood" stories dating back to Robert Samber's 1729 English translation of Charles Perrault's *Stories or Tales of Times Past, with Morals.* As of this writing, the collection features 16 complete versions, dating from 1729 through 1916. Both the various texts and rich and colorful illustration styles across several centuries are most enlightening. Children and adults no longer have to travel to London to the British Museum or to some other faraway site to see firsthand the literary past. They can simply plug into the Internet, locate the "Little Red Riding Hood Project," choose the versions they find especially engaging, and print them out. The World Wide Web address of the project at this writing is http://www-dept.usm.edu/~engdept/lrrh/lrrhhome.htm. A note of caution: As World Wide Web addresses have a habit of changing, the preceding address could easily change. Good Net surfing on the part of users will ultimately lead them to almost any resource. This author did not have the above address. He simply began using browsers and search tools such as Netscape Navigator 2.0 and Magellan, Excite, and Yahoo! and searched for fairy tales, especially "Little Red Riding Hood." It did not take long to find the USM Web site.

Fig. 3.3 *A Comparison of "Little Red Riding Hood" and "Lon Po Po"*

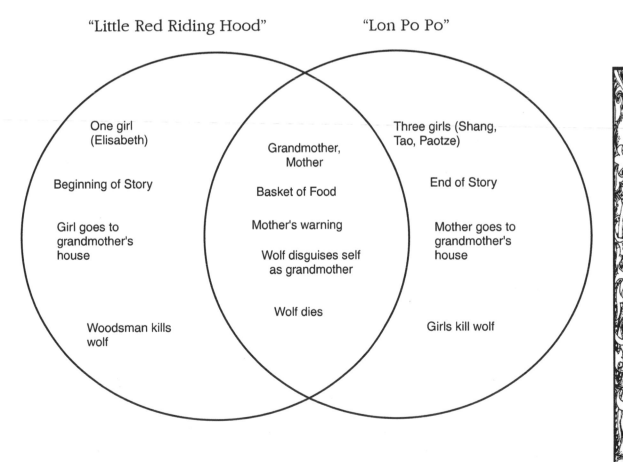

"Little Red Riding Hood"   "Lon Po Po"

One girl
(Elisabeth)

Beginning of Story

Girl goes to
grandmother's
house

Woodsman kills
wolf

Grandmother,
Mother

Basket of Food

Mother's warning

Wolf disguises self
as grandmother

Wolf dies

Three girls (Shang,
Tao, Paotze)

End of Story

Mother goes to
grandmother's
house

Girls kill wolf

Paired Reading

Pairs and small groups of students can experience the joys of reading aloud the plenitude of "Little Red Riding Hood" stories. Younger children will enjoy reading and retelling traditional versions of the tale, while older students may have more of a fancy for unusual variations, such as Lisa Campbell Ernst's *Little Red Riding Hood: A Newfangled Prairie Tale* or historical versions found on the Internet via the "Little Red Riding Hood Project." A vast array of "Little Red Riding Hood" stories and books are listed elsewhere in the chapter.

When students work in pairs, prereading activities may involve examination of the pictures accompanying the text for clues about the setting, the dominant characters, and other relevant clues to the best possible reading experience. Encourage students to be visual detectives and see how much of the story they can piece together from the illustrations alone. Also encourage students to write down two or three genuine questions they have about the version of "Little Red Riding Hood" they are preparing to read. For example, since there are many variations of the folktale, students may honestly ask and then seek to determine the fate of Little Red Riding Hood and her grandmother in the version they have. Do they die, or does the woodsman save them?

A reading and comprehension cycle can be established in paired reading. The first reader begins and reads aloud until a certain number of paragraphs or pages have been read. The second reader then summarizes what has been read. Next, the second reader goes back to the text and reads aloud the next passage while the first reader listens, paying careful attention to better summarize what he or she hears. At the next convenient stopping point, the first reader summarizes what has been read and then again assumes the role of the active reader. This cycle continues until the tale is finished.

When the story is completed, paired readers should go back to the questions they posed before reading to determine whether they found the information needed to satisfactorily answer their questions. There are innumerable ways students can respond to what they have read. They can assume the roles of characters and be interviewed by reporters with, perhaps, the first reader portraying the woodsman and the second reader portraying a television reporter covering the wolf slaying. Pairs may also work together to create their map of the story to demonstrate comprehension. Because of the simplicity of the tale and the specific reference to two separate paths to the grandmother's house, "Little Red Riding Hood" lends itself particularly well to map-making activities. Students can list the settings and the characters in the tale and draw the critical settings on their map. Next they can determine where to best place each of the characters on the map. (Story maps are illustrated in "The Frog Prince" chapter.) A rich variety of maps results when all the pairs in the classroom do this activity. Some pairs may only place the characters in their respective locations at the beginning of the story. Other pairs may represent Little Red Riding Hood's complete round-trip into the forest to her grandmother's cottage and back to her own home (assuming, of course, they read a version where she survives).

Pairs may also conclude their reading and rate the crucial characters—especially Little Red Riding Hood and the wolf—by devising their own five-point scale. They first generate a duality that forms a continuum from superior to inferior. One duality might be "hate-love," and another might be "good-evil."

LOVE   *HATE*

  (1)   (2)   (3)   (4)   (5)

Where on a five-point scale of the continuum of good and evil do students place Little Red Riding Hood? Where on the same continuum of good and evil do they think the wolf belongs?

LITERARY ELEMENTS AND "LITTLE RED RIDING HOOD"

The basic elements of literature such as plot, setting, point of view, characterization, and theme may be taught using "Little Red Riding Hood" as a model. Indeed, it is from their encounters with nursery-rhyme stories and fairy tales that most children first learn about and develop expectations about story plots. Children learn early that every story should have a beginning, middle, and end; that is, it should have a *plot.* The plot of a story is built upon key situations, usually conflicts, and a sequence of events. In "Little Red Riding Hood" both elements are clearly specified. A little girl is supposed to go to her grandmother's cottage some distance from her own home. As this situation or plot premise unfolds, a pattern of action develops. Little Red Riding Hood's mother strictly warns her to stay on the beaten path to her grandmother's cottage. This is the literary device of foreshadowing. Even very young readers and listeners understand that something dark and dangerous must be in the woods. The sequence of events in the tale follow an explicit set of steps. Little Red Riding Hood meets the wolf, and the conflict of the story is introduced. The wolf has evil intentions; he wants to eat the little girl, and he will use deceit and treachery to accomplish his aim. Because the little girl is human and the wolf represents the dark forces of nature, the conflict may be said to be person versus nature.

After the conflict of the story is introduced, the action of the story or the sequence of events builds quickly. Little Red Riding Hood takes a longer route to her grandmother's cottage while the wolf beats her to the cottage, eats the grandmother, and disguises himself as the grandmother. The exposition or telling of the sequence of the story then builds to the dramatic climax wherein the wolf eats (or attempts to eat, depending on the version read) Little Red Riding Hood and is promptly slain by the woodsman. The denouement, or summing up, of the tale occurs in many versions of the story as the grandmother, the young child, and the woodsman have a joyful reunion. Young listeners or readers know that evil has been expunged from the world and balance and goodness have returned. Of course, in Perrault's French telling no such reunion occurs. Little Red Riding Hood pays for her disobedience with her life.

From fairy tales, children also grow to expect that stories will have different kinds of *characters*. They know that there are heroes and heroines (protagonists) who triumph over villains and evil forces or spells (antagonists). In "Little Red Riding Hood" the characterization is explicit. The two primary characters are Little Red Riding Hood and the wolf. Although the mother, grandmother, and woodsman are integral to the plot of the story, they are really secondary characters who exist chiefly to help drive the story line. Little Red Riding Hood represents innocence and is the heroine or protagonist of the story, while the wolf is a villain, the antagonist who stands between the innocent heroine and her goal of taking good things to her sick grandmother. Students will note that most of the characters found in fairy tales are really closer to being caricatures than fully developed, multidimensional characters who have flaws as well as virtues and who experience doubt as well as certainty.

The *setting* of a story refers to both time and place. In adventure stories, especially survival tales, the place setting may be so vital to the story that it becomes a character in the story. The angry sea, the wild or the maniacal forest fire become the antagonist forces that threaten to destroy the protagonist. Fairy tale settings are usually less specific. The woods Little Red Riding Hood enters could be almost any woods. The exact time and place are deliberately vague so that the universality of the story can be realized. The cautionary tale can then be told to young children in any land and at any time. Laszlo Kubinyi's illustrations for Tom Robert's retelling of *Red Riding Hood* indicate a mid-nineteenth-century American setting, while Lisa Campbell Ernst modernizes the tale, setting it in the farm belt of the Great Plains of present-day America in *Little Red Riding Hood: A Newfangled Prairie Tale*.

Point of view refers to the narration of the story. Most versions of "Little Red Riding Hood" use the omniscient point of view wherein the narrator has the power to recount all the actions, thoughts, and conversations of the characters. The narrator, speaking from a third-person point of view, reveals the private thoughts of the treacherous wolf as he sweet-talks the naive Little Red Riding Hood into picking flowers and taking a longer path to her grandmother's cottage. The narrator has the power to foresee what is coming even as Little Red Riding Hood does not. The omniscient narrator also has the power to quickly move back and forth from one scene to another. While Little Red Riding Hood is gathering flowers, the narrator magically moves readers forward to the cottage where the wolf is busy gobbling up her grandmother. Most often, the narrator sympathizes with Little Red Riding Hood and paints the wolf as being evil and treacherous. In some recent versions of fairy tales such as Jon Scieszka's *The True Story of the Three Little Pigs* and Della Rowland's *Little Red Riding Hood/The Wolf's Tale*, the wolf is given the opportunity to tell his side of the story. He becomes the narrator and uses the first-person point of view to tell readers how he has been misrepresented in earlier tellings of the tale. He also attempts to build reader empathy for the injustices done to him.

Most fairy tales use narration as the primary means of moving the story forward. However, dialogue can also be a critical element of writing and storytelling. "Little Red Riding Hood" can serve as a model of how to write riveting dialogue. The verbal exchange between the little heroine and the wolf disguised as her grandmother is one of the most famous conversations in all of literature. No one who has ever heard the story can forget this exchange:

"Oh! Grandmother, what big ears you have."

"All the better to hear you with."

"What big eyes you have!"

"All the better to see you with."

"And, what big teeth you have."

"All the better to eat you with!"

These brief six lines of dialogue become the pivotal event in the entire tale, immediately leading to the climax of the story, the wolf's attack on Little Red Riding Hood, and to his subsequent demise.

The *theme* of "Little Red Riding Hood" is clear since the tale has been told for centuries to children as a cautionary tale, a warning not to disobey their parents. How this moral or message is transmitted, however, may vary. Key texts already cited in the chapter illustrate this point. The theme is explicitly stated by Trina Schart Hyman in her *Little Red Riding Hood*. On the last page of the book, a much wiser little girl thinks, I will never wander off the forest path again, as long as I live. There is no doubt left in readers' minds—no matter how young they may be. The theme is directly stated by the omniscient author speaking through the heroine's thoughts. James Marshall also makes the theme explicit in his *Red Riding Hood*. The narrator tells the reader that the little girl promises her grandmother never ever to speak to strangers again, and the story ends with a delightful final page. The simple line "And she never did" is hilariously punctuated with an illustration showing a chastened Little Red Riding Hood pushing away a seemingly friendly greeting from a huge alligator she meets on the wooded path on the return trip to her home. The theme of Ed Young's *Lon Po Po: A Red-Riding Hood Story from China*, although quite similar, is far less explicit. Young implies that children need to be wary of the dark forces in the world and to guard themselves against treachery. This theme, however, is only implicit. The story ends with the unpretentious reunion of three girls and their mother and the girls' simple account of the wolf's visit.

Frequent practice with identifying the elements in simple fairy tales allows students to develop the skills needed to approach and understand more complex literature as they mature. Teachers who want to learn more about such basic elements of literature as plot, setting, and point of view will find *A Critical Handbook of Children's Literature* by Rebecca J. Lukens (1995) especially helpful. Lukens uses children's literature classics such as *Charlotte's Web* to illustrate and explain the many elements of literature.

The following pages discuss author-illustrator Trina Schart Hyman and her approach to *Little Red Riding Hood* and other stories.

Little Red Riding Hood

by Trina Schart Hyman

I was a really strange kid. I was born terrified of anything and everything that moved or spoke. I was afraid of people, especially. All people—kids my own age, all grown-ups, even my own family. Dogs (until my parents bought me a puppy of my own), horses, trees, grass, cars, streets. I was afraid of the stars and the wind. Who knows why?

My mother is a beautiful woman with red hair and the piercing blue gaze of a hawk. She never seemed afraid of anyone or anything. It was she who gave me the courage to draw and a love of books. She read to me from the time I was a baby, and once, when I was three or four and she was reading my favorite story, the words on the page, her spoken words, and the scenes in my head fell together in a blinding flash. I could read!

The story was "Little Red Riding Hood," and it was so much a part of me that I actually became Little Red Riding Hood. My mother sewed me a red satin cape with a hood that I wore almost every day, and on those days, she would make me a "basket of goodies" to take to my grandmother's house. (My only grandmother lived in Rhode Island, three hundred miles away, but that didn't matter.) I'd take the basket and carefully negotiate the backyard, "going to Grandmother's house." My dog, Tippy, was the wolf. Whenever we met, which in a small backyard had to be fairly often, there was an intense confrontation. My father was the woodsman, and I greeted him when he came home each day with relief and joy.

I was Red Riding Hood for a year or more. I think it's a great tribute to my mother that she never gave up and took me to a psychiatrist, and if she ever worried, she has never let me know.

Text and illustration reprinted with permission of the author-illustrator Trina Schart Hyman. The text is from *Self-Portrait: Trina Schart Hyman* published by Harper & Row, 1981. The illustration, Fig. 3.4, is from *Little Red Riding Hood* published by Holiday House, 1983.

Profile:
Trina Schart Hyman

Trina Schart Hyman is one of the finest author-illustrators in children's literature. Her splendid retelling and illustration of *Little Red Riding Hood* won the *Boston Globe*-Horn Book and Golden Kite Awards and was a Caldecott Honor Book in 1984. The following year she received the Caldecott Medal for her illustration of Margaret Hodges's retelling of *Saint George and the Dragon*.

The artist grew up in the newly expanding suburbs of Philadelphia, Pennsylvania, during and immediately after the Second World War. Just beyond her neighborhood, vast tracts of farmland and woods could be seen and beckoned to her. A "queen" lived in the capacious farmhouse nearby and supervised the vast estates while her husband, the "king," was off slaying dragons and fighting great battles. Her parents read to her often, and she learned to read to herself at an early age. Trina was raised on myths, legends, and the tales of the Brothers Grimm. Her precocious art talent was also recognized and nurtured by her parents.

For a little girl used to self-portrayals of Little Red Riding Hood, and to reading tales of wonder and having a "queen" live just down the road, the rules of school and *Dick and Jane* readers with their cookie-cutter art were stultifying experiences. But Trina's parents never let her down or allowed her creativity to wither. For nine years, weekly Saturday trips to an orthodontist were turned into adventures by a magical father who took Trina to the Philadelphia Art Museum. There she fell in love with the rooms and hallways filled with great art.

Upon graduation from high school, she attended the Philadelphia College of Art. After marriage to Harris Hyman, Trina studied for a year at the Boston Museum School of Fine Arts before moving to Stockholm, Sweden, where she studied at the Konstfackskolan (School of Applied Art) and received her first commission to illustrate a children's book, *Toffe and the Little Car*. One of the high adventures of her young adult life was a 2,800-mile tandem bicycle journey through Sweden, Norway, and Denmark that she and her husband completed. It was on this journey that she heard the murmurings and laughter of trolls.

Returning to Boston, Trina received a commission to illustrate a children's book of Irish folktales for Little, Brown and Company. It was also at this period of her life that her daughter, Katrin, was born. After an unhappy move to New York City, Trina and her husband divorced, and she and Katrin moved along with friends to Lyme, New Hampshire, into a small stone house on the banks of the Connecticut River. There, and later in the larger farmhouse where she still lives, Trina raised her daughter and came into her own as one of America's premier illustrators of children's books. Two of those beautiful books are *Sleeping Beauty* and *Snow White*. During this highly productive passage of her life, she also became the art director of a brand new magazine, *Cricket*. In the ensuing

years, she has raised a daughter, become a grandmother, and continued to produce breathtaking images for children that illumine the words of folk stories and other literature. Trina celebrates and glorifies the human experience. She does not rob children of childhood; she makes it a place of wonder filled with good and evil and with strong, beautiful women and robust, courageous men.

Although she does not work with models, the illustrator does use in her creations her images and memories of relatives as well as familiar places. She writes in *Children's Book Illustration and Design* (Cummins 1992) that *Little Red Riding Hood* is a Valentine to her own childhood. Little Red Riding Hood is Trina as she was at four or five years of age, and the mother and grandmother are very much the way she remembers from that time in her life. She sets the story in a village and woods much like those she lives in and knows in New Hampshire, and the woodsman is a tribute to her kindly neighbor, an old Vermont farmer. Her trademark cat and kittens are all her own pets.

Little Red Riding Hood is a quintessential Trina Schart Hyman book. Art is everywhere, and the reader—young or old—is never shortchanged. Where other artists characteristically leave half-title and copyright pages blank, Hyman fills every page with color and pattern, if not complete paintings. Note the two-panel hinged picture frame in the border of the copyright page. Given her description on page 64 of her mother's lovely red hair, it is not unlikely that these are portraits of a young Trina and her mother.

The title page is actually a two-page spread featuring a lovely full-page romantic painting of the heroine safe in the domestic serenity of her own backyard, surrounded by gentle, loving pets (see figure 3.4). Hyman's sly sense of humor is immediately apparent. A close examination of the painting reveals that Little Red Riding Hood is intently reading a storybook—presumably her favorite—and the book jacket is none other than the same book the real reader is reading, Trina Schart Hyman's *Little Red Riding Hood*. One of her signatures, the bold use of line, is immediately obvious. In the same frontispiece painting, opposite the title page, the bold vertical and horizontal lines in the steps, fence, shutters, roof line, siding, and door frame immediately give power to the painting. Moreover, the lines in the painting complement and balance the more formal lines of letters that spell out the data on the title page. At the same time, on both pages, the use of nature's flowing shapes found in flowers, trees, plants, playful kittens, and birds along with the artist's use of rich browns, reds, yellows, and greens softens the angular effect of man-made lines. The overall result is romantic and inviting. Everything in the reader's view is vibrant and alive from the playful kitten to a winging bird in the distance. Little Red Riding Hood's mother is busy in the kitchen, even the potted geraniums are obviously healthy, and all in the world is well.

One of Trina Schart Hyman's hallmarks is the use of borders. Often she uses her borders to enhance and amplify the text and primary illustrations. She researches the flora of particular places and includes flowers and plants natural to the historical setting of each story. This is clearly evident in the illustrations done for books by Margaret Hodges set in England's distant past such as *The*

Fig. 3.4 "Little Red Riding Hood" by Trina Schart Hyman

Kitchen Knight: A Tale of King Arthur and *Saint George and the Dragon.* In *Little Red Riding Hood,* the borders are used to great effect in framing the text, both literally as well as subjectively in mood and tone. Hyman's borders revel in the glory of nature. Ferns, butterflies, Queen Anne's lace, red clover, ladybugs, wild strawberries, mushrooms, red apples, field mice, and spiders spinning intricate webs all thrive on these pages. Again, all is right with the world. There are no rotted flowers or dead trees and certainly no man-made litter. The robust natural world alternates with human artifacts such as Pennsylvania Dutch motifs and quiltlike textile patterns that suggest grandmothers, warmth, security, and intergenerational family love.

But Hyman's borders are far more than decoration. They are, in fact, windows that invite children of all ages to step through them and be transported to the incredible, sometimes frightening, but always rewarding world of fairy tales and make-believe. If we look just inside the frames, we will discover special truths as well as high adventure. Just as we know when the lights go down and the curtain opens in a theater or movie house that something wonderful is about to take place, that we are being transported to another world as if by magic, we also know that if we peer inside Ms. Hyman's borders, we will discover wonderful things.

Trina Schart Hyman's extraordinary use of light is also evident in her paintings for *Little Red Riding Hood.* A warm, dawnlike pink light suffuses the inviting kitchen of Little Red Riding Hood's cottage home. Even when she first meets the wolf in the glorious woods, sunlight filters romantically through the forest canopy. But as the true intent of the wolf becomes apparent, the light shifts and the woods seem less inviting. When the apprehensive child tiptoes into the open door of her grandmother's cabin, the natural light of day has lost its friendliness. It is stark, and it creates sharp, angular shadows, which, in combination with the dimness of the cabin's interior, create a sense of palpable fear. Grandmother's cabin is no longer a safe place for a child to be. The lighting portends something truly evil is inside; it is going to require great courage for Little Red Riding Hood to take each step forward.

Happily, for those who love folktales of all kinds, this marvelous artist who loves fairy tales and has believed in fairies, trolls, goblins, angels, and magic all of her life has illustrated and told many more tales from the Brothers Grimm. Just as Hyman uses borders to frame the story in *Little Red Riding Hood*, she uses stone arches, both humble and grand, as the visual framework to capture and glorify the magic of *The Sleeping Beauty* (Hyman 1977), the story of an evil curse cast by the thirteenth fairy in the Brothers Grimm tale of the princess who sleeps for 100 years. All Hyman's princesses are beautiful and strong; all the princes are robust and heroic. This is certainly true of the king's son and the future queen she creates in the Brothers Grimm's *Snow White* (Grimm 1974), translated by Paul Heins, which she believes is technically one of her finest books. She also created majestic and rich paintings of princes and future queens for Eric Kimmel's splendid retelling of the Brothers Grimm story of *Iron John* (Kimmel 1994).

Hyman also illustrated *Rapunzel: From the Brothers Grimm* and *The Water of Life*, both tales by the Brothers Grimm retold by Barbara Rogasky (Rogasky 1982, 1986). Both tales are beautifully and romantically realized through Hyman's paintings, and there is absolutely no blurring of the lines between innocence, goodness, and courage in the heroes and evil and deceitfulness in the villains. One of the most intriguing elements of the lesser-known tale, *The Water of Life*, is the expansion of the story to include the oceans or seas. Unlike so many landlocked European fairy tales set in castles and in deep, dark woods, this King Lear-like tale of three sons finds much of its action and resolution at sea.

Another collaboration with Rogasky yields some of Hyman's most joyous and personal creations. *Winter Poems* (1994) is a wonderful celebration of the simple yet profound joys one finds in the winter season. The poems of Emily Dickinson, John Greenleaf Whittier, Edna St. Vincent Millay, and many others celebrate the first snow, winter birds, and ice skating. In a warm introduction, Rogasky identifies herself, Trina Hyman, Trina's extended family, Trina's home, and numerous family pets as found in the glorious illustrations. The beauty of the New Hampshire countryside in winter and the wonder of family love are richly celebrated in Hyman's artwork for *Winter Poems*. No one save God creates snow quite as magically as Trina Hyman.

The most recent collaboration with Rogasky resulted in *The Golem* (Rogasky 1996). Hyman creates dark, mystical paintings for Rogasky's retelling of the Jewish tale of a nonhuman being, the Golem, created by Rabbi Judah Loew to protect the Jews of Prague from their enemies.

Three of Hyman's most distinguished collaborations have been with Margaret Hodges, and each is focused upon a tale of England's distant past. Hyman won the Caldecott Medal in 1985 for her heroic India ink and acrylic paintings that illustrate *Saint George and the Dragon* (Hodges 1985), Hodges's adaptation from Edmund Spenser's *Faerie Queen*. The artist's acceptance speech upon receiving the Caldecott Medal is most insightful in its explanation of how she works and particularly how she created the magical art for *Saint George*. The text of the speech as well as an excellent profile of the artist written by her daughter, Katrin, may be found in *Newbery and Caldecott Medal Books, 1976-1985* (1986, 264-74 and 275-78 respectively).

The Kitchen Knight is a retelling of an Arthurian legend of Sir Gareth's titanic battles with the Red Knight. Sweeping panoramas of battlefields and the grand English seascapes and landscapes open up this story far beyond the majestic court of King Arthur. The physicality and fury of jousts and battles are notable in the paintings. *Comus* (Hodges 1996) features children as heroes in a retelling of a masque (play) created by poet John Milton in 1634. Believed to be one of the oldest of English fairy tales, *Comus* is named for its wicked wizard who casts an evil spell over the child heroine, Alice. She must be saved by her two younger brothers, John and Thomas. Here, there are no comforting borders. Just as the dark paintings seem to spill over and beyond the physical page edges, the evil of Comus is manifest and seems to leap from the pages to ensnare even the reader.

Hershel and the Hanukkah Goblins (Kimmel 1989) is Eric Kimmel's Eastern European Jewish folktale. Hershel of Ostropol (located in what is now

Ukraine) was a popular folk hero in the nineteenth century. In this tale, goblins have terrified the people of a small rural village and have forbidden them to light even a single Hanukkah candle. Hershel's combination of courage and cunning is too much for the goblins, however, and peace and tradition are restored. Hyman's vibrant and joyful paintings for the book earned her a Caldecott Honor citation in 1990. She has created pen-and-ink drawings to illustrate a further collection of Hershel of Ostropol stories (Kimmel 1995).

Hyman's domain is not limited to folktales and fairy tales set in Europe. Surely, one of her most accomplished works is *The Fortune-Tellers*, Lloyd Alexander's deliciously witty tale, which Hyman visually sets in the country of Cameroon in West Africa. The illustrator writes in the dust-jacket notes that her ink, crayon, and acrylic paintings were especially crafted with her grandson in mind. She wanted to show him the beauty she discovered on her visits to his father's homeland. The faces and expressions of Alexander's characters are especially wonderful in these illustrations. The colors and patterns of the clothing are glorious, and Hyman captures movement and humor superbly in the paintings. Because of her lively and astonishing illustrations, it is impossible to view *The Fortune-Tellers* without a smile on one's face and joy in the heart.

Children today are most likely to recognize Hyman's rich palette of colors even though much of her early work consisted of superb black-and-white illustrations. Indeed, she related in *Something About the Author* (Commire 1987) that she considers her best work to be the black-and-white illustrations for Norma Farber's *How Does It Feel to Be Old?* (Farber 1979). Her daughter, Katrin, at age 10, served as the inspiration for the child in Farber's book about a child whose grandmother shares with her the wisdom of years. Hyman uses incredible overlapping, evocative drawings to portray the elderly woman's reflections of her life now and when she was young. The illustrator also uses black-and-white illustrations to bring to life Jean Fritz's popular biographies for young readers of American patriots Sam Adams and John Hancock. In both *Why Don't You Get a Horse, Sam Adams?* (Fritz 1974) and *Will You Sign Here, John Hancock?* (Fritz 1976), the artist's painstaking research and skillful black-and-white illustrations bring the architecture, costumes, means of transportation, and manners of another period to life for children so that they may better understand the real-life heroes who witnessed the birth of this nation.

The artist skillfully blends black-and-white and color illustrations in a wonderfully romantic interpretation of the holiday classic *A Child's Christmas in Wales* (Thomas 1985). She traveled to Wales to research the setting of Dylan Thomas's boyhood reminiscence. Another Christmas holiday masterpiece illustrated by Hyman is Charles Dickens's *A Christmas Carol* (Dickens 1983).

Just as previous generations of children learned of the great deeds, dark tales, and heroic actions that form much of the culture they inherit from images created by great illustrators such as N. C. Wyeth and Howard Pyle, contemporary children are also being introduced to the rich panorama of folk culture through the wonderful magic Hyman creates by putting pen and brush to paper.

RESPONDING TO "LITTLE RED RIDING HOOD"

The Jolly Postman

One of the most delightful book creations in the past several years is *The Jolly Postman* by Janet and Allan Ahlberg (1986). The book is wonderfully interactive. Riding his bicycle, a jolly English postman delivers letters to fairy tale characters that include the Three Bears, Cinderella, and B. B. Wolf, Esq. B. B. Wolf's letter is delivered in care of "Grandma's Cottage" and consists of a letter from the law firm of Meeny, Miny, Mo & Co. who inform Mr. Wolf that their client, a Miss Riding Hood, protests the wolf's wearing of her grandmother's clothing and orders Mr. Wolf to vacate her grandmother's cottage immediately.

Many opportunities exist for expanding and elaborating upon the ideas put forth in *The Jolly Postman*. Students can assume the roles of the characters who receive mail from the Jolly Postman and can create return letters for the Jolly Postman to pick up and deliver to others. B. B. Wolf's response to the firm of Meeny, Miny, Mo & Co. might look like the example on page 72.

The students might draw wolf paw prints beside B. B. Wolf's signature to complete their delightful letter. Of course, the story can continue. Harold Meeny of Meeny, Miny, Mo & Co. can next reply to B. B. Wolf's letter.

Creative students can write more letters for the Jolly Postman to deliver to fairy tale characters who do not receive mail in *The Jolly Postman*. For example, a Colorado elementary-school teacher has her students assume the characters of Hansel and Gretel. Since they did so much damage to the home of the alleged "witch," their father asks them to write letters of apology to the new owner of the cottage, the "witch's" sister. She gives them focal-point prompts, such as "What things are you sorry for?" and "How can you make amends?"

Students can also devise and present creative-dramatics improvisations involving the delivery of other goods and services using the prompts in figure 3.5, on page 73, for idea starters. Instruct students to choose one item from each column. Working in groups, they should create a three-minute pantomime or improvisation presenting a possible outcome based on their choices.

Harold Meeny, Attorney
Meeny, Miny, Mo & Co.
Deep Woods, Grimm City

Dear Mr. Meeny,

    I have received your RUDE, accusing letter. Enclosed please find the signed lease for this property. If this harassment by you and Miss R. Riding Hood does not cease immediately, I will instruct my attorney, Mr. Mal Practice, of the firm of Shy Ster, Mal Practice, and F. Lee Bailiff, to sue for damages.

Legally yours,

B. B. Wolf
Enclosure

Fig. 3.5. Black Forest Deliveries

Fairy Tale Characters	Item Delivered	How Delivered
Three Bears	Mail	Jolly Postman
Cinderella	Pizza	Storks
Snow White	Flowers	U.P.S.
Red Riding Hood	Furniture	Harley-Davidson
Jack and the Beanstalk	Baby	School Bus
Rapunzel	TV, Stereo	Semi Truck

Grammar

"Little Red Riding Hood" is so adaptable that teachers can even use the tale for some fun work with grammar. Just as reading and writing can be accentuated with fairy tales, grammar can be practiced along with good humor when teachers adapt the venerable "Mad Libs" game by using short pages from well-recognized fairy tales. A gifted student can also help by penning fairy tales "Mad Libs" fashion, which classmates can then use for grammar practice. Figure 3.6 is one example. To utilize "Little Red Riding Hood," place students in teams of two. Student A, concealing the written form from Student B, asks the partner to provide the words for the appropriate parts of speech where there are blank lines on the document. For example, Student A will ask Student B for a noun and then an adjective to complete the first two blanks of figure 3.6. Because Student B has no idea of contextual clues, random words are given. When the blanks are completely filled in, the incongruous and often hilarious completed passage is read by Student A. Roles can then be reversed and the game continued, using the same passage or a new one. The text materials are easy to create. Simply write down a passage from a fairy tale and then eliminate keywords, making sure to leave ample blank lines. Under each blank and line, note the part of speech that grammatically belongs in the blank space.

Fig. 3.6 "Little Red Riding Hood"

Once upon a _____ there was a _____ girl who was known to all as
                     noun   adjective

Little _____ Riding _____. Her _____ loved _____ Red Riding Hood very
        adjective   noun   noun   adjective

much. Indeed, _____ had made the red cape and _____ that the little girl _____
               pronoun   noun   verb

everywhere she went. _____ day when the grandmother was not well, Little
                          adjective

_____ Riding Hood's _____ packed a basket of good things to _____ and
  adjective   noun   verb

some herbal medicine and _____ the little girl to take the _____ to her
                          verb (past tense)   noun

grandmother who lived in the _____. She _____ Little Red Riding Hood not
                                noun   verb (past tense)

to _____ to strangers and not to _____ from the _____. _____
       verb   verb   noun   adjective

Red Riding Hood promised that she would do _____ as her mother told her to do.
                                              adverb

In the _____ a mean and nasty _____ waited for the little girl.
           noun   noun

He planned to _____ her and have both her and her _____ for his supper.
                 verb   noun

When Little Red Riding _____ arrived at her _____ cottage, she
                          noun   possessive noun

immediately noted that her _____ looked _____. She said, "My
                              noun   adverb

goodness, what _____ _____ you have, grandmother."
               adjective   plural noun

Her grandmother replied, "All the better to _____ you with."
                                               verb

From *From the Land of Enchantment.* © 1997 Jerry D. Flack. Teacher Ideas Press. (800) 237-6124.

WRITING AND "LITTLE RED RIDING HOOD"

Students may observe other people's originality by examining the delightful retellings of classic fairy tales such as those in the annotated list of "Little Red Riding Hood" books found at the end of this chapter and on the Internet at the "Little Red Riding Hood Project" Web site. Once students have read and enjoyed these creative tales, they will be motivated to create their own versions of classic fairy tales. Their own writings may take many forms as the following prompts reveal.

Fractured Fairy Tales

Even reluctant student writers show enthusiasm when they are asked to create fractured fairy tales. This writing activity is an excellent elaboration activity. (See Elaboration as a creative productive thinking construct in the chapter, "In the Kingdom of Ideas.") To set the stage for "fracturing," first give each student three or four index cards. On each card, he or she writes a simulated dictionary entry of a slang word or phrase. An example might look like this:

> Turkey (noun), someone or something that is bad (not good);
> e.g., That movie is a real *turkey*.

Collect all of the cards, alphabetize them, and create a slang dictionary that students can use as a kind of "hip" talk thesaurus as they rewrite classic fairy tales with modern—and invariably comic—turns (see figure 3.2, number three). The introduction of a "fractured" "Little Red Riding Hood" might read something like this:

> Like, once, ya know, there was this really outta sight, foxy chick. I mean, like she really knew how to groove. She had this one, I mean, really red set of threads. She really thought she was Suzy Cool when she wore those rags. I'm sure! For real, man! Well, like anyway, she had this granny, ya know, who lived out in the sticks. I mean, like doesn't it blow your mind, Madonna! Like this granny lady really got wasted one time, so Suzy Cool jumped in her bright red BMW and booked on over to granny's place. But, like, you see, she didn't get only 'bout halfway there when this mangy wolf, like, burns rubber in front of her on his slick Harley.

Jack Zipes's superb *The Trials and Tribulations of Little Red Riding Hood* contains two hilarious spoofs of "Little Red Riding Hood" penned by humorists James Thurber and Tony Ross that can serve as further inspiration for secondary students. Students of all ages can create contemporary "Little Red Riding Hood" raps modeled upon David Vozar's splendid example in *Yo, Hungry Wolf!* Artistically talented students can achieve visual humor by illustrating "Little Red Riding Hood," "Sleeping Beauty," or any other fairy tale in the fashions of the latest teen dress craze.

Additional Creative Writing Prompts

Mature creative writers may want to use the literary conceit of fast forwarding beyond the traditional tale's end. What happens after happily ever after? Writers select any future date in the life of Little Red Riding Hood and write from the point of view of the character's life when she is older and wiser. What future life hurdles must she overcome? What is she like as a mother with her own young daughter? In Shelley Duvall's Fairie Tale Theatre film version of the tale, the woodsman is a handsome and single young man whom Little Red Riding Hood grows up to marry.

Patricia Baehr's *The Search for Happily-Ever-After* (see annotation in Variations and Other Treatments in the "Cinderella" chapter) provides yet another model for extending fairy tales in writing. A contemporary young woman feels undervalued as the middle child in her family. She meets the talking rat from the "Cinderella" story and is off on a quest that allows her to meet other fairy tale characters in situations that extend beyond the confines and ages of classic fairy tales. Students can borrow Baehr's technique and fashion stories in which Little Red Riding Hood or other characters from the tale meet up with or intervene in the lives of contemporary children or adults. For example, invite students to write a story about Little Red Riding Hood's first day or week in a contemporary high school. Are there some wolves lurking about in the halls of George Washington High School? How does a teenage Big Red Riding Hood deal with them? Does she need a woodsman to rescue her this time?

Verse

Story is not the only form "Little Red Riding Hood" retellings and reflections can take. Fairy tales inspire poems too. Teachers may share with students verse written about fairy tale characters such as "The Grandmother" from Sara Henderson Hay's *Story Hour*.

The Grandmother by Sara Henderson Hay

You wouldn't think they'd let me live alone
Away out here in the woods, so far from town,
Old as I am, and winter coming on . . .
Still, I suppose, they've problems of their own.
They send the child sometimes, when it's not too
    late,
With an extra shawl, and a little basket of food.
I like to watch her skipping through the gate,
Bright as a robin in her pretty red hood.

I get so lonely, at the close of day,
Here by the fire, without a thing to do.
I've even thought of that poor mongrel stray
That skulks around, so miserable and thin.
Next time he scratches, I think I'll let him in,
And give him a warm bed, and a bone or two.[3]

Hay's poem may serve as a model for older students on how to use verse to explore the feelings and pursue the thoughts of characters found in fairy tale literature, especially minor characters who are not the primary focus in the original works.

Perhaps the easiest verse form for young students is the acrostic or personalized poem. A name or word is written on the page, vertically, one letter per line. Next, descriptions of the subject, words beginning with each corresponding letter of the subject, can be written on each line, horizontally, to complete the poem. Here, Little Red Riding Hood is herself the subject of a personalized or acrostic poem.

Little girl
Into the woods
Told to stay on the straight and narrow path
To grandmother's cottage . . . who
Lay ill in her bed
Everyone knew the girl because of her red cloak

Red Riding Hood they called her
Early one
Day she set forth . . .

Ruse was the tool of the
Infamous wolf who was a
Dastardly fiend
Intent on
No
Good!

Hiding in grandmother's clothes behind spectacles
On the other side of the woods, BUT . . .
Only until LRRH and the Woodsman
Did him in! YEA!!!

3. Sara Henderson Hay. *Story Hour* (Fayetteville, AR: University of Arkansas Press, 1982). Used with permission.

Another variation of acrostic poems occurs when the subject is placed in the center of a poem. Here, the word "WOLF" is written vertically and then used as the focal point for an acrostic poem the wolf himself might write:

Why me?
am I the **O**nly villain?
it gets **L**onely always
being the **F**all guy!

Students can also write limericks, epitaphs, or other humorous verse based upon a favorite fairy tale character. Here is a limerick the wolf of "Little Red Riding Hood" might have penned as he smugly zeros in on grandmother's cottage.

As a villain, I'm the greatest star.
I'm nastier than others by far.
My howl, I adore it,
My cunning, I love it!
Oh great! Granny's door is ajar!

"LITTLE RED RIDING HOOD" RESOURCES

"Little Red Riding Hood" is one of the most popular folktales in the world. Shared around the globe, parents have been telling the cautionary story to small children for hundreds of years. Two of the best known European versions come from France's Charles Perrault and Germany's Brothers Grimm. Ed Young's Chinese version of the story, *Lon Po Po*, won the Caldecott Medal in 1990 and has become extremely popular in school and library storytelling hours. Because of the story's universal appeal, humorists such as James Thurber and cartoonist Gary Larson have also created unique versions of the tale that may be enjoyed by secondary students. Here, both traditional print versions and variations are noted along with video re-creations of the "Little Red Riding Hood" story.

Traditional Stories

Coady, Christopher. 1991. *Red Riding Hood*. New York: Dutton Children's Books. Coady bases his retelling and illustrations on Charles Perrault's version of "Little Red Riding Hood." The rich, dark tones of Coady's palette along with heavily textured paintings create a palpable sense of foreboding. Fear is the dominant theme. Danger is everywhere. Evil is palpable. There is no redemption for the child in this cautionary tale. The wolf consumes both grandmother and child. No woodsman appears to save them. Coady's final page emphasizes the story's moral: "The sad story of Red Riding Hood has been a lesson to all little children."

Goodall, John S. 1988. *Little Red Riding Hood*. London: Andre Deutsch.
This splendid British import uses all animal characters in retelling the "Little Red Riding Hood" story. LRRH is a mouse who meets an assortment of helpful and friendly animals on her way to grandmother's house. A kind and gentlemanly frog, for example, helps her cross a stream. Alas, an evil wolf still lurks behind trees with villainy in his heart and mind. But fortunately for the heroine, a husky woodsman bear overhears LRRH's call for "Help!" (the sole word in an otherwise wordless picture book), vanquishes the wolf, and reunites grandmother and LRRH.

Grimm, Jacob. 1995. *Little Red Cap*. Trans. by Elisabeth D. Crawford. Illus. by Lisbeth Zwerger. New York: North-South Books.
The great Austrian illustrator Lisbeth Zwerger brings her talent to the Brothers Grimm's version of "Little Red Cap," which includes a gruesome end for the wolf. Zwerger's style of illustration is distinctive and uniquely atmospheric.

Hyman, Trina Schart. 1983. *Little Red Riding Hood*. New York: Holiday House. Caldecott Honor Book.
Hyman's rustic scenes transport readers to a time and place when and where fairy tales really could happen. Her splendid floral and patterned borders add significantly to the joy of the visual feast. The palette of colors and hues is splendid. (See profile of Hyman, her story about herself as Little Red Riding Hood, and an illustration from *Little Red Riding Hood* elsewhere in the chapter.)

Langley, Jonathan. 1996. *Little Red Riding Hood*. Jonathan Langley Nursery Pop-Up Book Series. Santa Monica, CA: Barron's Educational Series.
This small-size pop-up book for the younger crowd has delightful pull tabs, pop-ups, and lift-up panels to delight any reader, plus Langley's illustrations have a sassy sense of humor kids enjoy. In this retelling, LRRH's mother comes to the rescue and has little trouble wasting the pesky wolf with grandmother's frying pan.

Marshall, James. 1987. *Red Riding Hood*. New York: Dial Books.
There is a charming irreverence in all of Marshall's work, and those qualities are used to great effect in this telling of the classic story of the child who forgets her mother's instructions not to tarry or speak to strangers. Marshall's wolf is deliciously wicked and sly.

Mayer, Mercer. 1991. *Little Critter's Little Red Riding Hood*. New York: Random House.
The greatest fun of this charming little board book is found behind the small flaps on each page. They move the plot forward or reveal private thoughts of the characters. For example, LRRH stops and asks a beggar where the road goes. Early readers (or good listeners being read to) can lift the flap that serves as the blue cloak of the beggar, and in a flash the beggar's disguise reveals the dastardly wolf. A real charmer of a book for young readers.

McPhail, David M. 1995. *Little Red Riding Hood*. Favorite Tales from David McPhail Series. New York: Scholastic Cartwheel Books.
This small-size board book is perfect for young readers. McPhail's retelling and illustrations are charming. He puts some new twists in the story, such as having the wolf get stuck under the bed—with LRRH jumping up and down on him—that will tickle readers but not rob them of the classic tale's ability to cast a spell of wonder.

Roberts, Tom. 1991. *Red Riding Hood*. Illus. by Laszlo Kubinyi. Westport, CT: Rabbit Ears Productions. Note: Package may include accompanying narration by actress Meg Ryan and music by Art Lande on an audiocassette.
This retelling, based on the collected story of the Brothers Grimm, is set in what appears to be a nineteenth-century mill town and the dense wooded hills and cypress groves that surround it. The wolf is appropriately suave but nonetheless evil. Kubinyi's colored pencil illustrations are richly evocative. He uses a wide variety of visual perspectives to involve the reader or viewer intensely.

Scarry, Richard. 1993. *Little Red Riding Hood*. Little Nugget Series. New York: Golden Books.
Scarry's version of LRRH is done in a hand-size board book for young readers. The positive characters exude all the sweetness and charm typically found in Scarry's books for younger readers. Little Red Riding Hood is a white and yellow kitten. Of course, the woodchopper, a robust pig, dispatches the pesky wolf.

Thompson, Gare. 1997. *Little Red and the Wolf*. Illus. by Nan Brooks. Austin, TX: Steck-Vaughn.
This version of the classic story is designed for emergent readers. It is packaged with Michael K. Smith's *Wolves* (1997) in Steck-Vaughn's "Pair-It" series that introduces primary grade students to fiction and related nonfiction books simultaneously.

Variations and Other Treatments

Crump, Fred, Jr. 1989. *Little Red Riding Hood*. Nashville, TN: Winston-Derek.
The European history and orientation of many well-known "Little Red Riding Hood" stories excludes African Americans from the retellings. Fred Crump Jr. happily rights that omission. In this robust and funny retelling, LRRH is Sarah Jane Jimson, a bright and lovely African American seven-year-old. It is a glorious day in the woods, and Sarah Jane, unfortunately, dawdles along the way to her granny's home. That's the window of opportunity the mean old wolf needs. But all ends happily for Sarah Jane and Granny when an awesome woodcutter comes to rescue the day. A charming retelling that should be shared in all classrooms. The cartoon illustrations are bright, colorful, and witty.

Ehrlich, Fred. 1992. *A Class Play with Ms. Vanilla*. Illus. by Martha Gradisher. Hello Reading! Series. New York: Viking.

In this captivating early reader with pictures, Ms. Vanilla's class puts on a play version of "Little Red Riding Hood" for their elementary schoolmates. There is a great sense of esprit de corps as everyone in the class participates in the production with some students being trees in the forest while others move among them as the hunters. The big surprise comes at the curtain call, when the actor portraying the wolf is revealed on the final page. (It's the teacher, Ms. Vanilla.)

Note: Teachers who want to put on their own Little Red Riding Hood play may wish to consult Interact's *Little Red Riding Hood: A Mini-Musical for All Students*. The simulation can be ordered from Interact, 1825 Gillespie Way #101, El Cajon, CA 92020-1095. Phone: (800) 359-0961.

Emberley, Michael. 1990. *Ruby*. Boston: Little, Brown.

In this contemporary update, the inner city of Boston replaces the woods as a scary place, and Emberley's LRRH is Ruby, a book-loving little girl mouse who is taking cheese pies across the dangerous city to her ailing granny. Not surprisingly, Ruby forgets her mother's admonition to not talk to cats. A fat cat prepares to eat both Granny and Ruby for brunch until a *really big* dog, Mrs. Mastiff, changes the menu. Children will chuckle at Emberley's animal denizens of the inner city, especially a particularly scuzzy reptile hood.

Ernst, Lisa Campbell. 1995. *Little Red Riding Hood: A Newfangled Prairie Tale*. New York: Simon & Schuster.

No deep, dark woods here. The Great Plains with their ocean-size wheat farms are the setting for a modern-day heroine who sports a red-hooded sweatshirt. She pedals her coaster bike (red, of course) on the country paths to deliver wheat-berry muffins and lemonade. The wafting aroma of the muffins is just too much for the wolf to ignore, so he distracts LRRH and beats a path to find Granny—except this "frail, loony, muffin-hungry granny" is anything but a victim. At the tale's end, the wolf is reformed and helps out at the new business, Grandma's Muffin Palace. Readers of this delightful revisionist tale get an added bonus: a recipe for Grandma's Wheat-Berry Muffins.

Lowell, Susan. 1997. *Little Red Cowboy Hat*. Illus. by Randy Cecil. New York: Henry Holt.

The creative author of *The Three Little Javelinas* (Northland, 1992) again turns to the American Southwest for a revisiting of "Little Red Riding Hood."

Morris, Ann. 1987. *Little Red Riding Hood Rebus Book*. Illus. by Ljiljana Rylands. New York: Orchard Books.

Morris and Rylands combine their talents to make this book a special treat to decode. Pictures are occasionally substituted for words in this traditional retelling of the little girl who is cautioned not to wander off the path on the way to her grandmother's house. The same team also created the *Cinderella Rebus Book* (New York: Orchard Books, 1989).

Rowland, Della. 1994. *Little Red Riding Hood/The Wolf's Tale.* Illus. by Michael Montgomery. Upside Down Tales Series. New York: Carol Publishing.
Readers proceed halfway through the book hearing or reading the familiar tale of "Little Red Riding Hood." The wolf dies, and LRRH is reunited with her mother, promising never to talk to strangers or stray from the path again. But readers can then turn the book over and begin reading again to learn the wolf's side of the story.

Vozar, David. 1993. *Yo, Hungry Wolf!* Illus. by Betsy Lewin. New York: Dell.
"Little Red Riding Hood" is done as an autobiographical rap by the wolf in this fun and colorful book that also includes raps celebrating the wolf's famous encounters with the Three Little Pigs and The Boy Who Cried Wolf.

Young, Ed. 1989. *Lon Po Po: A Red-Riding Hood Story from China.* New York: Philomel.
Young won the prestigious Caldecott Medal in 1990 for this stunning variant of the "Little Red Riding Hood" story. Set in China where Young himself grew up, this story has many of the same features of the European "Red Riding Hood" tale but distinct differences as well. A wolf disguises himself as the grandmother of the three girls whose mother has left their home to take care of their real, ailing grandparent. Young uses watercolors and pastels to create the impressionistic illustrations that find their inspiration in ancient Chinese panel art. (See a Venn diagram comparison of *Lon Po Po* and Trina Schart Hyman's *Little Red Riding Hood*, fig. 3.3 on page 59.)

The Wolf's Tale

Readers who think the wolf takes a bum rap in LRRH will find at least two storybook resources that provide a better view of wolves. Della Rowland provides the wolf's viewpoint in *Little Red Riding Hood/The Wolf's Tale* (annotated above). Even better is *The Story of the Kind Wolf* by Peter Nickl, illustrated by Jozef Wilkon (New York: North-South Books, 1982). Stereotypes are exposed in this warm and revealing story. The owl is anything but wise, and the wolf is a kind doctor who takes care of all the creatures of the forest. For a selection of reference books about real wolves, please see "Giving the Wolf His Due" in the Happily Ever Afters section of this chapter.

Professional Reference Resource

Zipes, Jack. 1983. *The Trials and Tribulations of Little Red Riding Hood.* South Hadley, MA: Bergen & Garvey.
Folklorist Zipes shares 31 "Little Red Riding Hood" stories in this collection, which opens with a French version penned by Charles Perrault in 1697 and moves chronologically and geographically to include a contemporary Chinese version, "Goldflower and the Bear," published in 1979. Along the way, readers are treated to such unusual versions as Anne Sexton's poem and James Thurber's parody, both clearly intended for adult audiences. For the serious and gifted students of folklore and storytelling traditions, this is a must reference.

Videocassettes

Little Red Riding Hood. Shelley Duvall, producer; Graeme Clifford, director. Faerie Tale Theatre Series. Livonia, MI: Playhouse Video. 1983. 60 minutes. Videocassette. Shelley Duvall's Faerie Tale Theatre productions are clever live-action re-tellings of many classic folktales. However, "Little Red Riding Hood" does not translate as well to dramatization as other tales such as "Cinderella." Mary Steenburgen is a gifted actress, but she is still an adult woman attempting to portray a small child, and it just does not work. The writer's (or director's) attempt to turn the tale into a love story by having a handsome young apprentice woodsman save LRRH and her grandmother is also unconvincing. Malcolm McDowell is, however, appropriately villainous as the wolf.

Little Red Riding Hood. Bruce W. Smith, director. Happily Ever After Fairy Tales for Every Child Series. New York: Random House Home Video. 1995. 30 minutes. Videocassette.
"Little Red Happy Coat" is an Asian child who takes a basket of food to her beloved Poa-Poa (grandmother) in this animated film celebrating Asian culture. In the forest, panda bears eat bamboo, but such fare does not appeal to the fiercely hungry wolf. All is not lost, however, as a village herbalist comes to the rescue of Little Red Happy Coat and her grandmother. B. D. Wong is the voice of the wolf, and Vu Mai is the voice of Little Red Happy Coat. Other titles in the admirable multicultural treatment of classic fairy tales include "Beauty and the Beast," "The Frog Prince," and "The Emperor's New Clothes."

Red Riding Hood and Goldilocks. C. W. Rogers, director. Weston, CT: Rabbit Ears Storybook Classics. 1990. 30 minutes. Videocassette.
Sweet illustrations of both tales are complemented by actress Meg Ryan's narration. Somewhat jarring is the wolf's Count Dracula-like voice charac-terization. Intended for young audiences, the retellings are faithful to the original folktales. The film is not animated. Rather, a variety of camera angles and close-ups are used to create a video from still drawings of the two tales.

Happily Ever Afters

Giving the Wolf His Due

Aristotle described wolves as "wild" and "treacherous" as early as 350 B.C., and so through history popular culture has seen the wolf as an enemy of man. A great part of man's enmity toward the wolf is based on superstition and myth. With increased awareness and scientific knowledge, human perceptions of wolves have changed in recent years to the point where the wolf is now the symbol of nature, beauty, and courage for many Americans, especially those concerned with the human impact on the rest of the Earth's environment. Since the wolf receives such a bad rap in "Little Red Riding Hood," some teachers and students may well want to engage in reading and research that serves as an antidote to the negative stereotype of wolves in much of children's literature. Many outstanding resources can be used in studies of wolves. The following are but a few recommended student and teacher resources.

Brandenburg, Jim. 1993. *Brother Wolf: A Forgotten Promise.* Minocqua, WI: Northwood Press.
This is a gorgeous photographic essay on wolves in their own world and in their contact with men. Brandenburg provides an amazingly intimate and positive look at the lives of wolves.

Long, Kim. 1996. *Wolves: A Wildlife Handbook.* Boulder, CO: Johnson Books.
Long's book is especially good for student research projects. The book opens with an examination of the wolf as a devouring creature and a threat to humans as found in holy books such as the *Bible* and the *Koran.* Long also examines the wolf as revealed in Native American legends and wolves as found in literature featuring werewolves. The book also comprehensively explores scientific and ecological information about wolves.

Lopez, Barry Holstun. 1978. *Of Wolves and Men.* New York: Touchstone.
Lopez's book is a classic text on the study of wolves from almost every aspect. "Images of Childhood" is a chapter devoted to an exploration of the wolf as depicted in children's literature from Aesopian fables to Jack London's adventure stories. A superb read and a fine reference.

Wolfe, Art. 1995. *In the Presence of Wolves*. Text by Gregory McNamee. New York: Crown.
    Wolfe's nature photography is legendary, and this book affords spectacular, close-up views of wolves in the wild. The photography is nicely complemented with a selection of ancient and contemporary myths and legends about wolves.

Wood, Daniel. 1995. *Wolves*. Vancouver, British Columbia: Whitecap Books.
    "Only man has more complex social structure and a wider range of territory than the wolf." So begins Wood's highly informative and sympathetic photographic essay on wolves.

Creative Problem Solving

Creative and critical thinking may be activated through encounters with "Little Red Riding Hood" stories. For example, after students have learned a creative problem-solving model (see "Goldilocks and the Three Bears" chapter), they can practice with another fairy tale dilemma: What might Little Red Riding Hood have done if there had been no woodsman nearby when she had gone to visit her grandmother? Since the content of the tale is familiar, the students are free to concentrate on the creative problem-solving steps.

First, students can analyze the situation. What facts do they know about LRRH's situation? Second, they can define the key problem facing Little Red Riding Hood. Once the key problem has been identified, students can brainstorm ideas about how LRRH might save herself and her grandmother. Once they have a list of alternatives, the students next propose criteria to use in evaluating their alternatives. Criteria might include: Will the proposed solution be ecologically sound? Can the proposed solution be quickly implemented? The final stage should find the students formulating a detailed plan of action to implement their proposed best solution. Children and adolescents love these lessons and learn valuable problem-solving skills quickly.

"Little Red Riding Hood" Board Game

Students can create an original board game based on a specific fairy tale or fairy tales. For example, invite students to draw a map of the woods Little Red Riding Hood traveled through. Because the story involves a specific journey—a round-trip from the little girl's house to her grandmother's cottage—the notion of a board-game trek or expedition is appealing. Students may devise new traps for LRRH to fall into or avoid. The map can become the game board, and movement around the board may be controlled by each player's ability to answer questions related to the tale correctly. Of course, "chance" and "fate" cards and moves may also be invented for student-created board games.

Creative Drama

A tableau is a still-life scene depicting a moment in time, history, art, or literature. It may be compared to a stop-action shot in cinema. Representations of the Nativity that appear at Christmas are one type of tableau. The plural of tableau is tableaux. Ask student groups to dramatize five scenes from a classic fairy tale such as "Little Red Riding Hood" in five tableaux so that when revealed in sequence they tell the classic story.

ADDITIONAL RESOURCES

In addition to the fine references cited, profiles and critiques of Trina Schart Hyman and critiques of her work appear in the following books. Her address for the Zena Sutherland Lectures is also insightful.

Cullinan, Bernice E., and Lee Galda. *Literature and the Child*. 3rd ed. New York: Harcourt Brace, 1994. Profile of Hyman, p. 182.

Hearne, Betsy, ed. *The Zena Sutherland Lectures 1983-1992*. New York: Clarion Books, 1993. See Hyman's speech "Zen and the Art of Children's Book Illustration" (pp. 183-205).

Kiefer, Barbara Z. *The Potential of Picture Books: From Literacy to Visual Understanding*. Columbus, OH: Merrill, 1995. Profile of the illustrator, pp. 105-114.

Silvey, Anita. *Children's Books and Their Creators: An Invitation to the Feast of Twentieth-Century Children's Literature*. Boston: Houghton Mifflin, 1995. "Voices of the Creators: Trina Schart Hyman," pp. 338-39.

ANSWERS

1. Model D.
2. Model A.
3. Model C.
4. Model B.

REFERENCES

Ahlberg, Janet, and Allan Ahlberg. 1986. *The Jolly Postman*. Boston: Little, Brown.

Alexander, Lloyd. 1992. *The Fortune-Tellers*. New York: Dutton.

Commire, Anne, ed. 1987. *Something About the Author*. Detroit: Gale Research. Vol. 46: p. 107.

Cummins, Julie, ed. 1992. *Children's Book Illustration and Design*. New York: PBC Library of Applied Design, pp. 78-80.

Dickens, Charles. 1983. *A Christmas Carol*. New York: Holiday House.

Farber, Norma. 1979. *How Does It Feel to Be Old?* Illus. by Trina Schart Hyman. New York: E. P. Dutton.

Fritz, Jean. 1974. *Why Don't You Get a Horse, Sam Adams?* New York: Coward, McCann, & Geoghegan.

———. 1976. *Will You Sign Here, John Hancock?* New York: Coward-McCann.

Heins, Paul, trans. 1974. *Snow White by the Brothers Grimm.* Boston: Little, Brown.

Hodges, Margaret. 1985. *Saint George and the Dragon.* Boston: Little, Brown.

———. 1990. *The Kitchen Knight: A Tale of King Arthur.* New York: Holiday House.

———. 1996. *Comus.* New York: Holiday House.

Hyman, Trina Schart. 1977. *The Sleeping Beauty from the Brothers Grimm.* Boston: Little, Brown.

———. 1981. *Self-Portrait: Trina Schart Hyman.* New York: HarperCollins.

———. 1983. *Little Red Riding Hood by the Brothers Grimm.* New York: Holiday House.

Kimmel, Eric A. 1989. *Hershel and the Hanukkah Goblins.* New York: Holiday House.

———. 1994. *Iron John.* New York: Holiday House.

———. 1995. *The Adventures of Hershel of Ostropol.* New York: Holiday House.

Kingman, Lee, ed. 1986. *Newbery and Caldecott Medal Books, 1976-1985.* Boston: Horn Book.

Lukens, Rebecca J. 1995. *A Critical Handbook of Children's Literature.* New York: HarperCollins.

Rogasky, Barbara. 1982. *Rapunzel: From the Brothers Grimm.* New York: Holiday House.

———. 1986. *The Water of Life: A Tale from the Brothers Grimm.* New York: Holiday House.

———. 1994. *Winter Poems.* New York: Scholastic.

———. 1996. *The Golem.* New York: Holiday House.

Thomas, Dylan. 1985. *A Child's Christmas in Wales.* New York: Holiday House.

Chapter *4*

Creative Problem Solving with the Three Bears

CHAPTER PREVIEW

In this chapter a first-rate model for creative problem solving will be introduced and explained. Then the Three Bears (of "Goldilocks" fame) will apply the model to figure out what to do about the little girl intruder who has visited their cottage in the woods. Finally, readers will find an annotated list of first-rate "Goldilocks" storybooks, a recipe for porridge, and creative extensions to explore when using the classic tale of "Goldilocks and the Three Bears."

CREATIVE PROBLEM SOLVING: AN INTRODUCTION

Creative problem-solving (CPS) models are widely used in business and government today. They have tremendous power and applicability in the education sector as well. When schools provide young people with tools and strategies for solving problems, such youth are well on their way to building better tomorrows confidently.

There are many approaches to solving problems. Some people solve problems intuitively, while others rely upon past experiences and procedures (regardless of whether their time-tested tools are applicable to the new problem situation). One especially fine tool to use when confronted with dilemmas is CPS, which is an example of "structured problem solving." That is, the model is a systematic approach to problem solving that is learned, practiced, and brought to bear on new problems. It does not rely upon intuition or random choices. Creative and critical thinking—wherein creative thinking is associated with divergent thought processes and critical thinking is associated with convergent thinking—complement and enhance each other, and they are given equal weight in CPS. They are not considered to be in conflict. The CPS model has evolved over four decades of research at such institutions as the Center for Studies in Creativity (CSC)

89

at Buffalo State College in New York and at the Center for Creative Learning, Inc. (CCL) in Sarasota, Florida. The version of this evolutionary model that the author has found to be the most effective and easy to teach to students learning CPS for the first time is outlined in *Creative Problem Solving: An Introduction* (Treffinger, Isaksen, and Dorval 1994).

The CPS model is composed of six stages that fall into three components integral to creative problem solving. A visual overview of these components and steps appears in figure 4.1. In the past, CPS has often been learned and practiced as a linear, fixed sequence of steps. More recently, Donald Treffinger, Scott G. Isaksen, and K. Brian Dorval have advocated a more flexible CPS approach that views the three components and the six stages within them as independent modules that may be used or skipped as situations and conditions dictate. A problem solver can use all or some of the components and stages of the CPS model and may move from one component or stage to another smoothly. This kind of flexibility has the obvious benefits of maintaining the freshness and the practicality of the model.

The purpose of this chapter is to introduce children to CPS. Some educators may be most comfortable first teaching the model to students in a linear and sequential fashion, and then moving them to practices of breaking the model into components and stages for more flexible usage. Other teachers may wish to emphasize the flexibility of the components and stages at the outset. At present, there is not hard evidence to suggest one method is superior to the other.

Understanding the problem is one of the components of the CPS model. People can be most effective in solving problems when they truly understand the dilemmas or predicaments they are attempting to resolve. One example is the medical model. Physicians examine patients, make their diagnoses, and then prescribe treatments. Good medicine does not occur when a physician prescribes a treatment for pneumonia only to learn later that the patient needed to have his appendix removed. Wise problem solvers invest time up front noting all the vital ingredients and parameters involved in the dilemmas that confront them. Good problem solving occurs when caution and care are used to develop a good understanding of the problem.

One of the stages that facilitates understanding problems is *mess-finding*. In this CPS stage, students and problem solvers recognize that there is a problem, and they evidence "ownership" of the problem through their acceptance of the challenge to attempt solutions. It is perhaps important here to differentiate between teaching this CPS phase to students for the first time and recognizing mess-finding as it is typically used by people in their professional and personal lives. Once students learn and use the CPS model, they are likely to be on the lookout for unresolved problems and new opportunities for themselves in their schoolwork, jobs, or daily living. Both individuals and organizations seek better ways to use their resources and increase their opportunities for success.

Fig. 4 1. Creative Problem Solving (CPS) Model: Three Major Components and Six Specific Stages [1]

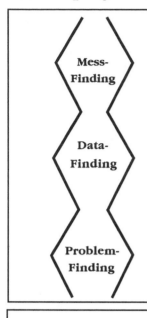

Understanding the Problem Component

D: Seeking opportunities for problem solving.

C: Establishing a broad, general goal for problem solving.

D: Examining many details, looking at the Mess from many viewpoints.

C: Determining the most important data, to guide problem development.

D: Considering many possible problem statements.

C: Constructing or selecting a specific problem statement (stating the challenge).

Generating Ideas Component

D: Producing many, varied, and unusual ideas.

C: Identifying promising possibilities—alternatives or options having interesting potentials.

Planning for Action Component

D: Developing criteria for analyzing and refining promising possibilities.

C: Choosing criteria, and applying them to select, strengthen, and support promising solutions.

D: Considering possible sources of Assistance/Resistance and possible actions for implementation.

C: Formulating a specific Plan of Action.

Source: Donald J. Treffinger, Scott G. Isaksen, and K. Brian Dorval. 1994. *Creative Problem Solving: An Introduction.* [Rev. ed.] Sarasota, FL: Center for Creative Learning. Used with permission.

---

1. Donald J. Treffinger of the Center for Creative Learning, Inc. (CCL) was especially helpful in providing advice and assistance in the preparation of this chapter. The author wishes to thank him and to acknowledge his generous sharing of the graphic found in figure 4.1. All the CPS books cited in the chapter may be ordered from the Center for Creative Learning, Inc., 4152 Independence Court, Suite C-7, Sarasota, FL 34234. Phone: (941) 351-8862.

There are some basic mess-finding questions that can be addressed when students are learning CPS. What problems are perceived? Do the students accept the challenge of problem solving? To return to the medical-model analogy, mess-finding is found in the physician's agreement to see a patient who perceives a medical problem. The physician is predisposed to help the patient. Once creative problem solvers acknowledge that problems exist and indicate their willingness to confront the problems and attempt solutions, they are likely to employ the *data-finding* stage of understanding the problem. Here, problem solvers collect all relevant data. Just as the physicians tackle medical problems by conducting physical examinations, creative problem solvers need to investigate all the possible factors related to potential problems they tackle. Teach young problem solvers to behave much like ace reporters. Reporters seek answers to the five *W*s plus *H*: *who, what, when, where, why,* and *how*. They also ask themselves what potential outcomes, opportunities, and obstacles they may encounter while problem solving. The *who* component of the five *W*s may be especially important in CPS as it determines "ownership" of the problem and potential solutions.

Problem-finding is another stage of the component of understanding the problem. Here, creative problem solvers typically create several potential problem statements that can be used to frame and direct their search for creative solutions. Good CPS problem statements often use these stems:

How might . . . ?   In what ways might . . . ?

Effective problem statements are characterized by clarity and are constructive. The clarity makes obvious the problem to be solved. Problem statements are constructive when they are focused and indicate the *positive* direction idea- and solution-finding will take. One good practice is to encourage students to consider several alternative problem statements when using CPS. Much of the generating of ideas and the focusing of questions is affected or skewed by the wording of the problem in the problem-finding stage of understanding the problem. In their problem-finding, physicians seek the best and most accurate diagnoses of their patients' health status. They may consider several alternative diagnoses given a particular patient's symptoms. The final diagnosis is their problem statement. Even then, they may recommend that further testing be done or that additional specialists be consulted to increase the probability that the final diagnosis or problem focus is correct.

Generating ideas is another fundamental component of the CPS model, and *idea-finding* is the most familiar, albeit misunderstood, part of creative problem solving. As an *idea-finding* tool, brainstorming is used with gusto. Problem solvers adopt Nobel Laureate Linus Pauling's dictum that "the best way to have a good idea is to have lots of ideas." This use of divergent thinking is widely recognized. The problem is that many people also believe brainstorming to be synonymous with the entire CPS model or process. The erroneous perception may be that one simply generates lots of wild ideas whenever problems arise. Such an assumption misses the critical point that both diverging (D) and converging (C) thought processes are used in every component and stage of CPS. Brainstorming is just one of many idea-generating tools. CPS is a comprehensive, structured, and complete model of problem solving that utilizes *both* divergent and convergent thinking throughout. Brainstorming is one possible tool that may be used by idea generators using the model.

The generating ideas component and idea-finding stage of CPS are analogous to the treatment recommendations of physicians. Once their diagnoses are sure, physicians may consider all the possible alternative treatments that are known to remedy the specified illnesses or injuries. In the idea-finding stage of CPS, participants use many of the tools of creative thinking identified elsewhere in this text. (See pp. 117-27, "In the Kingdom of Ideas" chapter.) Creative problem solvers use the creative productive skills of fluency, flexibility, originality, and elaboration and tools such as brainstorming, SCAMPER, and forced relationships.

Planning for action is another component of the CPS model. One stage of planning for action is *solution-finding*. In this stage, problem solvers select the most promising suggestions or ideas they have generated. Typically, criteria are chosen as a way of evaluating a list and paring it down to the most promising possibilities. Criteria may include such factors as cost, time, availability of resources, and the potential popularity or acceptability of proposed solutions. Typical questions generated and used in solution-finding include:

Which idea has the greatest probability of success?

Which idea can be implemented quickly?

Which idea will be the most cost effective?

When physicians engage in solution-finding, they may consider such qualifying criteria as the age, weight, and health of their patients. They have to take into account such factors as allergies patients have or possible negative interactions between newly prescribed drugs and other medications their patients use.

There is no single "right" procedure for evaluating ideas problem solvers have generated. Ideas can be ranked or prioritized using the familiar movie-rating or reviewing scheme: Ideas that appear to be terrific receive five stars, *****, while "duds" or "dogs" barely get one star, *. Alternatively, students could discriminate among their ideas by assigning traditional report card grades of *A, B, C, D,* and *F* to them.

When solution-finding becomes more complex and several student-generated ideas are reviewed across many criteria, a solution-finding grid may be used. On one axis of the grid the various criteria are listed; along the other axis, the best ideas are noted. Each criterion is then used to rank order all the posited ideas to determine how they measure up. Typically, forced rankings are used when grids are employed. A sample grid is shown in figure 4.2, where classic fairy tales, the "ideas" in this example, are evaluated across several criteria selected to gauge student attitudes and opinions. The "criteria" in the example pose these questions:

Which fairy tale is most easily remembered?

Which fairy tale is the funniest?

Which fairy tale is the scariest?

Which fairy tale is the most exciting?

Note that criteria questions are stated in the positive direction. Positive wording avoids the "double negative" confusion of attempting to answer such confounding questions as "Which tale is the best at being the least scary?" Note also that forced rankings have been utilized. The purpose in this example is not to synthesize several good ideas into one broad, comprehensive solution to a problem as is frequently the case in creative problem solving. Rather, it is to determine a clear winner to answer the question: "What fairy tale is most favored by the class?"

Acceptance-finding is a vital stage of the CPS component planning for action. Here problem solvers transform their best solutions into specific action steps. The action plan may involve immediate, short-term, and long-term outcomes. Once again, the medical model may be instructive as to how acceptance-finding works. A physician may need to immediately reduce fever, infection, or swelling before moving forward with even a short-term treatment or medical procedure. The physician may next prescribe pharmaceutical drugs to effect short-term patient cure but may additionally recommend an improved diet and exercise plan—preventive medicine—as a long-term solution to the patient's medical problems.

Two effective acceptance-finding tools are the reporter's five *W*s plus *H* and performance calendars. Problem solvers use who, what, when, where, why, and how to outline how a solution can best be implemented. Again, note that the *who* indicates ownership of both the problem and solutions and is a vital ingredient in decision making. The resulting plan states who will implement the solution, when and how it will be implemented, and so on. Performance calendars are simple laundry lists that order the steps that must be completed for the proposed solution to be successful. For example, a physician specializing in injuries to the

Fig. 4.2 Fairy Tale Solution-Finding Grid

	Easy to Recall	Funny	Scary	Exciting	Total
"Little Red Riding Hood"	5				
"Three Little Pigs"	3				
"Goldilocks and The Three Bears"	4				
"Cinderella"	2				
"Jack and the Beanstalk"	1				

eye gave this author a set of steps to follow that included first wearing an eye patch for 24 hours, next using prescription eye drops for five days, and, third, moving on to a second prescription drug after five days to effect long-term prevention of further damage to the injured eye. Performance calendars are simply the laundry lists people love to make to maintain order in their lives—not to mention to have the joy of crossing off completed tasks.

The CPS model is dynamic. Even after an action plan has been drawn up and implemented, good problem solvers will want to engage in periodic assessment and evaluation to be sure that the solutions chosen work effectively. The CPS model is an extremely effective tool with which to equip young people. Once students learn the model they can use it to confront problems that affect them in virtually any life arena. People routinely use CPS in the home, at the office, and in public sectors. A family can use the CPS model to plan a memorable vacation. A religious community can use CPS to develop a plan to build membership or increase stewardship. A business can use CPS to develop new clients and increase sales. Students can use CPS to increase scholastic success.

Students need frequent practice with CPS. The more experiences they have with using the CPS model, the more likely they are to employ it outside of the classroom. Practice may not make perfect, but routine practice certainly encourages wide and frequent usage and promotes more knowledge about the details, nuances, and principles of problem solving. Once students learn the fundamentals outlined in this chapter, they can easily move to the advanced applications of CPS outlined in such fine resources as *Assessing CPS Performance* (Treffinger 1994a), *Creative Problem Solver's Guidebook* (Treffinger 1994b), and *The Real Problem Solving Handbook* (Treffinger 1994c). These resources make the critical points that CPS is not always the sole or perfect tool to use in every situation. Problem solvers need to appraise tasks or problematic conditions and determine whether CPS is likely to be an effective means to manage the given situation. Moreover, even when parties determine that they do want to use CPS, they may not always apply the model in the linear sequence beginning with mess-finding and concluding with acceptance-finding. Students, for example, may not need to invest time exploring the component of understanding the problem when teachers prescribe the exact task they expect students to complete. Essentially, the problem really has been defined. If students decide that CPS can be an effective tool for them to use in completing the specified task, they can immediately invoke the model's generating-ideas and planning-for-action components and the stages therein.

Several years ago this author worked with a group of middle-school boys who used the CPS model in the well-known interscholastic Future Problem Solving Program.[2] These boys had placed first in the United States for two consecutive years in their division. At a luncheon following their recognition by the Michigan State Legislature, the state's director of gifted programs congratulated the youth on their accomplishments but wondered aloud if there was any carryover into their

---

2. Information about the Future Problem Solving Program (FPSP) may be obtained by contacting the organization at Future Problem Solving Program, 2500 Packard Road, Ann Arbor, MI 48104-6827.

"real" lives of the model they had used so well. Their responses were affirmative. One youth said, "I do not use CPS for everything I do, and even when I do use it, I sometimes skip steps that I don't need for that particular problem." The other youths confirmed his experience with their own examples. Like so many of life's tools and skills, once the basics are mastered, users can creatively apply, adapt, and use them effectively and efficiently as circumstances, needs, and desires dictate.

"GOLDILOCKS AND THE THREE BEARS": A PROBLEM-SOLVING OPPORTUNITY

Fairy tales provide a fun, safe, and creative content base for explaining, practicing, and mastering the CPS model. Young children can be motivated to listen intently to the reading of fairy tales when they know they have to help fairy tale characters such as Cinderella, Little Red Riding Hood, and the Three Bears solve problems. Older students will fondly recall their own first explorations into the world of fairy tale magic and can bring their newly found, "grown-up" sophistication to the CPS process when classic fairy tales are used as practice problems.

The example used here for an introduction to CPS is "Goldilocks and the Three Bears." There are countless versions of this classic English fairy tale. Depending on the age of students, teachers can read the tale directly to the children or ask student volunteers to piece together the story from memory. When and if disputes arise over remembered details, texts can be consulted to resolve questions and to note literal details. A resource list of "Three Bears" stories and other resources follows. One fine, humorous version of the tale is James Marshall's *Goldilocks and the Three Bears.* Marshall provides a humorous retelling of the tale that will delight modern audiences. He achieves humor without sacrificing the classic story line or the characters. The book earned Marshall a Caldecott Honor citation. An added bonus is that the book has been fashioned into a short, clever video presentation. Both the videocassette and other versions of the tale are described at the end of this chapter.

"Goldilocks and the Three Bears": Understanding the Problem

Mess-Finding

Is there a problem? Yes, someone has trespassed into the bear's home, and damage has been done to their possessions. Do students accept the challenge of problem solving? Yes, hopefully. The bears need their help! Moreover, the students will learn how to use vital problem-solving skills as a bonus. When students agree to help solve the bears' problem to better learn and practice problem-solving strategies, they are also acknowledging their willingness to "buy" into, or enter, the world of fantasy. There is a tacit agreement between the teacher or facilitator and the students that they will suspend belief for the duration of this problem-solving simulation. Here the students accept the notion of anthropomorphic bears and accept their problems as being real and worthy of a commitment of the time and effort required to create a solution.

Data-Finding

Students should review the story. They may even go to additional versions of the classic tale to find new clues that will ensure that they have garnered all salient facts and details they need to solve the dilemma the bears face. In most traditional fairy tale versions, Goldilocks is guilty of entering and breaking (Baby Bear's chair); hence students can pretend to be employed as newspaper reporters in pursuit of a hot news story and the answers to the five *W*s plus *H*. Students may note the following information in their problem-solving journals:

Who: Papa, Mama, and Baby Bear; Goldilocks

What: Home trespassed; porridge eaten or spilled; chairs sat in and broken; beds slept in; runaway girl

Where: Home in or on the edge of wooded area

When: Child entered cottage while the bears were out pursuing family-oriented recreation

Why: Goldilocks's curiosity, possible hunger, and eventual need for sleep

How: Goldilocks entered the house uninvited and escaped through an open window

It is worth noting at this point the critical importance of the answer to the question "Who?" The answer to that question leads to the issue of ownership, which, in turn, influences the formation of the problem statements generated. Traditional fairy tales tell the story from the bears' point of view. However, Alvin Granowsky (1996) tells the story from Goldilocks's perspective in *Goldilocks and the Three Bears/Bears Should Share*. Obviously, the bears and Goldilocks are going to have differing views about what constitutes "problems" and "solutions."

Problem-Finding

Students can help the bears by posing many possible problem statements, which may include:

How might Papa, Mama, and Baby Bear "Goldilocks-proof" their home?

In what ways might Papa, Mama, and Baby Bear outsmart any and all intruders?

How might the Three Bears prevent an intruder from using and possibly damaging their furniture?

In what ways might the Three Bears meet and make friends with Goldilocks and her family?

Generating Ideas

Idea-Finding

Students will be able to generate many ideas to help the Three Bears. Recall that the problem statement will determine the direction of responses. The following represent some ideas children may offer. Teachers may share one or more of the ideas to serve as a catalyst to student production of ideas.

> Outwit Goldilocks: Booby-trap the doors of the house (pails of water over doors, triggered to spill onto intruders).

> Call Rent-a-Wolf Security System.

> Buy new locks for the cottage.

> Forget security. Become more inviting to strangers who walk through the woods.

> Throw a "block party," and invite Goldilocks and her family.

> Be more concerned about break-ins. Call for a Neighborhood Watch meeting of all parents and cottage owners in the woods.

> Contact Little Red Riding Hood's grandmother and the woodsman to find out how they deal with intruders.

> Create the Goldilocks & Three Bears Nursery School.

> Stage an open house for all neighbors (including children) in the woods so that their curiosity about the bears' home is satisfied.

> Put porridge in the refrigerator and Please Do Not Sit or Lie Upon signs on all beds and chairs whenever the cottage is left unattended.

Planning for Action

Solution-Finding

After students have generated lots of ideas to help the Three Bears, move them further in the CPS practice to the solution-finding phase. There is no "right" way to evaluate the ideas generated previously. All the ideas can be posted on an overhead transparency, chalkboard, easel flip chart, or in some other fashion. Older students may want to use the stars system found in movie ratings to differentiate among ideas. Younger students may want to use letter grades, such as *A+* or *D-*, to the same end. A more involved form of solution-finding involves using a forced-ranking procedure. In this case, students generate three to five criteria they will use independently to rank order the ideas produced. Possible criteria might include:

> Which idea will be the most effective?

> Which idea will be the most fun to implement?

> Which idea promises the most excitement?

Next students survey the list of ideas generated and pare the entire list down to a more manageable 5 to 10 ideas. Ideas that are nearly identical can be combined. Ideas that have virtually no chance to succeed are eliminated. Students then place keywords from the remaining ideas on the horizontal lines on the left side of the grid. The criteria they have chosen are placed above the vertical rows of boxes formed by the grid. All the ideas are evaluated one criterion at a time as students work their way, from left to right, across the grid. Good ideas are first evaluated by the criterion "effectiveness." Which idea seems to have the greatest likelihood of being effective in helping the Three Bears resolve the stated problem? In the example shown in figure 4.3, five ideas are forced ranked by three criteria. The idea judged to be the most effective earns five points. The idea judged to be least effective receives one point. Students then rate the remaining three ideas, awarding four, three, and two points, respectively, in the order of next most effective to next least effective. Solution-finders next move on to the second vertical column and proceed to evaluate all five ideas by the "fun" factor or criterion. The procedure is carried forward until all ideas have been measured by all chosen criteria. Obviously, the forced-ranking grid system is time-consuming and not always necessary. It is only offered here as one example of how solution-finding can be operationalized. It is critical for teachers and students to recognize that it is an option that can be used, but it is not a mandatory CPS step or procedure. In real life, a particular idea's potential for success is often so evident from the moment it is suggested that problems solvers can immediately move forward to acceptance-finding without losing valuable time in fashioning a grid that would be superfluous.

Fig. 4.3. *"Three Bears" Solution-Finding Grid*

	Effective	Fun	Exciting	Total
Rent-a-Wolf	5			
Call a Neighborhood Watch meeting	2			
Booby-trap the doors of the house	1			
Create a nursery school	4			
Have an open house	3			

Acceptance-Finding

When students have selected the idea (or a combination of ideas) that promises to be effective, fun, and exciting, they can help the Three Bears devise an action plan using the five *W*s plus *H*. Or they can create a Performance Calendar that sets forth the first, second, third, and remaining steps to be taken to bring about a successful resolution of the identified problem. If the Three Bears decide to have an open-house celebration, they need to begin choosing a date, planning the party, sending out invitations, and ordering or gathering food. Their performance calendar might look like this:

1. Choose date for open-house party (Mama, Papa, Baby);

2. Decide upon refreshments (Mama, Baby);

3. Order invitations (Papa);

4. Decide on best games for visiting children to play (Papa, Baby);

5. Pick up and mail invitations (Papa).

The numbers indicate the order of the activities to be completed, and the parentheses note who will complete the tasks. Of course, the Three Bears could just as readily make use of the five *W*s plus *H* scheme to plan for their party. Under "When?" for example, they could fashion a time line for ordering and sending invitations. "Who?" might specify which family members will complete particular tasks.

Once students have assisted the Three Bears with their problem-solving charge, they can move on to practice the CPS model by helping other fairy tale characters confront and solve problems they face. For example, how might Little Red Riding Hood become more self-reliant and solve the problem of the pesky wolf without having to resort to calling on the woodcutter and even slaying the wolf? If all fairy godmothers were attending a faraway convention and were unable to help Cinderella, how might she rely upon her own inventiveness and resourcefulness to develop a means of transportation to go to the prince's ball? Suppose Jack (of beanstalk fame) is a peaceful kind of guy and does not believe in bringing harm to the giant. How might he improve the financial outlook of his mother and himself without having to steal from or slay the giant? When students work with fairy tales to learn and practice CPS, they will gradually realize the benefits, fluidity, and flexibility of the model. Cinderella knows well the "mess" she has been handed. She does not need to spend great amounts of time mess-finding, data-finding, or even problem-finding. If her life is to change, the problem has been predetermined: How might she go to the ball, dressed as a princess, and capture the eye and heart of the prince? Cinderella's entry point in CPS, therefore, is most likely to be generating ideas. She needs to engage in idea-finding to determine the best ways to go to the ball. Likewise, Hansel and Gretel do not need to spend large amounts of time taking stock of their precarious position. The wicked witch has already determined their basic problem: In what ways might they outwit the witch and survive? Through clever and imaginative steps, students can generate ideas and make action plans with gusto!

"GOLDILOCKS AND THE THREE BEARS" RESOURCES

The story "Goldilocks and the Three Bears" is available in many outstanding picture-book versions. The following list of readings first notes traditional versions of the story. Variations and other treatments that feature such twists as a bear cub entering a human household and the tale told from Goldilocks's point of view are also cited. Finally, cartoon and live-action video treatments of the story of a small child who encounters humanlike bears are noted. One of these filmed treatments is based upon James Marshall's illustrations in his version of *Goldilocks and the Three Bears* (1988).

Traditional Stories

Brett, Jan. 1987. *Goldilocks and the Three Bears*. New York: E. P. Dutton.
Brett's bears are so lovable and charming that young readers will want to join them for breakfast. Her characteristic borders provide humor, hint at events to come, and add further magic to the retelling of the tale.

DeLuise, Dom. 1992. *Goldilocks*. Illus. by Christopher Santoro. New York: Simon & Schuster.
DeLuise's humor and playful retelling of the old tales are matched point for point by the imaginative and fun-filled illustrations. Recipes for Goldilocks's porridge and corn muffins are provided along with one for Pasta E Fagioli, which the storyteller DeLuise claims to have been the true dish that Goldilocks sampled at the bears' cottage.

Langley, Jonathan. 1991. *Goldilocks and the Three Bears*. London: HarperCollins.
Langley's illustrations bring smiles as do his contemporary twists on the story. His Goldilocks is appropriately spunky and fun, and the bears are politically correct: On the morning in question, it was Father Bear's turn to cook porridge.

Marshall, James. 1988. *Goldilocks and the Three Bears*. New York: Dial Books.
There is great good humor in Marshall's tale of a spunky little girl who goes where she should not. The illustrations are so much fun that even secondary students will enjoy them. Marshall, who died tragically young, was a sort of Chuck Jones of children's book illustration; he was awarded a Caldecott Honor for this version of Goldilocks's story. These prim and proper bears are given a late Victorian or Edwardian style in dress and setting.

McPhail, David. 1995. *Goldilocks and the Three Bears*. David McPhail's Favorite Tales Series. New York: Scholastic.
Made just for little hands to hold, this charmer tells the classic story with right good humor and delightful and charming illustrations that portray Goldilocks as a hip little girl.

Ross, Tony. 1992. *Goldilocks and the Three Bears*. Woodstock, NY: The Overlook Press.
A delightful retelling of the tale. Ross has an eye for amusing detail and a sly sense of humor. His bears are white but do not live in the Arctic. Papa bear even wears glasses!

Stevens, Janet. 1986. *Goldilocks and the Three Bears.* New York: Holiday House.
Stevens's watercolors are as charming as her fresh retelling of the story. This talented storyteller and artist has a special way with bears as evidenced in her Caldecott Honor Book, *Tops and Bottoms* (New York: Harcourt, 1995).

Ziefert, Harriet. 1995. *Goldilocks and the Three Bears.* Illus. by Laura Rader. New York: Tambourine Books.
The split-page construction of this book makes it fun to read—an interactive treat for primary-age readers. The book design may serve as a model for older students who would like to fashion books of fairy tale stories for younger siblings or younger students.

Variations and Other Treatments

Ada, Alma Flor. 1994. *Dear Peter Rabbit.* Illus. by Leslie Tryon. New York: Atheneum.
Guess what? Goldilocks is actually the daughter of Farmer McGreggor, the near nemesis of Peter Rabbit. Behind-the-scenes adventures of Goldilocks and the Three Bears, the Three Little Pigs, Peter Rabbit, and Little Red Riding Hood are revealed through letters they write to one another. All is happy at the end with a party at Goldilocks's described by Red Riding Hood in a letter to her grandmother.

Ahlberg, Janet, and Allan Ahlberg. 1986. *The Jolly Postman.* Boston: Little, Brown.
Correspondence between Goldilocks and the Three Bears is featured in a charming, interactive book. Later, Goldilocks sends a Christmas card to Baby Bear in the Ahlbergs' *The Jolly Christmas Postman* (Boston: Little, Brown, 1991).

Granowsky, Alvin. 1996. *Goldilocks and the Three Bears/Bears Should Share.* Illus. by Anne Lunsford. Another Point of View Series. Austin, TX: Steck-Vaughn.
This treatment is yet another entry in the Another Point of View Series. The classic tale is told halfway through the book. Then readers flip the book over and read the story from the point of view of Goldilocks, who opines that bears are much less than the hospitable hosts they should be.

Petach, Heidi. 1995. *Goldilocks and the Three Hares.* New York: Putnam & Grosset.
In this whacky, contemporary version, hares (they're really rabbits) replace bears, and resident mice serve as a Greek chorus informing the audience about plot developments. Since hares live underground, a sort of modern-day Alice crawls down the hole that leads to the hares' residence and the predictable story of a family of three—Papa, Mama, and Baby—who jump in the van and go to get a taco and a McCarrot after Mama burns the porridge ("Why can't we have a microwave like everyone else?" Mama complains). A delightful spoof with entertaining contemporary touches children of all ages will enjoy.

Tolhurst, Marilyn. 1990. *Somebody and the Three Blairs.* New York: Orchard.
The Blairs are a picture-book family, and Somebody is a very curious little bear. Baby Blair's delight in Somebody's outrageous investigations in the Blair house adds a special charm to this reversal of the traditional story.

Turkle, Brinton. 1976. *Deep in the Forest*. New York: E. P. Dutton.
This wordless picture book features a young black bear cub who wanders away from his mother and explores a pioneer cabin set deep in the virgin woods of early America in this reversal of the classic story of humans and bears interacting. Turkle's frightened bear cub safely rejoins his anxious mother at the tale's end after raising much havoc in the pioneer cabin.

Videocassettes

Goldilocks. Shelley Duvall, producer; Gilbert Cates, director. Fairie Tale Theatre Series. Livonia, MI: Playhouse Video. 1987. 47 minutes. Videocassette.
This entry in the live-action Faerie Tale Theatre series features Tatum O'Neal as Goldilocks and Alex Karras as Papa Bear. Hoyt Axton and John Lithgow also appear in the clever filming of what happens in the bears' cottage after they awaken from their long winter nap.

Goldilocks and the Three Bears. Milan Klikar, director. Weston, CT: Weston Woods. 1993. 8 minutes. Videocassette.
This short, animated film uses the delightful words and art of the late James Marshall in an upbeat and funny Goldilocks story. The film is short enough to fit nicely into a class exploration of creative problem solving with the Three Bears.

Red Riding Hood and Goldilocks. C. W. Rogers, director. New York: SVS/Rabbit Ears. 1990. 30 minutes. Videocassette.
Actress Meg Ryan narrates both classic tales in the Rabbit Ears filming of lovely still paintings. The camera moves in for close-ups and uses a variety of angles, but neither tale is truly animated.

CPS RESOURCES

Many wonderful people in this country continuously research, debate, practice, and fine-tune CPS. They also write wonderful books and newsletters, make terrific presentations, and sponsor outstanding workshops and conferences. For more information on these many, varied activities, please contact one or more of the following groups:

Center for Creative Learning, Inc. (CCL)
4152 Independence Court, Suite C-7
Sarasota, FL 34234
Phone: (941) 351-8862; Fax: (941) 351-9061
E-mail: dontreff@netline.net

Center for Studies in Creativity (CSC)
Buffalo State College
Chase Hall
1300 Elmwood Avenue
Buffalo, NY 14222
Phone: (716) 878-6223; Fax: (716) 878-4040

Creative Education Foundation
1050 Union Road
Buffalo, NY 14224

Creative Problem Solving Group—Buffalo (CPS-B)
1325 North Forest Road, Suite F-340
Williamsville, NY 14221
Phone: (716) 689-2176; Fax: (716) 689-6441
E-mail: cpsbhq9@mail.idt.net

The Future Problem Solving Program, a highly worthwhile interscholastic program for school-age students, uses CPS. Teams of students first learn and then use CPS to grapple with hypothesized problems of the future, problems they are likely to confront as adult leaders 20 to 50 years hence. In addition to the problem-solving phase of the program, there are scenario writing and community problem-solving projects to engage students. For information, write:

Future Problem Solving Program
2500 Packard Road, Suite 110
Ann Arbor, MI 48104-6827

Happily Ever Afters

Porridge for Breakfast

An imaginative first-grade teacher in Leonidas, Michigan, saves the story of "Goldilocks and the Three Bears" until a fine winter morning. On a given date she urges all her students to eat a light breakfast at home the following day and reminds them to bring their teddy bears to school. She has hot cereal cooking in Crock-Pots when the children arrive the next morning. She serves them hot chocolate, reads "Goldilocks" to them as they tend to their individual bears, and caps off the experience by serving a breakfast of hot porridge to all.

Traditionally, the word *porridge* was used to identify the consistency of cereal rather than a specific grain. A thin cereal was known as gruel, while a thicker cereal was called mush. The thickest consistency was porridge. Porridge can be made with rolled oats or rolled wheat, hominy, rice, or cornmeal. When making porridge from scratch, it is best to use a double boiler to prevent sticking. Moreover, slow cooking enhances the taste of the cereal. Cereals may be cooked with milk in place of water or with a combination of water and milk to taste. Milk makes the porridge more nutritious. Dates, raisins, maple syrup, brown sugar, and nuts may be added to the porridge before serving.

A century past, porridge often had to be cooked for up to six hours. Today's instant oatmeal requires little more than hot water. For best results with porridge, follow the directions on boxes of hot cereals such as Quaker Oatmeal, Cream of Wheat, and Farina. The following recipe may also be fun to prepare.

Goldilocks's Porridge

2 cups rolled oats   4 cups milk (or water)
1 teaspoon salt

Bring liquid with salt to a boil in top portion of double boiler. Add rolled oats to rapidly boiling water, stirring constantly. Cook porridge for two to three minutes over direct heat. Return porridge to double boiler over boiling water, and cook on low to medium temperature for 30 minutes. Allow porridge to cool for several minutes before serving. Makes 5 (child-sized) portions. *Warning*: Do not leave the house unguarded or go for a walk while the porridge is cooling.

Fairy Tale Newspapers or Television News Hours

A fun elaboration activity or extension is to create a classroom newspaper predicated upon the events and characters found in fairy tales. Of course, with today's video-sound equipment, a "televised" news hour is also a possibility. News, features, reviews, editorials, advice and commentary, book or film reviews, and advertisements can be among the journalistic components utilized. For example, students might create a Goldilocks and the Three Bears newspaper that has a bold, trumpeting headline that reads: Blonde Runs Screaming from Cabin! The accompanying story can report the details found in the classic story. The newspaper editorial might carry this title: Let's Make the Woods Safe for All. Ann Landers or Miss Manners might describe the proper etiquette when visiting the homes of bears, and a feature could explore the question of whether children who wander the woods alone are "at risk." A display ad might promote Three Bear's Secure-Home Safety Devices. There is no end to the creative fun students can have as they flex their creative muscles to apply contemporary-media tools to classic fairy tale content.

Bear Research

Invite curious and highly motivated students to research the lives of bears around the world. Students who want to engage in further reading and research may be interested in locating the answers to some of these questions.

How do real bears create homes (dens)?

What are the different species of bears found in the world?

Choose one or more of the species of the world's bear population, and investigate its habits, characteristics, habitats, and degree of endangerment. One especially fine resource is *Investigating Science Through Bears* (Englewood, CO: Teacher Ideas Press, 1994) by Karlene Ray Smith and Anne Hudson Bush with illustrations by Sherri Keys.

Bears in Story and Art

What are the origins of "Goldilocks and the Three Bears"? Who first told the tale? Are there cultural variants of this story in the same manner that there are "Cinderella" and "Little Red Riding Hood" stories told around the world?

Some students may be fascinated by the work of illustrator Barbara Stone (see *In the Company of Bears*, written by A. B. Curtiss, and illustrated by Barbara Stone. Escondido, CA: Oldcastle Publishing, 1994), whose sole subject matter is polar bears. She paints polar bears in all kinds of climates (including the tropics) and situations (roller-skating, celebrating birthdays), but she paints only polar bears. Stone regularly visits Churchill, Manitoba, in Canada, where polar bears congregate every autumn waiting for ice to form on Hudson Bay. She also operates the Polar Bear Gallery, 470 Main Street, P.O. Box 2614, Longmont, CO 80502. Phone: (800) 728-6130.

A "Cool" Goldilocks

Create a new version of the "Three Bears" using polar bears as the subjects. The story would not be set in the woods because polar bears live in the Arctic where there is little or no vegetation. Mama Bear's breakfast that is either too hot, too cold, or "just right," would more likely be fish chowder than a porridge made from grain, and the most likely intruder would be an Inuit child. Ask imaginative children to "fool around" with the "Three Bears" story, substituting polar bears or panda bears for the black bears usually featured. "Ullu and the Three Bears," which follows, is a possible example.

"Ullu and the Three Bears"
by Jerry Flack

Once upon a time there was a little girl whose name was Ullu. She was the most beautiful child in her Inuit village, and all who lived there loved her very much. She brought great joy and happiness to her mother and father and her older brothers, but everyone in their village worried about Ullu because, to tell the truth, her curiosity just got the best of her sometimes; she would wander off from her home and the village and become lost— and the Arctic is a frightening and terribly dangerous place to become lost.

Ullu and her mother and father and all the other Inuits in her village were not the only Arctic families. Families of beluga whales, bearded seals, and Arctic char (fish) live in the Arctic Ocean, which is very, very large and extremely, unbelievably cold. Other families of caribou, reindeer, Arctic fox, and polar bears also live at the very top of the world in places with such names as Greenland, Siberia, Canada, and Alaska.

All the families in Ullu's village marked their calendars according to one of the most exciting days of the year, Christmas Eve. In the wintertime it is very dark in the Arctic North. For days, even weeks and months, the sun is rarely seen. Every year Ullu's parents dressed her as warmly as possible, bundled her in her warmest parka, mittens, and mukluks, and carried her outdoors in the early evening so that she could see Santa Claus and his reindeer climb up, up, and up into the dark night sky as they began their annual journey around the world to give presents to good children everywhere. Ullu marveled that Santa Claus had room in his old sleigh for so many presents. It must be bottomless, for she knew that Santa never returned home without making a final stop at her village to leave something special just for her.

Now, Ullu did not know it, but there was also a family of polar bears who lived not so far away from her village that looked up at the same Arctic sky and traced the graceful takeoff of Santa Claus on the special winter's night. There was a father bear whose name was Kavek, a mother bear whose name was Oona, and a very round and cuddly little baby bear, Olaf. The three bears hardly ever used those names, however. They were simply called Papa Bear, Mama Bear, and Baby Bear.

The family of three bears lived happily together in a house Papa Bear and Mama Bear made from great, big blocks of snow. It was a round house with a little door in front and a small circular hole cut in the dome ceiling to let smoke and steam escape when Mama Bear used the stove to cook breakfast or dinner. Their home was called an igloo, and it had just one great, round room where the bears lived when they were not swimming in the ocean or taking long walks across the great sheets of ice that lie quietly all around their home. In this room there was a kitchen where Mama Bear cooked breakfast on the stove and a table where Papa, Mama, and Baby Bear ate all their meals. (The bears had no need for a refrigerator since the Arctic is naturally cold.) There was also a sitting area with three chairs: Papa's great, big chair; Mama's medium-size chair; and Baby's little rocking chair. Baby Bear loved this area for this is where his papa and mama told him stories as he rocked in his much-loved rocking chair.

Finally, the igloo had a sleeping area where the bears each had a bed. Papa Bear's bed was huge and hard to lie on (Papa Bear had an old snowball back injury, and he needed lots of back support while he slept). Mama Bear's bed was medium-size and wonderfully soft. Its down feathers were especially light; she had wonderful dreams when she slept, always seeming to float on a cloud. Baby Bear's bed was the smallest, and it was not as hard as Papa's bed nor as soft as Mama's. The comfort of the beds was important to the Three Bears because they slept away much of the long, dark winter.

Just as the sun leaves the Arctic for much of the winter, it comes back and stays much of the summer, sometimes giving Inuit and polar-bear families abundant light and sunshine. Indeed, at the height of summer there is no nighttime, just days upon days when it never gets dark. Both Ullu and Baby Bear loved this time of year because it meant that they could go outdoors and play and play and play.

It was on one of these days, when the sun still shined at midnight, that Ullu came to the house of the Three Bears. You may remember that Ullu was a curious child, and one summer day when she was still much too young to wander beyond her village, she did just that. She forgot her parents' warnings, and she followed a path that led from her village out onto the great, vast plains where there was a great expanse, some remaining patches of snow and ice, and ocean as far as she could see.

Ullu was thrilled with all the new discoveries she was making in the land beyond her village. She saw an arctic fox teaching her young family how to hunt mice. Mother Fox warned Ullu that she should be a good girl and go back to her village, but just about that time Ullu spotted a thicket of berry bushes that she could not resist. She had had berry jam once, and it was so-o-o-o delicious. And to tell the truth, her wanderings were beginning to make her hungry. But these berries were hard and green and not at all sweet, so Ullu strayed even farther from her village, hoping to find something that would taste very good.

Much of the year, the bear family followed much the same schedule as the sun. As spring and summertime came each year, they spent more and more time away from their winter home and slept less. They spent their long days fishing and hunting seals and gathering sweet berries that they stored so that they would have plenty of good food to last them through the long winter months when the sun went south. Even on long work days the bears always began their day by having a bowl of Mother Bear's fish porridge. Mama Bear's porridge was so good that it filled Baby Bear full up to his very top every day. Papa Bear always had his porridge in a great, big bowl. Mama Bear had her porridge in a medium-size bowl, and Baby Bear had his own bowl that was just the right size.

It was one of these late spring or early summer days when the Three Bears had no more than sat down to their morning meal than Papa Bear burned his tongue on Mama Bear's wonderful but hot porridge. "Mama Bear, this porridge is too hot," Papa Bear said. "Baby Bear will burn his tongue on it and cry."

"Oh, dear, we don't want that to happen," said Mama Bear. "I have a good idea. We need fresh moss for our supper soup. Why don't we all go for a nice walk while our porridge cools and gather our supper moss." So that was just what they did.

The Three Bears were not far from their home when Ullu happened upon it. Normally, she would never have gone into a strange house, but the open door seemed to welcome her and the wafting aromas of Mama Bear's fish porridge reminded her that she was very, very hungry. She forgot all her mother and father had told her about good manners and boldly approached the bears' igloo. Just before entering the igloo, Ulla did call out, "Is anybody home?" Hearing no response, Ullu boldly entered.

It was one of the prettiest homes Ullu had ever seen, and the table was most inviting with its three bowls of delicious fish porridge just waiting for someone such as a pretty young Inuit girl to try them. So that was just what she did. She first picked up Papa Bear's spoon and sampled the fish porridge in his great, big bowl. But it was too hot and nearly burned her tongue. Next she tried Mama Bear's bowl of porridge, but—quite the opposite—it was too cold for her. Finally, she picked up Baby Bear's spoon and promptly discovered that the porridge in his bowl was just the right temperature and just the right amount to fill her tummy, and she ate every last drop.

No longer hungry, Ullu began to explore the home of the Three Bears. She thought Papa Bear's huge chair looked very inviting, but as soon as she climbed up into it, she discovered that it was much too big and much too hard for her. It was not at all comfortable like her daddy's lap, which was her favorite place to sit— something she was missing more with the passing of every minute. Next Ullu tried the Mama Bear's chair, but it was also too big for her and so soft that she almost became lost in it. So she tried Baby Bear's little rocking chair: It fit her just right and was great fun to rock back and forth. But

then, just as suddenly as she had found the inviting igloo, she heard a loud "crack!" followed by an even louder "bang!" and she found herself sitting on the floor surrounded by the pieces that were all that remained of Baby Bear's chair.

Falling on your bottom and breaking a chair and being so very far from home doesn't feel good, and Ullu was more and more feeling like a nap would be just the right thing for her, so she carried Papa Bear's footstool over to the biggest bed, stretched as far as she could, and crawled on top of Papa Bear's bed. She knew in an instant that this bed was too hard. She would never get to sleep on that bed! She climbed down from the biggest bed, collected the footstool, and climbed with much less effort into the medium-size bed that looked soft and inviting. But it was too soft. Indeed, it was so soft that Ullu had to work really hard to climb out of Mama Bear's bed. By the time she laid down on Baby Bear's bed she was pooped! It felt so-o-o-o-o good that she immediately fell fast asleep.

The Three Bears, meanwhile, had had especially good fortune and found not far from their igloo a great patch of tasty fresh green moss just perfect for Mama Bear's moss broth. The walking and gathering of moss had increased the appetites of all three bears, so they headed home for breakfast in great anticipation. No sooner had they crossed the threshold of their beloved home than all three knew another polar bear or something even more fierce had been in their igloo. Papa Bear saw his spoon was not where he remembered leaving it and excitedly said, "Someone's been eating my porridge." Mama Bear echoed Papa Bear's words exactly. But Mama and Papa Bear still had fish porridge in their bowls. Baby Bear looked at his empty, overturned bowl and cried, "Somebody's been eating my porridge and ate it all up!"

In a flash of the eye, the bears could tell that somebody had also been in their living room. Papa Bear's favorite pillow for his bad back was askew. "Somebody's been sitting in my chair," he growled more fiercely than before. Mama Bear's chair still looked most soft and inviting, but her knitting was not where she remembered leaving it, and she also gasped, "Somebody's been sitting in my chair." But the most disconsolate utterance came from Baby Bear. "Somebody sat in my rocking chair and broke it all to bits!" he wailed.

Mama Bear rushed over and put her arms around Baby Bear to comfort him. As she brushed away the tears on his snow-white face with her gentle paws, Mama Bear cooed: "Hush, Baby Bear, don't you worry. Papa Bear can fix your rocking chair."

By that time, Papa Bear's attention was elsewhere. His footstool was not where he left it. Somebody had moved it over beside his huge bed, and the patchwork quilt Mama Bear had made and Baby Bear had given him on Father's Day was rumpled. Papa Bear was really steaming mad now. "Somebody has been sleeping in my bed!" he bellowed. Mama Bear and Baby Bear certainly heard his outburst, and they rushed to see the condition of their own beds. There was a little depression right smack in the middle of Mama Bear's bed. She knew it had not been there before for Mama Bear always made her bed first thing every morning—even before she started making fish porridge for her family's breakfast. Mama Bear's surprise wasn't announced with a ferocity that matched Papa Bear's roar, but it was still a loud complaint: "Somebody's been sleeping in my bed too!"

Baby Bear had the biggest surprise of all that morning, for when he walked to his bed, there was somebody in it. Baby Bear gasped, "Somebody's been sleeping in my bed, and she's still here!" Of course, all the roaring and bellowing and bear activity finally woke Ullu from her deep sleep. Ullu did not like to be awakened from her wonderful naps even under the best of circumstances—such as ending a nap to observe Santa and his reindeer take off from the North Pole in the late afternoon every December 24th—and she was really unhappy to awaken to such awfully loud and fearsome noises in a place that did not appear at all familiar to her.

Ullu had seen the great white bears before but only from great distances and always in the satisfying and protective arms of her beloved father. Now here she was in a strange place with three of them staring down at her and not a single smile on any face. And, oh, my, were they ever big! Faster than anyone could say "aurora borealis" Ullu was out of Baby Bear's bed, out the bears' igloo door, running for her life across the great tundra, and headed to her own home. Ullu was no farther than a mile from her home when she heard—and then saw—her father calling for her: "Ullu." "Ullu." "Ullu."

"Here I am, Daddy!" she yelled as she rushed even faster to be picked up and hugged and kissed by her father.

"Where have you been, Ullu? Your mother and I have looked for you everywhere."

Much of that whole day, Ullu told of her adventure over and over again, first to her parents and then to her grandparents and even to other villagers. And she continued to tell the story year after year. When she was all grown up and herself a mother, she told her children the story of the Three Bears and the beautiful igloo where they lived. She grew even older and told the story to her grandchildren. Her youngest granddaughter, Urilu, loved the story so much she begged her grandmother to tell the story over and over again. But one thing was sure. As often as Ullu told of her adventures that remarkable Arctic day long ago, she never, never, ever went off exploring alone again.

And the great white bears? Papa and Mama Bear both shared their fish porridge with Baby Bear that fateful day. After breakfast, Mama Bear made up all the beds as Papa Bear repaired Baby Bear's rocking chair, making it as good, if not better, than before. When all their work was done, and the igloo resettled, Papa and Mama Bear sat down in their chairs, and Baby Bear crawled up on his Papa's lap—for the glue on his chair was still drying—and they all agreed that it had been a most unusual day.

Although the beautiful little girl from the Arctic and the Three Bears never saw one another again, both the Bear family and Ullu lived quite happily ever after.

◆ The End ◆

REFERENCES

Granowsky, Alvin. 1996. *Goldilocks and the Three Bears/Bears Should Share*. Austin, TX: Steck-Vaughn.

Treffinger, Donald J. 1994a. *Assessing CPS Performance*. Sarasota, FL: Center for Creative Learning.

———. 1994b. *Creative Problem Solver's Guidebook*. Sarasota, FL: Center for Creative Learning.

———. 1994c. *The Real Problem Solving Handbook*. Sarasota, FL: Center for Creative Learning.

Treffinger, Donald J., Scott G. Isaksen, and K. Brian Dorval. 1994. *Creative Problem Solving: An Introduction*. [Rev. ed.]. Sarasota, FL: Center for Creative Learning.

Chapter *5*

In the Kingdom of Ideas

CHAPTER PREVIEW

Creativity is the encounter of the intensively conscious human being with his world.

—Rollo May

This chapter is filled with ideas to help teachers spark the creative thinking of students. Brainstorming, creative productive thinking, and several advanced creative-thinking tools such as SCAMPER are explained and highlighted by using such diverse fairy tale characters as Hansel and Gretel, Sleeping Beauty, Little Red Riding Hood, Goldilocks, and the Three Bears. A brief biographical sketch of the Brothers Grimm is included along with several Happily Ever Afters. Outstanding collections of fairy tales are then listed and annotated.

Anyone who has witnessed a child playing with an empty box realizes the wisdom of Rollo May's words. What is needed in education is the surety that the creative encounters students have with their world are not left to chance. Educators should establish classroom climates in which creative thinking and problem solving are cultivated and treasured. When teachers use creative-thinking strategies in classes, they typically note several things. Students who have previously been reticent or bored in class become excited about learning. Student interaction and cooperation improve significantly. Self-esteem swells in all students but especially in those students who have previously believed they could never master the one "right" answer as quickly or as often as others. Student enthusiasm for class often increases as discipline problems decrease. Student attendance may even improve! Teachers also find that they enjoy teaching more when they revitalize their teaching strategies to include plenty of creative opportunities and outlets for their students and themselves. One of the absolute truths about creative behavior is that it invariably makes people feel better about themselves and their environment.

115

CREATIVE THINKING

Creative thinking is the key subject of this chapter. Such classic creativity tools as brainstorming and the creative productive thinking elements of fluency, flexibility, originality, and elaboration are defined and their use is demonstrated through the use of a variety of fairy tale characters and situations. Teachers should note that all these tools are generic skills that may be applied to virtually any content matter. SCAMPER, for example, is as useful to inventors and artists as it is to storytellers or authors of modern fairy tales.

BRAINSTORMING

Brainstorming is most frequently used by groups of people working together to generate ideas and solve problems, but the rules of brainstorming are useful for individuals to employ as well. Brainstorming as a process was created by Alex F. Osborne (1963) and described in his creativity classic *Applied Imagination: Principles and Procedures of Creative Problem Solving*. Osborne suggests four guiding rules people should activate when seeking ideas: (1) criticism is ruled out, (2) wild ideas are welcomed, (3) many ideas are sought, and (4) combinations and improvements are gladly received. The best-known criterion among these four guiding points is the deferment of criticism. Osborne and others do not suggest that evaluation is not a component of creative-thinking processes. Realistic evaluation of ideas and plans is vital to the success of any venture. Rather, Osborne and other creative problem solvers suggest separating creative problem solving into at least two stages. Brainstorming is used in the first stage, often referred to as *ideation*, where the primary goal is idea generation. Critical thinking is saved for the decision-making stage of problem solving.

Students quickly learn the rules of brainstorming, but they need encouragement and frequent practice to greatly increase the quantity and quality of ideas generated in brainstorming sessions. Many students will quickly adopt a mode of not censuring other students' ideas but may continue to place limits on their own creative potential through the use of internalized self-criticism. They limit their own creativity—and ultimately their group's creativity—if they withhold ideas they perceive to be unworkable or too frivolous. Gently remind students that in the ideation phase of problem solving the primary goal is to generate as many ideas as possible, and brainstorming is the best way to achieve that goal. Teachers can emphasize the highly dynamic and interactive nature of the rules of brainstorming. Ruling out criticism of others *and* oneself leads to a dynamic atmosphere in which good ideas multiply and grow. One person's "wild" or "freewheeling" idea sparks another person's thinking, which, if verbalized, ignites still another person's imagination. Thus, not only are more ideas brought forth, but unusual combinations and adaptations emerge.

A princely tip: Employ the talents of an artistically talented student in the classroom. Ask the student to make a poster highlighting brainstorming's four essential rules. The resulting poster, perhaps illustrated with fairy tale characters, can be prominently displayed in the classroom as a continual reminder of brainstorming strategies.

CREATIVE PRODUCTIVE THINKING

Mirror Mirror
And the Queen spoke to the
mirror on the wall
Asking it to list the creativity
components, one and all.
The mirror returned its message
after a thoughtful and considered duration:
"Fluency, flexibility, originality, and elaboration!"

Fluency

Once students understand the format for brainstorming, they can use this ideational technique to explore the four components of creative productive thinking: fluency, flexibility, originality, and elaboration. One way to introduce students to the concept of fluency is through the use of a language analogy. What does it mean to speak French, Spanish, or German fluently? It means being able to speak many of the words and phrases of the language with ease. Fluency, as it pertains to creativity, is the ability to produce many ideas comfortably. Fluency skills can be enhanced and improved using any of the following activities. For ease of implementation, all ideas in this chapter have already been converted to "student talk." Remind students to fully employ all the rules of brainstorming when responding to these fairy tale prompts.

- List all the funny names you can think of for Cinderella's stepsisters.

- List all the things you can think of that Little Red Riding Hood might have been carrying in her basket of goodies for her grandmother.

- Spells, potions, and incantations figure into many fairy tales. Read Shakespeare's Witches' Scene from *Macbeth* (Act IV, Scene I). This is one recipe for a witches' brew. If you were going to make a potion or an evil brew, what are all the slimy, creepy critters and things you might want to include? If time permits, pantomime or improvise your own witches' scene, demonstrating the making of your brew and the spells cast.

- In 10 minutes or less, working together, fill in as many spaces as you can in the fairy tale grid, figure 5.1. Each entry must begin with the corresponding letter in the left column from the words *fairy tales*. Note: It is not necessary for all the names and items to correspond to classic fairy tale subjects.

- Create an acrostic fairy tale poem. Write the names of fairy tale titles, characters, settings, or words and phrases associated with fairy tales one letter at time, vertically, down the side of a piece of paper. Next, think of characters, concepts, and commonly found objects in fairy tales or fantasy literature. The beginning letters of these words and phrases should correspond to the vertical column of letters first written. Write these words horizontally on the appropriate lines. Presto! You have created a fairy tale poem. "Fairy Tale" is the completed poem. Can you complete the poem "Frog Prince" on page 119?

Fig. 5.1. Fairy Tale Grid

	Boys' Names	Girls' Names	Items of Clothing	Foods	Flowers and Plants
F	Frog Prince				
A				Apple	
I					Iris
R		Rapunzel	Red Cape		
Y					
T					Thorn Hedge
A		Aurora			
L			Lace Gown		
E					
S		Sleeping Beauty			

F	fantasy	T	_____
A	abracadabra	H	_____
I	invitation to the ball	E	_____
R	Rumpelstiltskin		
Y	youthful hero-Jack	F	_____
		R	_____
T	Three Little Pigs	O	_____
A	Alice in Wonderland	G	_____
L	Little Red Riding Hood		
E	elves	P	_____
S	Snow White	R	_____
		I	_____
		N	_____
		C	_____
		E	_____

From *From the Land of Enchantment.* © 1997 Jerry D. Flack. Teacher Ideas Press. (800) 237-6124.

Teachers, please note that another example of an acrostic fairy tale poem is found in the "Little Red Riding Hood" chapter of this book.

Fluency prompts and activities should be given to students often so that exercising creative thinking and brainstorming become regular features of how students think and respond. But the activities do not need to take up the valuable classroom time necessary for basic-skills development and practice. Wise teachers keep a brightly colored folder (for ease in locating) of fluency prompts handy and ready to use as time fillers when there are gaps in the daily schedule or just a few minutes to fill productively before a class or the end of the school day. Fluency prompts also make great wake-up prompts on those occasions when students are lethargic. Conversely, fluency prompts can even be used to quiet a noisy and rambunctious group of students at the start of a learning session. Simply convert a fluency exercise to a silent, individual exercise. Invite students to respond individually to fluency prompts by writing their ideas in their journals. For example, students can silently spend two minutes creating names for the seven dwarfs in their journals while the teacher takes roll or confers with individual students in a more peaceful and tranquil environment.

Flexibility

The second component of creative productive thinking is flexibility. Another analogy may prove useful in introducing the concept of flexibility. Ask students to think of different uses for steel. Steel girders help support buildings in part because of their strength and solidity. But steel can also be used to make wire

that is highly flexible and able to take many shapes. Flexibility is the opposite of rigidity. Flexibility, as it relates to creative thinking, is the ability to generate many *different* ideas and products. The creative mind characterized by flexibility seeks many varied answers or solutions. Flexible thinkers go beyond the bounds of conformist thinking as they seek and consider alternatives others fail to note. This does not mean that they ignore or break appropriate rules for safety or conduct. Flexible thinkers use rules as guidelines, not as straitjackets that will curb creative thinking. Where fluent thinking seeks many ideas, flexible thinking pursues uniquely *different* ideas. The following prompts are examples of fairy tale challenges to help develop the flexibility of students' thinking.

♦ Describe at least three different things Little Red Riding Hood might have done to save herself and her grandmother had the woodsman not been close by. Each solution should approach the problem from a different angle. That is, a solution should not just be a slight variation on a previous answer.

♦ Make up as many different common words as you can from the phrase *once upon a time*. For example, the words *one*, *Tim*, *count*, and *pot* are found in the phrase.

♦ Create three categories: fairy tales, characters, animals. As fast as you can, name a fairy tale. Next cite the central characters found in it, and, finally, change your thinking again and recall any animals featured in the fairy tale. As soon as you finish with one fairy tale, move on to another tale and again name the characters and animals associated with it. Keep on categorizing fairy tales until time is called. Here are two examples. How many fairy tales can you characterize in 15 minutes. Get ready, set, GO!

Fairy Tales	Characters	Animals
"Jack and the Beanstalk"	Jack, Mother, giant	cow, Milky-White
"Hansel and Gretel"	father, stepmother, children, witch	birds (eat the bread crumbs)

♦ The number 3 is a magical number in fairy tales: 3 wishes, 3 bears, 3 trips up the beanstalk. See how many *different* ways and how high you can count using only the number 3.

$$3 \div 3 = 1 \qquad\qquad 3 - [3 \div 3] = 2$$

$$3 = 3 \qquad\qquad\qquad \text{m m} = 4 \text{ humps from two 3s turned on end}$$

$$3 + 3 - [3 \div 3] = 5$$

♦ Suppose that a new fairy tale emerged about a young girl who awoke one morning to find her hair had turned purple. List the consequences of this event. What are some of the many benefits she might derive from her changed condition? What are some problems she may experience?

Originality

Originality is the ability to generate unique, clever, and unusual responses to prompts or tasks. Original thinking involves perceiving and responding to the world in fresh, new ways. Ideas or products suggested by students need not be new to the world, but they should represent new or original thinking by the students. The following prompts from fairy tales can serve as catalysts to students' originality of thought.

◆ Create a totally new fairy tale for a book of contemporary fairy tales. Invent a hero, and use as many of the highlighted items that follow as possible in the story: parking meter, black leather jacket, copy of *Newsweek*, Los Angeles Dodger baseball cap, vitamin capsule, Big Mac, purple vase, cowboy hat, airplane ticket.

◆ Be Futuristic! Create a science-fiction fairy tale fusing two literary genres. Use the plot and possibly the characters from a classic tale such as "Hansel and Gretel," but change the narration, dialogue, and setting to reflect some future time and place, say, Mars in A.D. 2107. *Note to teachers*: This activity functions equally well as an individual creative-writing assignment or as a group creative-dramatics improvisation.

◆ Think up new names for classic fairy tale and nursery-rhyme characters. The names should not be common names such as John or Susan. The names need to reveal something about the characters or their unique situations. Here are a few examples of existing and newly created names of classic fairy tale characters.

Old Names	New Names
Three Little Pigs	The Porcine Brothers
Rapunzel	Pretty Miss Longhair
Little Red Riding Hood	Missy Redcap

◆ Design an original, high-fashion ball gown or a wedding gown for Cinderella and appropriate formal wear for Prince Charming.

◆ When Snow White moved in with the Seven Dwarfs and started keeping house, she found that the storage room of their cottage really needed a thorough cleaning. The following were among the items she found in storeroom.

1 suit of armor	2 china chamber pots
3 boxes of marbles	1 broken spinning wheel
20 spools of thread	1 large, black kettle
1 straw broom	1 pierced tin lantern
1 rat trap	48 playing cards (the 4 queens missing!)
7 half-used candles	1 toy top

None of the items Snow White found may be discarded, given away, or sold. Because she is a highly imaginative person, Snow White wants to find entirely new uses for the items, singly or in combination. Please help Snow White. Think of new uses for all the items. You may change the composition of the items—say, melt the candles—and you may combine items in, for example, an invention that uses the toy top, the marbles, and the spools of thread.

Elaboration

Elaboration involves the addition of significant detail to basic ideas. Elaboration is the process of exploring alternatives that enhance ideas or make products more complex and intricate. A fine idea might be the suggestion that classrooms be made more accessible for students with disabilities. Elaboration of that kernel idea might involve the added suggestions of placing Braille labels on cabinets to accommodate blind students and lowering activity tables to accommodate students in wheelchairs. The following prompts will provide students with opportunities to develop and practice the skill of elaboration.

♦ Create and add three new characters to any existing fairy tale or nursery rhyme. Describe the new characters and how their addition would change the basic story. For example, what changes might occur if the fairy tale became "Snow White and the Ten Dwarfs"? What new twists might occur in "The Six Little Pigs"?

♦ Build a fairy tale. First, each person in the class or group should write a common noun such as balloon, basket, broom, or butterfly on a slip of paper. One person collects the slips of paper and places them in a hat or fishbowl. All persons in the group form a circle and number off. The story building begins when the first player selects a slip from the hat or fishbowl and uses the word contained on his or her slip in the tale's first sentence, which that student makes up. (Of course, the story always begins with the words *Once upon a time.*) Next, the second player selects another slip of paper, repeats what the first player has said, and adds a new sentence to the story, incorporating in his or her sentence the word he or she has drawn. The story building continues until everyone has had a turn, each successive participant repeating everything that has been said before and adding a new line which includes the word drawn. Just as the first player began with "Once upon a time," the final player concludes this storytelling activity with ". . . and lived happily ever after."

♦ Choose a character for a modern-day fairy tale—say, an animal that is an endangered animal species or a technology whiz kid. Brainstorm all the attributes, traits, and characteristics that help to develop the character as fully as possible. Traits might include faith, courage, cunning, wisdom, patience, and the like. Try to brainstorm at least 25 traits. Select the best, most descriptive, and appropriate traits, and elaborate on the original image or perception of the character. Write a character sketch that fully describes the character. Now create the settings, conflict, and additional characters needed to complete an original, contemporary fairy tale.

♦ Hans Christian Andersen's "The Little Match Girl" is a tragic tale about society's indifference to a starving child. Sadly, it is not so difficult to find contemporary parallels. Abused and homeless children and families do exist in lands of plenty. Using your elaboration skills, create a modern parable or fairy tale that will alert people to the tragic consequences that arise when defenseless children suffer neglect. When your story is completed, consider donating it to one of the many sponsoring institutions and social agencies that are concerned with the well-being of children.

♦ Suppose there had been a fire a long time ago and it had destroyed almost all of the possessions of the Brothers Grimm. Pretend you are a history sleuth. You find the following scraps of charred paper—all that remains of their writing. Elaborate on each basic idea. What might the whole stories have been like had they survived?

> She whose foot this golden slipper fits . . .
>
> Looking-glass that talks . . .
>
> Poisoned apple . . .
>
> Miller's daughter spins straw into gold . . .
>
> Little house made of gumdrops and sugar cakes . . .
>
> Beautiful girl pricks finger on spindle . . .
>
> Wolf's belly filled with stones . . .

♦ Be an illustrator. A major publisher of children's literature is producing a new anthology of classic fairy tales. You have been asked to submit a sample of your artwork so that the publisher may determine if you are the best artist to illustrate the entire book. You have the same three options all other competing illustrators have. Draw a character or scene from "Cinderella," "The Frog Prince," or "Rumpelstiltskin." Choose one of the options, and create the best drawing you can. Remember, the book-illustration contract is worth a lot of money, and the publisher will be looking for elaboration or attention to detail in choosing the best illustrator. *Note to Teachers*: Prior to using the following exercise, cut striking and attractive photographs and drawings from magazines, travel brochures, junk mail, and other media resources. The pictures may be artists' drawings or photographs. The photographs or drawings can be of people, animals, objects, or scenery. Clip only a portion of the picture—half of a ship or a person's face or the corner, roof, or foundation of a building—and affix any part of the picture to a larger piece of paper so that the photograph occupies no more than half of the paper surface. The pictures do not need to be centered. Indeed, interesting drawings often result when the partial photograph or drawing is placed nearer the top, bottom, left, or right margin of the paper. Prepare a sufficient number of these partial pictures so that each student has at least one choice. Students use crayons, markers, and other media plus their own skills of elaboration to visually tell "the rest of the story." The following prompt works well with these "unfinished" pictures.

◆ MGM will be filming a new movie with a fairy tale theme. You have been hired as the set designer. Unfortunately, the producer is a rather difficult person with whom to work. She never gives much direction, preferring that people who work for her think for themselves. She is also busy and rarely available for answering questions. She has only left you a stack of unfinished pictures and the direction to use your own imagination and elaboration skills to complete one of them. She's now in Rangoon—finishing another movie—so you are on your own. From the stack of unfinished pictures, select one that interests you. Complete the picture by adding all the significant detail that you believe would add up to an interesting visual scene or story.

CREATIVE-THINKING AND PROBLEM-SOLVING TOOLS

Just as the farmer's daughter used the three golden gifts of the apple, comb, and spinning wheel to free the prince from the clutches of the evil troll princess who resided in the castle *East of the Sun and West of the Moon* (Hague 1980), teachers can employ three golden ideas to liberate students' creative potential. Students can be freed from the grasp of the terrible trolls of lackluster and unimaginative thinking through the use of these three golden gifts: *attribute listing*, *forced relationships*, and *SCAMPER*. Each of these tools builds upon the creative-thinking products students have first developed using brainstorming, fluency, flexibility, originality, and elaboration in their creative thinking.

Attribute Listing

Attribute listing is an excellent tool students can learn when they want to modify existing objects, ideas, or institutions and create and synthesize new ideas, inventions, and solutions. Attribute listing moves beyond creative thinking in isolation. It is a tool that good problem solvers use to help them redefine situations and reinvent products. The technique is simple and easy to learn. Problem solvers first analyze a product, institution, or complex ideas, noting all the attribute or component parts. An inventor might note that a school desk has at least three separate attributes: frame material, seat, and writing surface. Next, the inventor brainstorms all the possible values of each attribute listed. The school-desk inventor notes all the possible materials that might be used in the frame of a school desk, such as wood, metal, and molded plastic. The inventor also identifies possible values of a desk seat (e.g., foam rubber, contoured wood) and writing surfaces (e.g., slate, heavy-weight plastic). Students then think of creative ways to improve the attributes of an object by manipulating or altering its component parts. Often, only one attribute needs to be changed or improved to produce a new product or idea. The following example illustrates how attribute listing may be employed using fairy tales as the item or artifact in need of improvement.

Classic fairy tales often project stereotypes that may be harmful. The problem: How might new fairy tales be created that would be less dependent upon stereotypes? First, examine the attributes of classic fairy tales. They typically feature villains, heroes, and spells or magic. When these attributes are examined, several values of each may be noted. For example, heroes are typically handsome, courageous, and virtuous. Villains are often portrayed as being physically unattractive. Moreover, villains cast evil spells or place obstacles in the path of heroes that can only be overcome using magic or special powers. By noting the attributes and values of fairy tales first, students can then analyze them and manipulate the elements to create fresh, new tales absent of stereotypes. The example shown here examines fairy tales broadly. The same procedure could be used with a single example. Attribute listing can also be applied to a single fairy tale, such as "Hansel and Gretel." Two disturbing elements of "Hansel and Gretel" are the abandonment of the children and the extremely negative portrayal of the stepmother. Students can examine "Hansel and Gretel" by inspecting the attributes of the story and by exploring creative ways to change the elements within it to fashion a more agreeable story.

Attributes of Fairy Tales	Typical Values of the Attributes	Ideas for Improvement
1. Villains	Evil, ugly, physically deformed	Create villain who is physically attractive
2. Heroes, heroines	Handsome, beautiful, virtuous	Create heroine who has a scarred face or a hero with a serious character flaw
3. External potions, charms, spells	Poisoned apples, 100 years of sleep	The "potion" is the character's inner resources (e.g., courage, sense of honor)

Forced Relationships

Sometimes good ideas appear when we least expect them. Forced relationships plays upon this notion of serendipity. It gives good fortune a gentle nudge. When people are problem solving, inventing, or creating, an entirely new idea or approach may occur when two or more seemingly unrelated words, objects, or ideas are brought together in such a way so as to "force" a relationship between them. Forced relationships may be employed in a variety of ways. One simple technique is to share randomly selected words such as *swan* or *ferocious* with students and invite them to incorporate the words into a solution to the problem at hand. The forced-relationship technique is highly effective in a brainstorming session when students appear to reach a lull or plateau, apparently running out of ideas. The infusion of a forced relationship almost always opens up the floodgates of creative thinking, and new, previously unimagined ideas surge forth. The stimuli used in forced relationships may be verbal or visual, abstract or concrete as the following fairy tale forced-relationship sample exercises illustrate.

♦ Help Rapunzel get out of the tower. Browse through a collection of catalogs, such as the *Neiman-Marcus Holiday Book* or the *Disney Catalog*. What items can you find in the catalogs that might help Rapunzel solve her problem? Do any catalog items suggest novel solutions?

♦ There is no woodsman nearby today, and Little Red Riding Hood finds herself in grandmother's cottage with a most suspicious looking "Granny." Consider these three words: *swan*, *mirror*, and *ice*. Can you think of a clever and effective way—based upon one of these words—for LRRH to dispatch the guy in grandmother's nightclothes?

♦ Beast wants to break the evil spell cast upon him. Look to other fairy tales for ideas. How did Rapunzel, Snow White, and Hansel and Gretel solve their problems? Can Beast use any of their ideas or strategies?

SCAMPER

SCAMPER is an acronym created by Bob Eberle (1982) that serves as a powerful creative thinking tool. Whenever people seek creative ideas and solutions to problems and they seem to run out of good ideas, they can always remember to SCAMPER. The SCAMPER technique serves to remind students to always consider all dimensions and possibilities inherent in a problem, situation, or solution under consideration. Briefly summarized, SCAMPER poses these questions.

S	Substitute	What might you substitute? Where might you go instead? What else could you use?
C	Combine	What things or ideas might you combine? Which things might you put together in a new way?
A	Adapt/Adjust	What adjustments might you make? Are there any adaptations you might employ?
M	Modify	What might you alter or change?
	Magnify	What might you enlarge, increase, strengthen?
	Minify	What might you lessen, weaken?
P	Put to Other Uses	What new uses, purposes might be realized? Is there a new way of perceiving this object or idea?
E	Eliminate	What might be removed, excluded, omitted?
	Elaborate	What detail might you add or superimpose?
R	Reverse	What might occur if you inverted the components, elements? Changed their order?
	Rearrange	What new sequence or order might be attempted? How might the elements be laid out anew?

Just as teachers may ask a student to create a poster illustrating the guidelines for brainstorming in the classroom, so, too, they may want to invite another student to create a colorful SCAMPER poster for the classroom to serve as a daily reminder to SCAMPER whenever new ideas and solutions are sought. Invite students to practice SCAMPERing with the following "Goldilocks and the Three Bears" fairy tale prompt. This activity works especially well when students are practicing creative problem solving with "The Three Bears" characters elsewhere in the book.

Apply the SCAMPER technique to this situation: NASA has commissioned your class to rewrite "Goldilocks and the Three Bears" in a manner and style appropriate for children living in a space colony in the year 2095. The simple plot and basic characters should remain the same. A lost girl invades the home of three bears who are away briefly. All other conditions may be altered to "futurize" the classic tale. SCAMPER for ideas. The following possibilities illustrate avenues your own thinking may take.

S   Substitute protein pills for porridge?

C   Combine your knowledge of space and astronomy with your knowledge of the tale? You know the story takes place in a woods. Where in space might the new setting be located?

A   Could you Adapt the architecture of the bears' domicile to reflect a futuristic type of residence?

M   Could you Modify the narration and dialogue to be reflective of possible twenty-first-century speech? What technological words or slang might be used?

P   Could you add humor to the story by portraying Goldilocks as a new visitor to the planet who Puts to Other Uses the beds and chairs in ways quite different from those the bears know or understand?

E   What details could you Elaborate upon at the beginning of the story that would immediately reveal to readers the tale's futuristic setting?

R   Could you Reverse or Rearrange key elements in the tale's final scenes to provide a new, humorous twist in telling the story?

THE BROTHERS GRIMM

The Brothers Grimm are the most famous human names associated with fairy tales. Jacob (1785-1863) and Wilhelm (1786-1859) Grimm were born only a year apart and were the two eldest sons in a family of five boys and one girl. Their father, Philipp Grimm, held an important civil-service job as clerk of the German town of Hanau in the kingdom of Hesse-Kassel. The brothers were not only close in age, they were apparently nearly identical in interests and temperament, sharing their lives and work almost as twins. The two brothers followed the tradition of their father and studied law at the University of Marburg, but neither pursued legal or civil-service careers. They became interested in philology, the

study of the authenticity and preservation of languages. They were not, as some may suppose, primarily tellers of children's stories. Jacob Grimm's work with sound changes in languages was so important that his scholarly procedures came to be known as Grimm's law and remain in use by linguists even today. Together, the brothers sought to create a fundamental dictionary of the German language that was such a monumental task that it was not finally completed until the middle decades of the twentieth century. Because of their intense interest in the history and evolution of their native language, it is not surprising that they would come to study folktales as literary artifacts of German. Beginning in 1812, the brothers published *Children's and Household Tales*, of which Wilhelm became the primary editor, especially after 1815. The tales became enormously popular and underwent subsequent revisions and additions, coming to be known as *Grimm's Fairy Tales* by 1822. The seventh and final edition, overseen by the brothers themselves, was published in 1857. Again, the scholarship of the Brothers Grimm was evidenced by their fairy tale collections. The scientific procedures they used in collecting and recording German fairy tales became the standard used by folklore specialists around the world.

The Brothers Grimm were only slightly older than Hans Christian Andersen, and, as was his life, theirs were often disrupted by the political strife, warfare, and shifting national alliances of nineteenth-century Europe. In 1833, for example, both brothers lost their jobs at the University of Gottingen, and Jacob was exiled from the German state of Hanover because they protested the revocation of the nation-state's liberal constitution by the new king, Ernest Augustus.

Except for Jacob's travels throughout Europe for scientific research, the Brothers Grimm lived and worked side by side throughout most of their adult lives. Wilhelm married and became the father of three children. Jacob never married and made his home with Wilhelm's family. Although the younger of the two brothers, Wilhelm died first, in 1859. Jacob died in 1863. The brothers spent the last two decades of their lives working in Berlin at the invitation of the king of Prussia, Frederick William IV.

The Brothers Grimm are responsible for the preservation and popularity of such classic fairy tales as "Hansel and Gretel," "The Fisherman and His Wife," and "Rumpelstiltskin." Their retelling of "Little Red Riding Hood" is noted for its more "child-friendly" resolution wherein a woodsman saves both the child and her grandmother—as opposed to Charles Perrault's French version of the tale in which both characters perish.

There are many collections of the complete 210 tales authored by Wilhelm and Jacob Grimm. The following editions are widely available.

Grimm, Wilhelm, and Jacob Grimm. 1992. *The Complete Fairy Tales of the Brothers Grimm*. Trans. by Jack Zipes. New York: Bantam Books.

   The translation is based upon the seventh and final edition of *Children's and Household Tales* published in 1857 by the Brothers Grimm. Zipes's introductory essay, "Once There Were Two Brothers Named Grimm," is especially insightful and revealing.

—————. *The Complete Grimm's Fairy Tales*. n.d. Illus. by Josef Scharl. New York: Pantheon Books.

This contemporary reprint of the 1944 edition of 210 ageless tales from the Brothers Grimm is translated into English by Margaret Hunt. The place of storytelling in world culture is examined in the introduction by Padraic Colum and in later commentary provided by renowned folklorist Joseph Campbell.

FAIRY TALE COLLECTIONS

In this chapter many fairy tales have been used to illustrate the diversity of creative-thinking skills teachers can share with young people. Therefore, it is fitting that the books celebrated in this chapter should be anthologies that contain extremely well-known fairy tales. All the fairy tales used for illustrative purposes throughout the book may be found in these anthologies.

Andersen, Hans Christian. 1991. *Hans Christian Andersen Fairy Tales*. Illus. by Lisbeth Zwerger. Saxonville, MA: Picture Book Studio.

Eight of Andersen's literary fairy tales—including "The Emperor's New Clothes," "The Princess and the Pea," and "The Little Match Girl"—are beautifully illustrated by Austrian artist Zwerger, a winner of the Hans Christian Andersen Medal.

Cresswell, Helen. 1993. *Classic Fairy Tales*. Illus. by Carol Lawson. New York: HarperCollins.

Nine classic fairy tales—including "Sleeping Beauty," "The Frog Prince," "Goldilocks and the Three Bears," and "Little Red Riding Hood"—are skillfully retold by Cresswell and handsomely illustrated with Lawson's full-color paintings.

Ehrlich, Amy, ed. 1985. *The Random House Book of Fairy Tales*. Illus. by Diane Goode. New York: Random House.

Nineteen of the most popular European classic fairy tales—including "Little Red Riding Hood," "Snow White," "Cinderella," "Rumplestiltskin," and "Puss in Boots"—are faithfully retold by Ehrlich. Good's lavish illustrations appear on virtually every page.

Eisen, Armand, and Shelia Black, eds. 1992. *A Treasury of Children's Literature*. Illus. by Lynn Bywaters et al. Boston: Houghton Mifflin.

More than 30 classic fairy tales, fables, and poems are visually highlighted by 16 illustrators. Tales include seven each from the works of the Brothers Grimm and Hans Christian Andersen.

Hayes, Sarah. 1993. *The Candlewick Book of Fairy Tales*. Illus. by P. J. Lynch. Cambridge, MA: Candlewick Press.

"Cinderella," "Hansel and Gretel," "Beauty and the Beast," and "Snow White and the Seven Dwarfs" are among the tales expertly retold and enhanced by Lynch's wonderful pencil-and-watercolor illustrations.

Lang, Andrew, ed. n.d. *The Blue Fairy Book*. Illus. by H. J. Ford and G. P. Jacomb Hood. New York: McGraw-Hill. (Reproduction by Dover, 1966.)
Between 1889 and 1910, Scottish writer Lang edited a dozen collections of fairy tales, each of which used a color in the title. They were enormously popular with children and remain in print today. The first volume was *The Blue Fairy Book*, which includes such classics as "East of the Sun and West of the Moon," "Cinderella," "Beauty and the Beast," "Snow White and Rose Red," and "The Master Cat or, Puss in Boots."

———. 1993. *The Rainbow Fairy Book*. Illus. by Michael Hague. New York: William Morrow.
Hague, a popular book artist, illustrates 31 stories found in Lang's 12 colored fairy tale books. Featured are such popular European tales as "Rapunzel," "Cinderella," "Hansel and Gretel," and "Jack and the Beanstalk" as well as tales from Zimbabwe, India, and China.

Lurie, Alison, ed. 1993. *The Oxford Book of Modern Fairy Tales*. New York: Oxford University Press.
This fine collection of tales runs the gamut from Nathaniel Hawthorne's "Feathertop" (1846) to "The Wife's Story" (1982) by Ursula Le Guin. In between are "modern" fairy tales by such notable authors as Oscar Wilde, James Thurber, Charles Dickens, Howard Pyle, Joan Aiken, and Jane Yolen.

Happily Ever Afters

Celebrating Family Romance

Romance plays a big role in fairy tales. A lovely princess and a handsome prince meet, fall in love, marry, and live happily ever after. As an elaboration exercise, write an original fairy tale about a romance in your family. First, interview your parents, grandparents, or another couple you love. How did they meet, court, and wed? Use the data you gather to weave a modern-day fairy tale that celebrates a love story in your family. Use the stock phrases of fairy tales such as *Once upon a time* and *They lived happily ever after*. Be sure to place some hurdles in the path of the young lovers. There are no dragons skulking about these days, but perhaps your grandparents or parents were kept apart by geographical distances or military service. The completed fairy tale makes a wonderful anniversary present from you to people you love and treasure!

Creating New Fairy Tales

All the elements of creative productive thinking may be used when students write (or improvise in creative drama) completely new fairy tales. Fluency is exercised when students generate many ideas for plot possibilities, characters, and settings (both time and place) characteristic of fairy tales. A grid such as the one shown in figure 5.2 may be fashioned from all the responses students name. Note that students should generate many more options than shown in the grid. Flexibility and originality are demonstrated when students make different and unusual connections among the many possible combinations of plots, characters, and settings to fashion their own original fairy tale. Finally, elaboration is brought to bear upon the task of developing their kernel ideas for new tales into fully developed stories with well-described characters and settings, dialogue, and appropriate narration.

Fig. 5.2 Creating New Fairy Tales

Plot	Character	Setting: Place	Setting: Time
Theft of priceless object	Small child	Dark, dense forest	Midnight
Twins separated at birth	Elderly woman	Castle	Long ago
Furious snowstorm	Princess	Cottage in forest	Dawn
Wedding of royalty	Prince	On board a sea vessel	The future

Creating New Fairy Tales: Two Presents

One way to demonstrate to students that they already have internalized and know the structure of fairy tales is to ask them to invent a brand-new fairy tale. Review the basic components of fairy tales, citing or calling upon students for examples of major fairy tale characteristics and motifs. Fairy tales almost always begin with the phrase *Once upon a time*, which indicates that the time setting is in an unspecified past time. There is a crystal-clear plot with an obvious beginning, middle, and end. Often, though not always, the action of the plot involves three journeys, three trials, or three central characters, such as the Three Bears and Three Little Pigs. The characters are invariably good and bad people. Royal birth or great wealth are no guarantees of either rectitude or happiness. Virtuous characters, often poor or maltreated at the outset of the fairy tale, are invariably rewarded at the end of the tale.

Once students have a strong sense of fairy tale writing structures, here is one prompt that almost always produces fresh and original fairy tales from young writers. Bring two wrapped packages to class. They should be dramatically different. One should be beautifully and elegantly wrapped and topped off with a gorgeous bow. The second present should be humbly wrapped, perhaps in newspaper or a plastic grocery sack and tied with simple kite string. Show both presents to the students, and invite them to make up an original fairy tale.

One student group fashioned an original tale that appropriately began "Once upon a time. . . ." The heroine is a little girl who lives in a beautiful mansion on the highest hill in the richest part of her city, Anytown, USA. But all the luxury that surrounds the little girl does not bring happiness. She is lonely. Now, the little girl has two grandmothers. One is very rich; she travels the world seeking the most expensive toys and dolls she can find for her granddaughter. The second grandmother is very poor; she is also an invalid. She must spend the entirety of her meager income on food and medicine. It is Christmas, and the little girl receives two wrapped presents. Inside the exquisitely wrapped box is a beautiful doll from China dressed in the finest and richest silks imaginable. The doll is so dazzling that the little girl forgets the other package waiting for her under the tree. She takes her new doll to her room and shows the doll all her splendid toys. Soon, however, the excitement created by the new doll fades, and the little girl becomes lonely again. Then she remembers the other gift, the humble package left under the Christmas tree. She returns and opens the present to find a box filled with hundreds of pieces of paper, all with fine, old-fashioned writing. This is the gift of her second grandmother. Every piece of paper tells a wonderful story. The little girl sits down and begins to read the stories. The first story relates her grandmother's first remembered Christmas. It is such a wonderful story that the little girl thinks she can smell the wonderful aromas of the old Christmas kitchen of her grandmother's childhood. There are other stories of her grandmother's childhood, and there are stories of her father's childhood too. There are even stories of the little girl herself; stories from a time she does not remember. The little girl falls in love with the stories that she knows she will read again and again. She also comprehends the great present her grandmother has given to her. She will never be lonely again, for she has the gift of stories.

Creativity is not just something that a few lucky people possess. It is a way of life. The climates and environments teachers and parents build to foster that creative growth are vital, life-giving, and life energizing. Creative growth is a grand endeavor worthy of the best possible efforts.

REFERENCES

Eberle, Bob. 1982. *Visual Thinking: A SCAMPER Tool for Useful Thinking*. Buffalo, NY: D.O.K.

Hague, Kathleen, and Michael Hague. 1980. *East of the Sun and West of the Moon*. Illus. by Michael Hague. New York: Harcourt Brace Jovanovich.

Osborne, Alex F. 1963. *Applied Imagination: Principles and Procedures of Creative Problem Solving*. New York: Charles Scribner's Sons.

Chapter **6**

"The Emperor's New Clothes" and Student Productions

CHAPTER PREVIEW

The use of the newspaper format as a teaching and learning tool is explored in the context of one of Hans Christian Andersen's most popular tales. Ideas for storytelling and creative dramatics production along with a brief profile of Andersen are also shared.

"THE EMPEROR'S NEW CLOTHES"

One of the most common plot elements of fairy tales features the ashes-to-glory rise of oppressed, victimized, and innocent characters. Hans Christen Andersen's "The Emperor's New Clothes" is a rare exception. In this famous story, the flamboyant, vain ruler of an empire is stripped of his wealth, pride, and—quite literally—his clothes. Indeed, the lasting appeal of this fairy tale is most likely found in watching the high and mighty fall from grace. The biggest man on the block—indeed, the kingdom—gets the pie in the face. The tale ends with the common people having a great and robust laugh at the emperor's very considerable expense.

Students and teachers do not have to go far to find the emperor's modern counterparts. Rock-music stars, politicians, and professional athletes almost continuously supply the media with contemporary reenactments of "The Emperor's New Clothes." In *The Principal's New Clothes*, Stephanie Calmenson informs readers that one need not even be famous or wealthy to fall prey to the trap of personal vanity.

"The Emperor's New Clothes" moves in the direction of satire more closely than any other well-known fairy tale. Because of the many levels of duplicity found in Andersen's biting tale, teachers can make many connections with theories and creative-teaching strategies explained in other chapters in this text. For example, the levels of moral development as set forth by Lawrence Kohlberg and explained in the "Jack and the Beanstalk" chapter play out beautifully in "The Emperor's New Clothes." All but the most innocent child tell lies about the emperor's clothes. Of course, the crooked tailors not only lie, but they also engage in fraud. Students can explore the motives of all the characters found in Andersen's story from the point of view of their moral reasoning.

In this chapter, however, "The Emperor's New Clothes" is used as a possible catalyst for student designed and produced media and drama productions. Included is the description of a fairy tale newspaper. Further, students can move from print media to the production of a television news program based on "The Emperor's New Clothes." The products and activities described can serve as learner-response models to other fairy tales and other kinds of literature.

THE NEWSPAPER AS A LEARNING TOOL

The newspaper is a terrific teaching tool and learning resource for bright, talented, and eager students of all ages. The newspaper format and structure are familiar to most students and can easily be modeled and adapted to serve as an outlet for students' creative products. Newspapers also offer a wide array of tasks and need many talented people, including cartoonists, reporters, designers, organizers, managers, and a host of other personnel. Given the variety of roles found in newspaper production, virtually any learning style can easily be tapped.

Students can exercise creative and technical writing skills by producing fairy tale newspapers based upon "The Emperor's New Clothes" and other famous fairy tales. What kinds of newspaper news items, weather forecasts, sports reporting, advice columns, classified and display advertisements, and stock-market reports can be fashioned from the magic cloth of fairy tales?

The first thing for students to do is to choose a name for their newspaper. If the accent is on the tales of the Brothers Grimm, the *Black Forest Times* may be a suitable name. When "The Emperor's New Clothes" is the focus, the *Empire Inquirer* or the *Emperor's Daily Mirror* could be possible names. Positions and responsibilities on the newspaper need to be chosen or assigned. Reporters, columnists, editors, cartoonists, typists, advertising managers, and other roles need to be filled. Next, the staff of the *Emperor's Daily Mirror* or any other newspaper need to determine the stories, feature articles, and events to be covered.

The lead story in the *Emperor's Daily Mirror* will most likely be a report of the emperor's naked stroll through the streets of his dominion. A headline might read:

Emperor Bares New Fashion;
Wily Weavers Wanted

Reporters for the *Emperor's Daily Mirror* go beyond the headlines and write creative news stories about the imagined events and happenings of fairy tales. Encourage students to read the lead news stories in the *USA Today* or any regional newspaper. Alert them to the reporter's use of the six journalistic questions, the five *W*s plus *H: who, what, when, where, why,* and *how.* Direct them to take notes on how each of these questions has been answered by the reporter. Next ask students to review Hans Christian Andersen's "The Emperor's New Clothes" from the point of view of an ace reporter. What facts, characters, and events supply answers to the five *W*s in the tale of the vain ruler? Their news stories should answer the six journalistic questions, be written in the third person, and emphasize the importance of their subjects and the events. Even if all students do not assume the roles of reporters, all can benefit from writing a news story to summarize the critical events and theme of a fairy tale as one fine way to demonstrate comprehension.

A related, real-life news story did come to light in the summer of 1996. An Associated Press news story dated September 6, 1996, from Copenhagen, Denmark, read: Fairy Tale Writer's Letter Is Valuable. The story reported the discovery of a four-page letter Andersen wrote in 1859. The story also noted that letters penned by Andersen have sold at collectors' auctions for as much as $1,725. The newly discovered letter is not for sale, however; it is the property of the Andersen Center at the University of Odense in Denmark. Andersen scholars will be able to access the letter to learn more about a poor shoemaker's son who rose to fame as the creator of literary fairy tales.

Students who are not reporters can assume other roles in the newspaper simulation. Editors can pen editorials about such things as the need for greater licensing restrictions on traveling tradespeople as a guard against future swindles at the royal court. Another editorial may question the wisdom of a ruler who thinks only of his own fashion and ignores the needs of the empire. Yet another editorial may underscore the strong moral message to be gained from a thoughtful analysis of the events of the tale.

Without doubt, this special edition of the *Emperor's Daily Mirror* needs a political cartoon or two relative to the motives and behaviors of the emperor, his advisers, the general public, or the rascally swindlers posing as weavers. Columnists can provide insights and advice on a wide array of matters relating to Andersen's "The Emperor's New Clothes." Miss Manners can write about the proper thing to do when the emperor appears on the streets without any clothes. Ann Landers may applaud the good parenting skill of the father who listened to his innocent son when he uttered, "But the Emperor has no clothes on!" A world-affairs columnist can reflect on the impact the emperor's embarrassing stroll is likely to have on the international community of kingdoms and empires.

Another role to be fulfilled is that of the unhappy citizen of the empire who strongly believes new ordinances need to be passed to outlaw nudity in the streets and, hence, pens a letter to the editor about this grievance.

The class meteorologist supplies the *Emperor's Daily Mirror* weather map and report. The weather must be mild if the emperor can appear out of doors wearing so little. The stock market report and business stories should be fascinating. Will there be a rush to buy or sell fabric and clothing stocks?

What kinds of community announcements, crime reports, and television programming will be found in the *Emperor's Daily Mirror* on the day the emperor's walk is news? Display and classified advertisements can be developed by the advertising and commercial art departments of the newspaper. Perhaps rival tailors will take out a full-page display advertisement to hawk their elaborate royal costumes.

The travel writer for the *Emperor's Daily Mirror* may write that there has never been a better time for residents of the empire to visit adjacent kingdoms. She may write about the incredible beauty to be found in forests visited by Little Red Riding Hood and Goldilocks. Another of her colleagues is responsible for using the names of fairy tale characters, places, and objects to construct crossword or word-search puzzles for the newspaper's readers who enjoy puzzles.

Reporters and newspaper officials need not stop with the emperor's tale. The events and occasions found in other fairy tales and even nursery rhymes can find their way into the *Emperor's Daily Mirror.* For example, the newspaper might carry an obituary about a citizen of the neighboring kingdom who met with a dreadful accident.

■ Noted Citizen Killed
H.T. Dumpty perished yesterday in a dramatic fall. Efforts by the King's Guard to save him failed. What's left of Dumpty's remains may be viewed today at Fairyland Funerals.

A classified advertisement might read:

> Wanted: One dwarf, must sneeze, must live and work with six others. Needs to whistle. Contact: S. White.

Wedding stories and reports may be used as models for writing about the royal weddings of Cinderella and Sleeping Beauty, which are taking place in neighboring kingdoms.

A science report may highlight ongoing research into events taking place in rural areas of the empire, beyond the emperor's capital city. Such a story can be reported in the science news pages.

Blind Mice Studied at Empire State University

Agricultural experts at Empire State University as well as local optometrists are examining a trio of rodents without tails to determine what caused them to attack a farmer's wife in one of the rural regions of the empire. Scientists want to know why the rodents went blind and started chasing the terrified woman and whether this was an isolated incident or the beginning of a new plague.

Forced Relationships

Several creative-thinking strategies are highlighted in Chapter 5, "In the Kingdom of Ideas." One of those strategies is forced relationships. Forced relationships involves the pairing of two or more seemingly unrelated words, objects, or ideas together in the hope that a "forced fit" of unusual combinations will spark new and original ideas. Some forced relationships are as easily employed as choosing a word at random from a dictionary and determining how its sound or meaning might prompt a new solution to a problem at hand. Other forced relationships are more complex and may use other creative-thinking tools, such as attribute listing (also described in Chapter 5). In the following example of a complex application of forced relationships, a group of middle-school students first use attribute listing to note the characteristics of fairy tales and school newspapers; then the students make forced relationships between the two seemingly different kinds of writing formats, as shown in figure 6.1.

The problem the students face is stated as follows: You have been studying fairy tales. You are also responsible for writing and publishing the school newspaper this semester. How might you combine your knowledge of fairy tales with your understanding of school newspapers to create the best, most original school newspaper ever? In this instance, key attributes of newspapers are listed across the top of the matrix and key attributes of fairy tales are listed vertically on the left side of the matrix. Students then move across the top of the grid, first asking themselves what attributes they can borrow from fairy tales to report sports. Most fairy tales have at least one evil character. How might this attribute be applied to sports reporting? One idea students suggest is to invent an evil or "mean" character who can be employed to explain school losses in sporting events. Moving on, students decide that there is too much evil or bad news reported in the media, and perhaps they should provide an antidote by focusing upon positive news happenings. Building on one another's ideas, they also decide to take the idea of "good news" further by having a creative tale in the features section of the school newspaper exploring the notion of what might happen if everything a so-called evil character touched or did had positive consequences. Many other creative ideas occur to students as they work across and down the grid, making unusual and creative connections between two seemingly unrelated things—fairy tales and newspapers.

Forced relationships as a creative-thinking tool or device may be employed any time students need to seek fresh and original ideas and products. For example, when students are planning a museum as described in the "Beauty and the Beast" chapter, they can easily substitute the attributes of museums for the attributes of newspapers listed in figure 6.1 and make original links and connections between the attributes of fairy tales and museums. Is the notion of forced relationships far-fetched? Not in the least. One example: The legendary University of Notre Dame football coach Knute Rockne developed his revolutionary "four horseman" backfield shift after observing intricate movements among chorus-line performers in a stage show. (For more information on the Knute Rockne example and other illustrations of unusual, forced relationships, see Roger von Oech's *A Kick in the Seat of the Pants* [New York: Harper & Row, 1986]: p. 28.)

Fig. 6.1. A Forced Relationship: Newspapers and Fairy Tales

Newspaper Components Fairy-Tale Components	Sports	News	Clubs	Games, Puzzles, and Creative Writing
Evil Characters	Create a "mean" character to explain all our losses.	Emphasize good news; eliminate gossip.	Sponsor a dance or school party based on dragons, etc.	Write a story in which everything the evil person touches turns to good; create a word search with evil characters.
Handsome Princes, Beautiful Ladies	Draw a cartoon of the football team as handsome princes.	Find and write about daring rescues students have been involved in.		Create a serial about a modern-day heroine and all her problems in middle school.
Animal Characters	Create a new sports mascot to cover a particular sport (e.g., B. B. Wolf reports baseball).	Begin a column about students' pets.	Design a nosy animal character who finds out about school activities and describes them.	Have a wise owl create fun math games to help students with math.
Happy Endings	Emphasize the good, even when our team loses.		Write features about clubs that are doing good things for people and the school.	Sponsor a contest to see who can say the most good things about the school, such as an essay contest: "Why I like my teachers."

Dress the Emperor!

A grand way to "cover" the emperor is with newspaper costumes. Break students into teams of four or five students. Provide each team with a supply of newspapers. Sunday editions of the newspaper work well because of the wide use of color inserts and color comics pages. Also provide teams with a generous supply of toothpicks, safety pins, tape, or other "fasteners." In every team, one student volunteers (or is drafted) to portray the emperor. Teams then have 20 minutes to create newspaper costumes that fit their emperors. When the masterpieces are complete, all the emperors show off their new garments in a parade of the emperors. Of course, the crowns, trains, and even royal trumpets of emperors may also be fashioned from newspapers.

Electronic Journalism

Are newspapers soon to be history? Will electronic media totally replace print journalism in the near future? Cable and network television gather and distribute news instantaneously for a population that increasingly seems to prefer its information delivered live, as it happens, and complete with full sound and color. Using video equipment, teachers and students may want to convert many of the newspaper activities described above into "on-the-air" television newsmagazine activities. Classified and display advertising can be converted to live commercials. Editorials are spoken to the camera. News events are covered with improvised re-creations. The newspaper costumes can be the "fabric" of the emperor's new clothes, and the parade of nobles before the citizens of the empire may be filmed as a lead news event in a video news format. The weather report can be given live at the scene of the emperor's parade.

Students and teachers may employ electronic software programs in the creation of fairy tale newspapers and electronic news programs. One dynamic and widely used program is *HyperStudio*, which is so popular with educators that there are at least two magazines devoted to up-to-date information on classroom applications. For complete information on *HyperStudio*, contact Roger Wagner Publishing, Inc., 1050 Pioneer Way, Suite P, El Cajon, CA 92020, or see the Internet at http://www.hyperstudio.com. Another popular media program is *Print Shop Delux*, produced by Broderbund. It is available from Broderbund Software, 500 Rosewood Boulevard, Novato, CA 94948 and at http://www.broderbund.com. See *HyperStudio*, *Print Shop Delux*, and additional software in stores specializing in educational software or from mail-order catalogs such as Educational Resources, 1550 Executive Drive, P.O. Box 1900, Elgin, IL 60121-1900. Phone: (800) 624-2926. New software programs and technologies are evolving so fast that readers are strongly advised to consult electronic educational resource companies, local merchants specializing in educational software, and school-district or public-library media specialists for the most up-to-date programs to help students realize the best media production programs possible.

HANS CHRISTIAN ANDERSEN

Hans Christian Andersen is one of the most famous names in all of literature. The great Danish writer was born into abject poverty in 1805 in the Danish city of Odense. His mother was a serving maid, and his father was an impoverished shoemaker. Hans Christian was only 11 years old when his father died. At age 14, when Danish boys were confirmed in the church and began to assume adult roles, Hans Christian went to Copenhagen, Denmark's capital city, to seek his fortune.

There, the youthful Andersen eventually found work at the Royal Theatre and, more importantly, discovered a mentor in Jonas Collin, one of the theatre's directors. Collin arranged for Andersen to gain an education, but some of his school experiences were brutal.

Andersen's writing was published as early as 1822. He was a prodigious author who wrote poetry, plays, travel books, and novels, but his fairy tales for children—such as "The Princess and the Pea," "The Ugly Duckling," and "The Emperor's New Clothes"—are what earned him lasting fame in world literature. Andersen's first collection of tales for children, *Fairy Tales, Told for Children*, was published in 1835. Andersen's tales are not always happily-ever-after stories, however. Many end in tragedy, perhaps the most famous of which is "The Little Match Girl." Andersen was never fearful of exploring deep feelings of loss and sadness in children's literature. He identified with poverty, and his tales are rich and evocative because he was not afraid to show loss and suffering, fears that may indeed haunt childhood minds but were, at the time, rarely explored in children's literature.

Andersen's own life seemed to be equal mixtures of joy, triumph, and sadness. His mother, father, and grandfather were all reduced to incredible poverty and died in mental despair. Denmark was often at war during his adult years; he lost both Danish and German friends. He was disheartened when critics disliked his work, and while he counted real princes and princesses and many famous cultural figures such as Charles Dickens, Jenny Lind, and Elizabeth Barrett Browning among his friends, he never appears to have developed a great or lasting love relationship with another person. He received a pension from the Danish government and hence was spared the pauper's lives of his parents, yet he never realized great wealth from the popularity of his writing. Although he traveled widely and stayed in palaces, Andersen never truly had a home of his own.

Andersen died in 1875. He has been described as the last great teller of fairy tales, following as he did, chronologically, both Charles Perrault and the Brothers Grimm. He was not merely a collector or recorder of folk and fairy tales, someone who would simply write down fairy tales exactly as they had been told for generations. Andersen was instead a remarkably creative writer who invented many tales and took other tales he had heard in childhood and reinvented them into magically fresh stories. Moreover, some of his tales, such as "The Little Mermaid," were truly original. In the 1837 preface to *Fairy Tales, Told for Children*, Andersen wrote that "The Emperor's New Clothes" was based on a Spanish story credited to Prince Don Juan Manuel, 1277-1347.[1]

Andersen was a meticulous writer who rewrote all his tales until he was satisfied with the stories, which he believed should be read aloud to sound as if they were being told rather than read. Although Andersen's tales are European in origin, he speaks to common emotions such as love and courage, which may explain the universal popularity of his tales and their easy translation to such other media as film, ballet, and even sculpture.

---

1. Andersen's "Preface" is found in *Hans Christian Andersen: The Complete Fairy Tales and Stories*, translated from the Danish by Erik Christian Haugaard (New York: Doubleday, 1974). For additional information on the life of Andersen, students may wish to consult Carol Greene's *Hans Christian Andersen: Teller of Tales* (Chicago: Children's Press, 1986).

READ ALOUDS, STORYTELLING, AND CREATIVE DRAMA

Read Alouds

"The Emperor's New Clothes" lends itself well to oral reading, storytelling, and dramatization. Fairy tales are definitely meant to be shared communally; they began in oral tradition. Only after centuries of oral telling were they gathered and printed by people such as Charles Perrault, the Brothers Grimm, and Hans Christian Andersen. Students of all ages enjoy read alouds. This writer notes every semester the joy even graduate students experience from having stories read aloud in classes. Fairy tales offer great opportunities to both read aloud to students and to help them become good oral readers and storytellers themselves.

The multiple versions of each of the fairy tales accentuated in the various chapters of this text afford teachers and students multiple versions of tales such as "The Emperor's New Clothes." Students can select a particular title, examine it carefully to determine the different character voices required, practice the reading several times, and finally read it aloud to their peers or even to other classes, especially classes of younger students. Middle-school students will delight in some of the humorous variations of "The Emperor's New Clothes" and other classic tales, such as Dom DeLuise's *King Bob's New Clothes* and Stephanie Calmenson's *The Principal's New Clothes*.

Readers' theater presentations are also easily adapted using the many fairy tale titles listed and annotated in this book. One or more students supply the narration, but other students join in reading the dialogue between the various characters such as the Emperor, his prime minister, and the crooked and conniving pair of weavers in "The Emperor's New Clothes."

Storytelling

Rich storytelling opportunities abound in fairy tale explorations with students of all ages. Older students can select stories, learn them well, practice telling the stories to their peers, and ultimately tell stories such as the "The Emperor's New Clothes" to a wide variety of audiences, including family members, peers, and younger and older classes of students.

The following steps will help teachers and students prepare and deliver satisfying storytelling experiences.

1. Select a favorite fairy tale or story, such as "The Emperor's New Clothes," for telling. Read the story over and over.

2. Determine the structure and sequence of the story, and learn it well.

3. Try telling the story aloud, paying attention to repeated phrases and actions.

4. Reread the story after a first telling to determine if any significant details were omitted.

5. Develop appropriate and different voices for some or all of the story's characters.

6. Commit to memory critical speeches (e.g., "This cloth is magic. Only those worthy of your kingdom can see it."). Retell the rest of the story in your own words.

7. Place picture notes and keywords on small cards as aides to recall specific beginnings, endings, and the sequence of story events (e.g., prime minister, then councilor, and finally the Emperor go to see the progress of the weavers).

8. Practice telling the story out loud, on cassette tape, and before a mirror.

9. Choose natural gestures, facial expressions, and props to heighten the storytelling experience for listeners.

10. Practice, practice, practice. Tell the story to everyone who will listen, including the family cat. (Practice eye contact when telling the story to the cat too.) (These storytelling tips are based on the advice of professional storyteller John Stansfield, P.O. Box 588, Monument, CO 80132. Phone: 800-484-6963, ext. 8253.)

Teachers and students may be reluctant at first to engage in telling stories, believing they are not real storytellers. Nothing could be farther from the truth. Everyone who describes the latest movie, replays Sunday's football game, or retells a classic family story about Aunt Hattie's peculiar holiday visitor is telling stories. Be sure that students' first fairy tale or folklore storytelling experiences are positive. Make sure the location for shared storytelling experiences is quiet, comfortable, and as stress- and interruption-free as possible. Build the confidence of young storytellers, too, by having them first tell stories in pairs and then in small groups or teams before telling a story to an entire class. Indeed, the best storytelling experiences most people have encountered are small groupings around a campfire or one-on-one experiences with Grandma or Santa Claus.

There are many fine resources teachers may consult about the art of storytelling. *Storytelling Activities* by Norma J. Livo and Sandra A. Rietz (Englewood, CO: Libraries Unlimited, 1987) provides especially useful tips for telling family and folktales. *Telling Your Own Story* by Donald Davis (Little Rock, AR: August House, 1993) is user friendly and has a wealth of practical suggestions and strategies for beginning storytellers. Robin Moore provides similar recommendations, particularly for family storytelling, in *Awakening the Hidden Storyteller* (Boston: Shambhala, 1991).

Another source of ideas for storytelling is Interact's *Folk Tales*, a simulation in which students learn the art of storytelling. For more information, contact Interact, 1825 Gillespie Way, Suite 101, El Cajon, CA 92020-1095. The National Storytelling Association (P.O. Box 309, Jonesborough, TN 37659) published *Many Voices: True Tales from America's Past* (1995) as a way of bringing American history alive for young people. The 36 stories span the history of America from colonial times to the present era. Students who become "hooked" on storytelling as a result of their encounters with classic fairy tales may well discover a whole new world of storytelling treasures in this fine resource. A teacher's guide for *Many Voices* is also available.

Creative Drama: Stories into Plays

Students can use any of "The Emperor's New Clothes" resources (pp. 147-48) and dozens more like them to create their own Hans Christian Andersen fairy tale dramatizations. There is no limit to the ways students can costume and improvise their own presentations. "Once upon a time" is automatic "poetic license" to re-create fairy tales at any time and with richly varied characterizations. Students can take wonderful clues from the many superb illustrations by S. T. Mendelson and Janet Stevens who use animal characters such as gorillas and lions to retell "The Emperor's New Clothes." (See p. 147.) Stephanie Calmenson employs human characters as Andersen did, but she sets her retelling in a contemporary public school governed by a principal with a taste for flamboyant clothes.

Students can use either human or animal characters in dramas they create. Just as students may collaborate on a class newspaper project, so can they combine forces and talents to put on a dramatic presentation of a fairy tale such as "The Emperor's New Clothes." Some students will be lead actors, playing such roles as the emperor and the crooked tailors. Other students can be costume and set designers and producers. These same students can then easily fill the nonspeaking crowd roles of observers witnessing the Emperor's parade. Of course, the production needs a director and, if a script is used, a prompter.

An encounter with "The Emperor's New Clothes" is a splendid opportunity for students to design sets, costumes, and masks. Wonderfully creative theater artifacts can be designed and fashioned by students of all ages. A number of outstanding books for children and young adults give step-by-step directions for planning and preparing costumes for plays, pageants, and costume parties. The following annotated list is but a brief sampling of such resources.

Resources for Making Costumes, Masks, and Drama Sets

Baker, Wendy. 1994. *The Dressing Up Book*. New York: Thomson Learning.
Believe it or not, Cinderella can have a gorgeous ball gown made of nothing more than a trash bag and pieces of colored cellophane. Baker shows young people how to make sensational and virtually cost-free costumes, masks, wigs, shoes, hats, and other accessories in this charming book with bright and cheerful color photography.

Hershberger, Priscilla. 1993. *Make Costumes for Creative Play*. Danbury, CT: Grolier Education.
Children can create dragon, witch and wizard, mermaid, and knight costumes if they follow Hershberger's easy directions for dramatic and colorful costume creations. The author-designer is especially good at showing how to turn stock items such as old pants and old washcloths into great costumes.

Owens, Cheryl. 1993. *My Costume Book*. Boston: Little, Brown.
Among the costumes Owens shows students how to make is that of a mythical mermaid. Patterns, easy-to-follow instructions, and ample color photographs illustrating a variety of costumes are shared in these pages.

Wallace, Mary. 1996. *I Can Make Costumes.* New York: Firefly Books.
> Children learn how to easily build their own enchanted castles from cardboard appliance boxes and fashion bristol board crowns for fairy tale re-enactments in this colorful and easy-to-use resource book. Many colorful photographs illustrate both instructional steps and final products.

Wilkes, Angela. 1996. *Dazzling Disguises and Clever Costumes.* New York: Dorling Kindersley.
> In this large-format book, Wilkes demonstrates how to make 50 super masks, magical jewel boxes, knightly armor, and other accessories that can be used by students to gloriously re-create fairy tales in their own theater productions.

Creative-Drama Schedule

Dramatic presentations offer students opportunities to learn how to set schedules, budget time reasonably, and achieve goals of instruction. A creative-drama schedule should consider these benchmarks.

1. Choose a tale for dramatization such as "The Emperor's New Clothes."

2. Divide the labor and responsibility among actors, directors, and the producers of sets, costumes, and so on.

3. Determine whether to prepare a formal script with lines to be memorized by lead actors or to create a staged improvisation. In the latter, students learn the characters and sequence of events so well that they are able to re-create the story "live" for an audience without the benefit of memorized lines, much as a single storyteller retells a story many times.

4. Identify the most likely audience for the dramatic presentation. Dramatic performances may be presented to any number of audiences: preschool and primary classrooms, senior citizen facilities, and so on.

5. Create costumes, props, and sets; actors learn parts.

6. Practice, practice, practice.

7. Dress rehearsal.

8. Performance.

Of course, scripted and improvised plays are not the only form dramatic presentations may take. Equally good approaches involve the use of individual and paired student monologues and dialogues based upon selected excerpts from the "Emperor's New Clothes" or a variety of other favorite fairy tales. Pantomime works, especially for audiences that are familiar with the tale.

"The Emperor's New Clothes" lends itself well to the use of shadow puppets. A particularly outstanding resource for teaching with shadow puppetry is *Worlds of Shadow: Teaching with Shadow Puppetry* by David and Donna Wisniewski (Englewood, CO: Teacher Ideas Press, 1997). This book discusses using cut-paper designs for puppets. Wisniewski is well known for his cut-paper technique, having recently won the 1997 Caldecott Medal for the book *Golem* (NY: Clarion Books, 1996), which contains his illustrations. The classic fairy tales "Goldilocks and the Three Bears," "Little Red Riding Hood," and "The Three Little Pigs" are all gloriously explored with stage directions, puppet patterns, scripts, and other essentials for great puppetry presentations.

"THE EMPEROR'S NEW CLOTHES" RESOURCES

There are many versions of Hans Christian Andersen's classic story of a ruler's vanity and the trouble it brings down upon him. Happily, a number of wonderful artists have illustrated the tale in delightful ways, including the use of wonderful animal characters. This eliminates a potentially "delicate" problem attendant to Hans Christian Andersen's tale. It is no special trick to "undress" animal characters. Humans present a quite different problem. The following traditional and contemporary versions of the tale represent a sampling of the many tellings students, teachers, and parents will find in library collections and in bookstores. Any of the tales cited make excellent fare for reading aloud, storytelling, and theatrical presentations.

Traditional Stories

Andersen, Hans Christian. 1985. *The Emperor's New Clothes*. Retold by Janet Stevens. New York: Holiday House.
>Stevens has a wonderful way with animals as evidenced by *Tops and Bottoms*, her 1996 Caldecott Honor picture book (Harcourt, Brace, 1995). Her touch does not fail her here either. A robust pig is the vain emperor who is waited upon diligently by a pair of penguins as the royal attendants. The crooked weavers are two sly foxes, and the prime minister is a camel. A little bear is the cub who finally tells the truth, exposing the emperor in more ways than one! A totally delightful book for children of all ages.

————. 1991. *The Emperor's New Clothes*. Retold by Riki Levinson. Illus. by Robert Byrd. New York: Dutton Children's Books.
>Andersen's tale of the vain and pompous emperor is retold and beautifully illustrated using all animal characters. Not surprisingly, the emperor is a lion, and the tailors are sly, cunning foxes. An innocent young kitten yells, "The Emperor is naked!" The opulence of the king's palace and the splendor of the king's vanity-filling possessions are wondrously conveyed in Byrd's watercolor illustrations.

————. 1992. *The Emperor's New Clothes*. Retold and illustrated by S. T. Mendelson. New York: Stewart, Tabori, and Chang.
>In Mendelson's retelling, the setting is Middle Eastern, and all the characters are animals. The emperor, a gorilla, holds fast in sumptuous surroundings, and the tailors are rats. The vanity and pomposity of the emperor is palpable in Mendelson's exquisite paintings.

Variations and Other Treatments

Calmenson, Stephanie. 1989. *The Principal's New Clothes*. Illus. by Denis Brunkus. New York: Scholastic.
This humorous, updated version of Hans Christian Andersen's fairy tale outlines events in the life of the principal of P.S. 88, Mr. Bundy, a vain dresser who meets a pair of tailors—Moe and Ivy—who are more than his match.

DeLuise, Dom. 1996. *King Bob's New Clothes*. Illus. by Christopher Santoro. New York: Simon & Schuster.
The same witty and slightly irreverent team that gave the world an Italian-flavored *Goldilocks* (Simon & Schuster, 1992) returns with this new look at the clothing problems of Discombobulated XVIII, called King Bob for short. Children will chuckle as King Bob's vanity leads him to the inevitable culmination of the tale.

Collections

Andersen, Hans Christian. 1974. *Hans Christian Andersen: The Complete Fairy Tales and Stories*. Trans. by Erik Christian Haugaard. New York: Doubleday.
Haugaard's translations from the Danish are considered by many critics to be the best English-language versions extant. The collection includes "The Emperor's New Clothes."

———. 1991. *Hans Christian Andersen Fairy Tales*. Illus. by Lisbeth Zwerger. Saxonville, MA: Picture Book Studio.
Many of the most famous of Andersen's tales, including "The Emperor's New Clothes," are illustrated by a winner of the prestigious Hans Christian Andersen Medal, the highest international award one can receive in the field of children's literature.

Videocassettes

The Emperor's New Clothes. Shelly Duvall, producer; Peter Medak, director. Faerie Tale Theatre Series. Livonia, MI: Playhouse Video. 1984. 54 minutes. Videocassette.
Alan Arkin and Art Carney are shameless scalawags as would-be tailors who sucker the foolish and vain emperor of Hans Christian Andersen's story, portrayed hilariously by Dick Shawn. The fashions and sets depict the style of Louis XIV's eighteenth-century French court. This is one of the funniest and most lavishly produced entries in the quite special Faerie Tale Theatre Series.

The Emperor's New Clothes. Robert Van Nutt, director. Westport, CT: Rabbit Ears Storybook Classics. 1990. 30 minutes. Videocassette.
With a perfectly regal tone, Sir John Gielgud narrates Hans Christian Andersen's story of the vain and pompous Emperor. Van Nutt's illustrations capture the pomp and circumstance of a grand and imperial court of the Renaissance. Appropriately royal music is supplied by trumpets.

Happily Ever Afters

A Royal Coat of Arms

Obviously, someone as grand as an Emperor needs a royal coat of arms. Utilizing the coat-of-arms framework in figure 6.2, invite students to create original designs for a royal coat of arms for the Emperor. Students should submit their designs along with a letter explaining to the Emperor the particular merits of their design.

Planning a McDonald's Happy Meal

Pretend that the parade of the Emperor has passed by, and all the family are hungry, so everyone heads to McDonald's for lunch. The kids, of course, want to have a Happy Meal. Pretend that the McDonald's Corporation has invited you to create a great new Happy Meal based on a classic fairy tale. Use all your creative strengths to design a terrific Happy Meal. Choose a favorite fairy tale from Hans Christian Andersen, such as "The Emperor's New Clothes" or "The Little Mermaid," as your focus, and complete as many of the following tasks as you can.

- Design one or more sides of a Happy Meal box, bag, or other style of the packaging container.
- Write some jokes, riddles, or questions about the fairy tale to be printed on the Happy Meal box.
- Design a maze that one or more fairy tale characters must negotiate.
- Invent a catchy slogan about the chosen fairy tale that could be used to market the new theme on posters, billboards, and in radio and television advertisements. Example: Jack's Ma Doesn't Know Beans About Giants!
- Compose or recall a simple melody (e.g., "My Bonnie Lies Over the Ocean") to go with the words of the slogan or jingle.
- Invent a series of simple toys appropriate to the selected fairy tale that might be placed in Happy Meal boxes.
- Plan, produce, and share a video commercial for the brand-new fairy tale Happy Meal you create and share with classmates. Also, create a full-page display advertisement announcing the new Happy Meal that will appear in the *Emperor's Daily Mirror*.

Fig. 62 A Royal Coat-of-Arms

Good News/Bad News

Newspaper humorists such as Dave Barry find humor in all manner of situations. Use the territory of "The Emperor's New Clothes" to write a series of Good News/Bad News one-liners that a syndicated humor columnist might use for his or her weekly entry in the *Emperor's Daily Mirror.* Summing up his day, the Emperor might share his good news/bad news day with the Empress.

"The good news is that my suit of clothes is finally finished."

"That's wonderful, dear," remarked the empress.

"No, the bad news is that they're invisible."

"Oh, that's too bad, dear."

"The good news is I have cancelled tomorrow's parade."

"That's very good news, dear."

"No. The bad news is I caught cold today and have to stay in bed tomorrow."

When the good and bad news from "The Emperor's New Clothes" is exhausted, move on to other fairy tale characters and situations to discover additional good news/bad news stories.

Oprah Meets the Emperor, the Tailors, and Other People Who Gripe

A CNN program to cover the human drama behind the story "The Emperor's New Clothes" is not the only television drama that may unfold in the classroom. One of the less fortunate communications developments in the past decade has been the proliferation of daytime talk shows, hosted by celebrities such as Oprah Winfrey, on which people whine and complain about how mistreated and misunderstood they are. The same guests who pillory their own families and neighbors also come up with mind-boggling excuses and rationalizations to justify their own questionable behaviors. Rather than bemoan that such television fare has become something of an American institution, teachers can seize the opportunity to have students create a parody of daytime talk shows. Their host may be Oprah or another well-known talk-show moderator. The opening guest can be the Emperor (dressed in a bathrobe, of course). He can relate how he has been swindled and embarrassed and is generally misunderstood. The follow-up can be Oprah's interview with the two tailors. What excuses do they offer for why they have been misrepresented over the years by Hans Christian Andersen's account of their efforts? Other characters can surface as talk-show guests. How does the Emperor's wife feel about his preoccupation with clothes? What feelings of neglect and jealousy bother the Emperor's teenage daughter or son?

Of course, the fun need not end with characters representative of "The Emperor's New Clothes." Cinderella's stepsisters surely have a story to tell, as do the much-maligned wolf and Snow White's stepmother. Invite students to survey famous fairy tales and imagine which characters might make colorful subjects for daytime talk-show appearances and revelations. Students can then work up a script of introductions and questions for the talk-show host to use as well as responses the guest can make. Be sure to videotape the resulting student production for showing to future classes when fairy tales are examined.

Chapter *7*

The Frog Prince: Thinking and Problem Solving with Art

CHAPTER PREVIEW

In this chapter a number of different products are suggested and patterns are provided for teachers as support in creating innovative, visual interpretations of fairy tales for their students. Books, mobiles, story maps, and other products that further extend the possibilities of successful art adventures for students are recommended, and several fine versions of "The Frog Prince" are listed and annotated. As the chapter centers on artistic expression, a number of superb picture books about key fairy tales that are not featured in one of the nine chapters of this book are noted.

THINKING WITH PICTURES

Today's youth are perhaps the most visually stimulated generation in history. Media and art are everywhere in the environment. It has been said that the best art in America today is found in children's picture books. While the point may be debatable, anyone who has taken even a casual stroll through the picture-book section of fine bookstores and libraries knows that the statement is not mere hyperbole. Picture books today are magnificent. They are portable art museums. Beautiful books of fairy tales and other folk literature illustrated by Trina Schart Hyman, Jerry Pinkney, Paul O. Zelinsky, Margaret Early, and Fred Marcellino stimulate, delight, and challenge the minds and visual sense of today's youth. The creativity, maturity, and versatility found in today's picture books represent just one splendid facet of this incredibly creative atmosphere. Elementary-grade teachers are familiar with the rich bounty of writers and illustrators; but middle-grade teachers may not be as well acquainted with this treasury of picture-book literature. But middle-level teachers can and should capitalize on the rich

and glorious collection of mature and sophisticated contemporary picture books that abound. For one thing, the wit and humor found in both the text and illustrations of works such as Jon Scieszka and Lane Smith's *The True Story of the Three Little Pigs* (Viking, 1989) and *The Stinky Cheese Man and Other Fairly Stupid Tales* (Viking, 1992) are tailor-made for middle-grade students.

Increasingly, too, educators (Ernst 1994; Hubbard and Ernst 1996) are coming to realize how many students are spatial and visual learners and that powerful learning occurs when teachers allow students opportunities to learn visually as well as verbally.

An exemplary literature curriculum program for gifted, talented, and creative students encourages these youths to read widely, critically, and creatively. Talented young people should learn in an environment saturated with a wide array of fine picture books and other visual stimuli. Young people do not automatically select the best literature available; teachers and parents need to introduce them to great picture books. Just as gifted students should read widely enough to become author conscious, they should also sample picture storybooks well enough to become aware of great illustrators in children's literature. That is, they should have wide exposure to superior picture books and be able to recognize the art of such illustrators as Jan Brett, Lane Smith, and Ed Young.

Talented students also need to be taught to read critically. When picture books are considered, students need to develop the skills that enable them to be discriminating readers, to be able to distinguish between original, superbly well-illustrated books and those that use stock drawings or follow unimaginative formulas. The education of gifted students is more complete when fine picture books are included in the curriculum. Visual literacy is developed when teachers skillfully use exemplary picture books. Students come to know the language of illustration—including line, color, and perspective—as a part of developing aesthetic judgment and taste.

These same students also need to read sophisticated picture books that force them to read creatively. They need exposure to imaginative picture books that serve to surprise them, perhaps even shock them, to think about their world in new ways. Creative readers especially vault beyond the printed page. Literature is not an end point; superb words and pictures serve as the grist for students' own thinking and as the catalyst for their own creative production. One example of children working as creative readers and producers is a pair of fifth-grade Minnesota students who, after reading a traditional version of "The Frog Prince," adapted the tale to a brand-new setting with different characterizations plus glorious illustrations. Ken is a prince turned into a frog. Only Barbie (of Barbie Doll fame) can kiss the frog and make him Ken once again.

Ultimately, creative and talented students should move from being consumers of superb picture books and become producers of their own illustrated works. The art products they create can be as varied as the imagination. Middle- and secondary-school students can create illustrated big books of classic fairy tales for use by teachers and students in elementary-school classrooms. Youthful authors and illustrators can also employ their creativity to extend a story beyond its original ending. Jon Scieszka and Steve Johnson move the story of "The Frog

Prince" beyond its traditional ending in *The Frog Prince Continued* (Scieszka 1991). Older, mature students can transpose classic fairy tales to settings and circumstances that evoke serious contemporary issues, such as violence toward women and children, illiteracy, and the menace of teenage gangs. How might "The Frog Prince" be transformed in an inner-city environment in Los Angeles or New York City?

Students can also tell and illustrate exciting moments and challenges in their own lives that have fairy tale connections or allusions. Have they ever felt like the princess and been sorry they promised something to another person or, conversely, had things denied them that had been promised? Have they had a scare in a foreign place such as did Goldilocks? Have they ever had a "Cinderella" experience, such as placing first in a contest in which nobody thought they even had a chance of recognition?

Of course, a book does not have to be the final product of explorations into the world of fairy tale illustrations. Students can create cartoons, such as figure 7.1, shared by middle-school student Chris Hickerson of Colorado Springs, Colorado.

Fig. 7.1. Student-Created Cartoon by Chris Hickerson

The directions and examples that follow demonstrate that fairy tales may be illustrated with mobiles, cubes, and other works of art.

Using exemplary picture books with fairy tale content, other illustration and design media such as movie posters of *Beauty and the Beast* and *Cinderella,* and lavishly illustrated catalogs such as the Disney Catalog, teachers may impress upon students that there are infinite possibilities for creating their own visual media. Options may include their own fairy tale pop-up books, fairy tale mobiles, or Venn diagrams (see definition and completed example on p. 59 in the "Little Red Riding Hood" chapter) comparing two characters or two different versions of "The Frog Prince."

THE ART OF STUDENT ILLUSTRATION

The old saying "a picture is worth a thousand words" is the essence of illustration. It is the task of the illustrator to read the words and determine the style of pictorial representation that best conveys the ideas and emotions of the story. Color, shape, line, and medium—such as watercolor, colored pencil, oil, or collage—create different tones and effects. The art of illustration is the marriage of text and graphics on the page. The illustrator or book designer asks: Where would the picture be best on the page? What type size and style are best suited to the story and the action within the story?

Graphic design and illustration are powerful teaching tools in the classroom. Young students who have not yet mastered fluency in writing may use illustration to demonstrate knowledge of story concepts and ideas. Older students profit from opportunities to develop their abilities to present information visually, especially as the world grows increasingly dependent upon communicating ideas and concepts through visual images. Too often it is considered "babyish" to engage students in visual art projects in the secondary grades. However, in today's sophisticated world of technology, a picture does the work of a thousand words. Students operate at the highest levels of thinking and derive great pleasure when they create visual expressions of concepts.

The following descriptions, examples, and patterns will help teachers encourage students of all ages to create their own art products. Story maps, story cubes, mobiles, storyboards, books, and bookbinding are highlighted here as is the concept of artistic style.

Story Maps

In literacy terminology, a map, or web, is a visual representation of what has been learned in an encounter with new information. The act of constructing a map or web is called mapping or webbing. One type of web is a story map, which helps students recall, organize, categorize, and assimilate the important elements of a story, such as characterization, setting, and plot. In figure 7.2, a combination of elements is used. The picture of the frog and the placement of the crown on the letter *P* add interest for viewers. Students may choose to add the princess and interior scenes from the castle.

Fig. 7.2 *"The Frog Prince" Story Map*

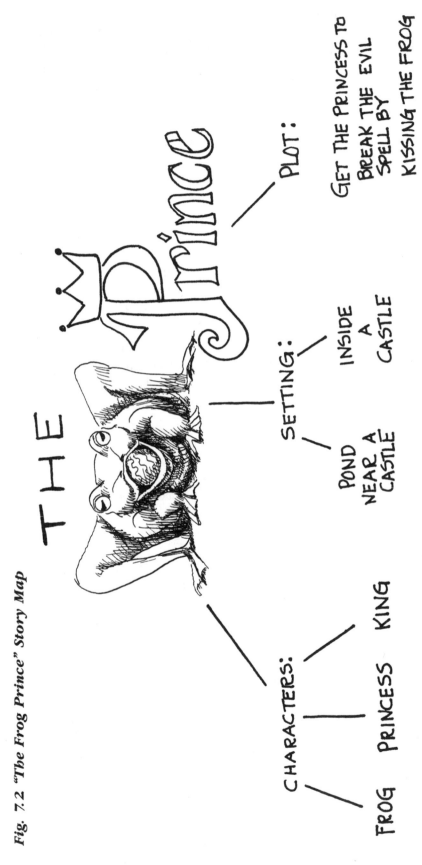

THE Prince

CHARACTERS:

FROG PRINCESS KING

SETTING:

POND NEAR A CASTLE

INSIDE A CASTLE

PLOT:

GET THE PRINCESS TO BREAK THE EVIL SPELL BY KISSING THE FROG

From *From the Land of Enchantment.* © 1997 Jerry D. Flack. Teacher Ideas Press. (800) 237-6124.

Webbing or mapping is not limited to story elements. Students can also create character maps that pictorially record the traits and sometimes the experiences of one or more characters in a story. Graphic symbols such as a lily pad or a golden ball may be used to represent such characters as the Frog Prince and the princess in "The Frog Prince."

An especially fine resource for teachers who want to learn more about mapping with children's literature is *Webbing with Literature: Creating Story Maps with Children's Books,* second edition, by Karen D'Angelo Bromley (Needham Heights, MA: Allyn and Bacon, 1996).

Story Cubes

Story cubes are essentially three-dimensional story maps. Figure 7.3 is a pattern that may be used as shown or enlarged using a photocopying machine. Heavy paper stock should be used, and careful attention should be given to crisp creasing of the fold lines. Have students draw the illustrations on the cube before assembly. It may be wise to have students assemble a trial or practice cube to aid them in planning the placement of drawings on their final products. Students can use story cubes to reduce the content of fairy tales and other literary selections to six key characters, events, and settings to demonstrate comprehension. Story cubes also make fine props for storytelling. Students rotate the cube as a guide to their own storytelling of the "The Frog Prince" or another favorite fairy tale.

Mobiles

Mobiles are popular three-dimensional art forms in many elementary classrooms, but their value cannot be fully appreciated without introducing Alexander Calder, their inventor. Calder explored many types of art: toys, graphic work, tapestry, jewelry, theater sets, wire sculpture, and wood sculpture. He is best known for his mobiles. His inspiration came from Chinese wind bells and eighteenth-century toys that demonstrated the planetary system. Calder wrote, "When everything goes right a mobile is a piece of poetry that dances with the joy of life and surprises" (Lipman 1989, 261).

After sharing information about Calder (found in numerous biographies, art books, and encyclopedias) and the basic design of mobile construction, present students with a large selection of found materials, different gauges of wire, and appropriate tools, such as wire cutters and pliers. Emphasize balance and design. The power of suggestion can be mighty. An eighth-grade teacher in Memphis, Tennessee, moves her students away from the "coat hanger" look of mobiles as book reports by using the term *wind harps*, which prompts the creation of sophisticated mobiles by her language-arts students. (See figure 7.4, on page 162, for an example.)

Fig. 7.3. "The Frog Prince" Story Cube

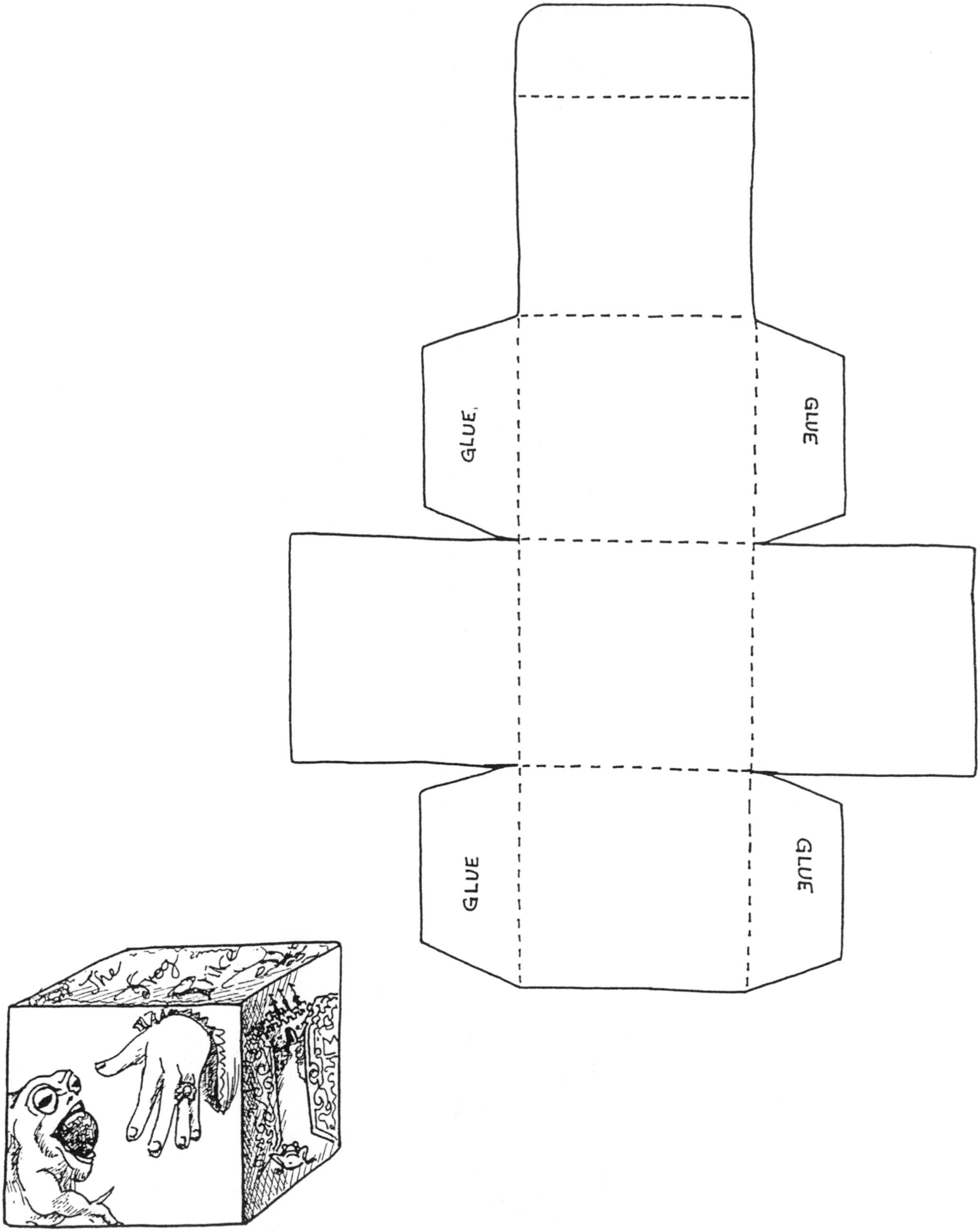

GLUE

GLUE

GLUE

GLUE

From *From the Land of Enchantment.* © 1997 Jerry D. Flack. Teacher Ideas Press. (800) 237-6124.

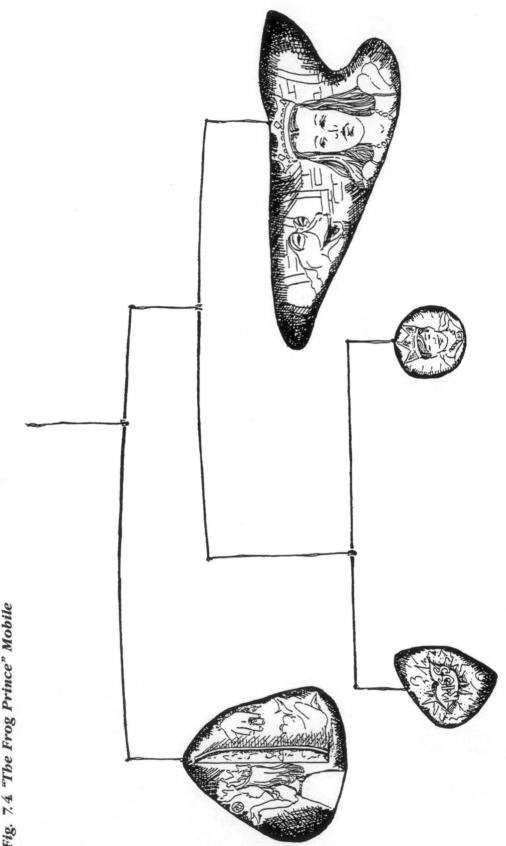

Fig. 7.4 "The Frog Prince" Mobile

Artistic Style

Artistic style is important in defining ideas and concepts of text. To understand how individual artists use such art elements as color, line, shape, and hue, present the works of several different artists to students and accent the style of their respective works. Then have students select a famous artist and illustrate one or more scenes from "The Frog Prince," as in figure 7.5, or another fairy tale. Would Pablo Picasso model the story after his famed painting *Guernica?*

Fig. 7.5. "The Frog Prince" Artistic Style: Pablo Picasso

What style might Georges Seurat have emphasized in a painting of "The Frog Prince"? How might Marc Chagall illustrate the story? Use the focus of a fairy tale such as "The Frog Prince" to aid students in understanding artistic style. (See a discussion of artist Trina Schart Hyman's artistic style on pp. 65-70 in the "Little Red Riding Hood" chapter.)

Storyboards

Storyboards are invaluable planning tools for artists whether they are illustrating a storybook or creating a video. Their sequential nature allows the artist to plan for the story action and audience interests. Figure 7.6 represents the beginning of a storyboard for "The Frog Prince."

Fig. 7.6 "The Frog Prince" Storyboard

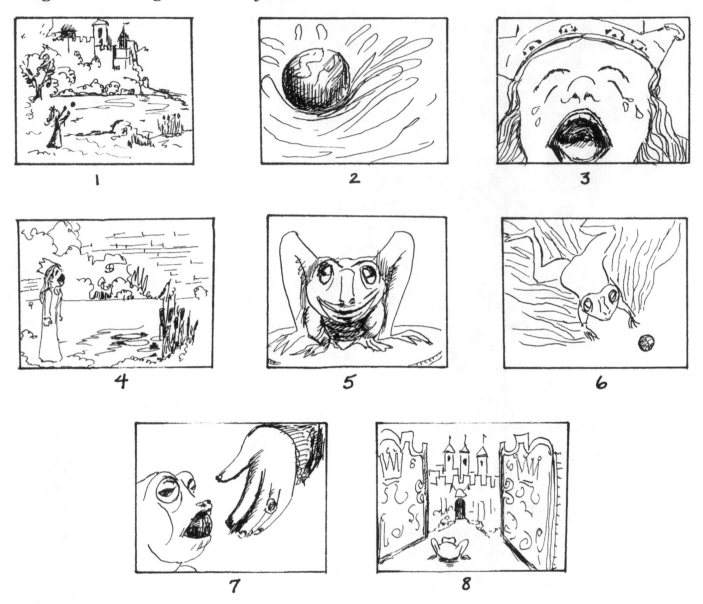

Notice the contrasting distant and close-up views. All distant or all close-up images would be boring for the viewer. Frames three and four illustrate the distress of the princess after losing her golden ball. Which is the most effective? Why? In the third frame some of the princess's face is absent from the picture. Find other examples of this kind of cropping or bleeding off the page in illustrated fairy tale books. These thumbnail sketches are small and provide little detail. However, they do provide the illustrator with an overview of the project in its planning stages.

MAKING BOOKS

Handmade books are fun to create and a treasure to keep. Appropriate for all ages and all curricula, they can be kept simple or made to be complex, sophisticated art products. Here, accordion books, books with doors, and pop-up books are explained.

Accordion Books

The simplest book to make may be the accordion, or concertina book, so named for the way the paper is folded. Figure 7.7 demonstrates how a simple accordion book is made. A sheet of 8½-by-11-inch paper cut in half may be folded to make a seven-page book with a separate title page.

Fig. 7.7. "The Frog Prince" Accordian Book (Simple)

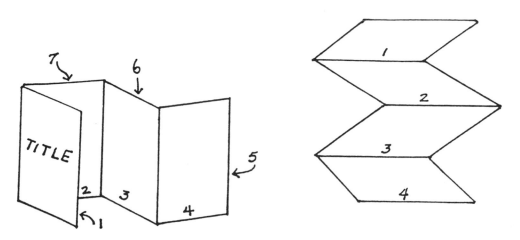

Variations on this simple method are endless and can produce charming and rewarding products for students. Figure 7.8 is an 8½-by-11-inch sheet of paper that has been folded in half rather than cut. Although the cuts in figure 7.8 are geometrical, they can be any shape, including forms found in nature, such as tree limbs.

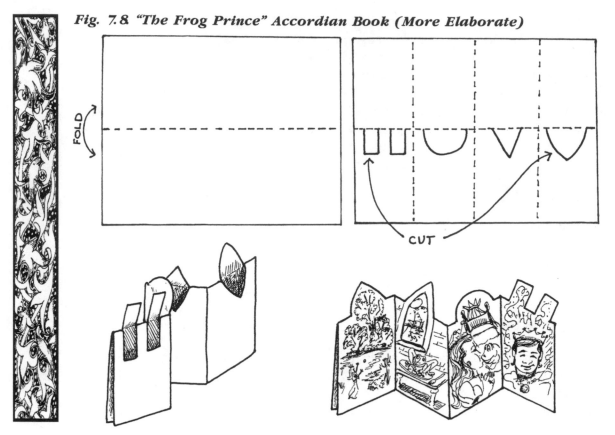

Fig. 7.8 "The Frog Prince" Accordian Book (More Elaborate)

After the cuts are made, fold the paper, popping up the cut sections. While the students experiment with accordion books, remind them to consider what they previously learned about illustrating, such as including both close-up and distant views.

Books with Doors

Books that include doors that open in their design have a great attention-gaining device. Figure 7.9 demonstrates how to make these books. Students need to plan for the inside picture since it will be on the inside page. Such drawings should be done after the cutting and folding.

As previously mentioned, folds should always be crisply creased. If students plan to have openings on both sides of their books, they must be certain that the openings do not line up with one another or the result will be a hole in the book.

Pop-Up Books

Pop-up books delight all readers. The principle of design is the same regardless of whether pop-up books are simple or complex. Figure 7.10 features a simple, single-fold pop-up book. Invite students to experiment with a variety of designs and share their results. Figure 7.11 demonstrates increased design complexity as well as how "The Frog Prince" may be incorporated into the design. To use the pop-up book technique in accordion books, the pop-up cuts are made in the folds of the book.

Fig. 7.9. "The Frog Prince" Book with Doors

Fig. 7.10. "The Frog Prince" Pop-Up Book. Top Row: Simple. Bottom Row: Other Types of Pattern Cuts.

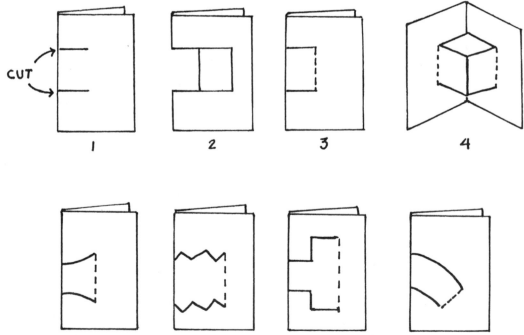

Fig. 7.11. "The Frog Prince" Pop-Up Book (More Complex)

Book Binding

Open-spine binding is the easiest way to put a hard cover on handmade books. Cut two pieces of cardboard or mat board slightly larger than the paper sheets of the book. Cut two sheets of paper or cloth one inch larger than the boards. See figure 7.12. Center the board on the cloth, leaving ½ inch of space around the outside borders. Cut off the corners at a 45-degree angle, taking care to leave a small bit extending beyond the corners. Fold paper or cloth as shown, using crisp creasing. Remove board, and use a finger or paper towel to spread the glue evenly on the paper or cloth. If the glue is not spread evenly, glue ridges associated with kindergarten school art will result. Replace board, centering in the folds, and fold the edges down and secure.

Attach the book pages using the end pages. Note that this must be planned in advance so that no illustration or text appears on these end sheets. Spread glue evenly on the backside of the covers almost to the edge. Center the end sheets over the backside, and press down.

Little extras can further increase the visual appeal of these books. Students might want to try different types of art papers, colored inks and pen tips, rubber stamps with metallic stamp pads, and small found objects. Ribbons, string, or small fasteners can be used to hold the covers together.

Some final tips: When making books with large groups, have book boards and paper precut to appropriate sizes. Supply scraps of paper for experimenting. For very young students, separate workstations may be beneficial. Always be sure to practice all processes before having students create their own books.

Fig. 7.12 Book Binding

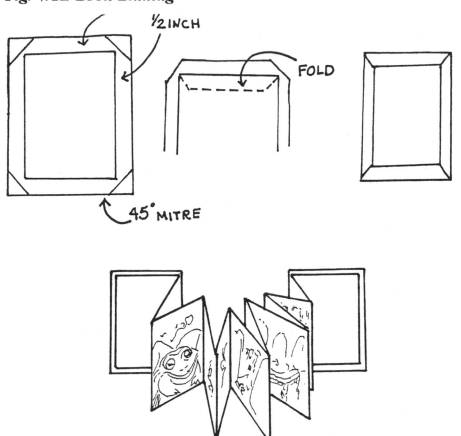

Other Book Patterns and Resources

Three especially fine resources for further ideas in helping kids create their own books are listed here.

Johnson, Paul. 1992. *A Book of One's Own: Developing Literacy Through Making Books*. Portsmouth, NH: Heinemann.
Johnson brings his success with developing children's writing and visual communication in British education to America. He includes many models for constructing books of every kind.

———. 1993. *Literacy Through the Book Arts*. Portsmouth, NH: Heinemann.
Johnson extends the wonderful discussions plus teaching tips he first shared in *A Book of One's Own*.

Zike, Dinah. *Big Book of Books and Activities*. San Antonio, TX: Dinah-Might Activities.

Zike's book is a real teacher pleaser because it is so full of great patterns, directions, and ideas. It may not be easy to find in stores, however. Current address as of this writing is: Dinah-Might Activities, P.O. Box 39657, San Antonio, TX 78218.

BOOKMAKING SCHEDULES

There is no set schedule for students to follow to have positive and successful art adventures with fairy tales, but the following benchmarks may be both practical and helpful whether students are creating fairy-tale cubes, pop-up books, or mobiles. The following benchmarks, however, may be useful to share with students.

1. Think of a variety of fairy-tale topics or subject possibilities that you might illustrate. For example, in the story "The Frog Prince," can you think of five characters or scenes or a combination of the two that would make appropriate panels or components in a "Frog Prince" mobile? How about your own illustrated biography of Jacob and Wilhelm Grimm? If you wrote a 10-page biography of their lives, which parts would you want to illustrate?

   [*Note to teachers:* ABC books may also appeal to students. Challenge them to create 26 drawings to represent 26 special events, places, and characters from the world of fairy tales. Because there are so many letters involved with the production of alphabet books, a class book made up of 26 pages, each from a different student, often works well.]

2. Decide whether to work alone, with a collaborator, or as part of a team of writers, but remember that decision making plays an important role in any art project. Will you work best alone or with a partner? Remember, when books are handmade, only one of you will be able to keep the final product.

   [*Note to teachers:* The first critical choice students have to make is whether to work solo or in collaboration with others. Caution students that the more people involved in a team project, the more difficult it may be to accomplish tasks and successfully create a first-rate product. Ownership of the final product can become an issue too. Students need to be advised that only one partner or team member will be able to keep the final product unless multiple copies are made. One of the advantages of computer-generated text and artwork is that this problem is overcome. Multiple copies can be generated from the same software file.]

3. Research the subject matter. Find out as much as possible about a given tale, character, or storyteller so that the pictures you make are accurate portrayals of times, places, and people.

[*Note to teachers:* If students are going to set the story of "The Frog Prince" in, for example, the Old West or the state of Mississippi during the Great Depression, they need to be accurate and their illustrations should be authentic. Students need to do adequate research for their art projects. Art is more than just drawing! Similarly, if they are going to create a picture-book biography of the Brothers Grimm, they need to find out something about the fashions of nineteenth-century Germany, the hair fashions of the day, and other vital details. Did either brother wear glasses? What kinds of towns and countrysides did they visit, live in, and describe? What are the physical features of Germany's Black Forest?]

4. Develop a storyboard. If you are going to design and produce a multiple-page book, you may want to create a storyboard, which is a sequence of thumbnail sketches placed in the chronology of the story. A storyboard will help you determine the number and kinds of illustrations you will need for your book.

   [*Teacher questions posed may include:* "What things need to be illustrated?" "Where will a picture work better than a word?" "How many illustrations will you need?"]

5. Consider such elements of art illustration as shape, color, line, texture, and space. Also decide how the text of your book will be displayed. Will you hand print the text or use a word processor? If you use a word processor to produce text, what font size and style will you choose? But remember that you want your reader to read your story, not be distracted by many different styles of lettering. Some fonts may be decorative, but they may also be hard to read. If readers must struggle to read because the text fonts are too fancy, they may not read all the content of your book.

   [*Note to teachers:* Art elements can be discussed and illustrated through exemplary picture books obtained from the school media center or public library. Students may want to think about such things as page layout. What role does white space play in picture-book design? Students also need to consider the size and font for the print in their artworks. When using computers for text generation, it is often wise to remind students not to go "overboard" in choosing different types of fonts and font sizes for their text.]

6. Choose the medium for the illustrations. What medium or media will you use to illustrate your book? There are limitless possibilities. In past decades, fairy tales were primarily illustrated with black-and-white pen-and-ink drawings. Today, artists use everything from torn-tissue-paper collage to watercolors to computer-generated art to illustrate classic fairy tales.

   [*Note to teachers:* Throughout the visual-arts component of the study of fairy tales, continually show models of the limitless variety of media that can be employed by illustrators. Artists use collages (wallpaper scraps, feathers, colored tissue paper), pencil drawings, crayon, charcoal, chalk, paint (oil, watercolor, tempera, gouache, and acrylic), pastels, pen and ink, quilt squares, woodcuts, tissue paper, photography, and a host of

other media. Computer graphics also offer great opportunities for illustrating books and generally allow for easy duplication. The current popularity of pop-up books will not be lost on students. They will be intrigued by the remarkable creativity found in book production. One of the advantages of providing students with a wide variety of picture books, posters, and three-dimensional items from fairy tales is that the sharing allows them to witness the countless examples of design and to determine the kind of look they want their own books and other products to have. Invite students to choose any medium that suits their stories, personal tastes, or particular skills of illustration.]

7. Develop a production plan. Practice illustration, and determine how much time it takes you to create a single illustration (e.g., double-page watercolor) for your book. Next, determine how many double-page illustrations your final book will contain. Finally, compute how long it will take to fashion a complete picture book.

   [*Note to teachers:* Time management is definitely one of the skills accented in the creation of art projects. Students need to budget class time wisely. A fairly strict time line with mandatory checkpoints often proves useful in keeping students focused and on task over a period of several weeks or even months, and it avoids the inevitable disappointment procrastinators will almost certainly experience otherwise. Frequent journal entries also help students note at the end of each work session what they have accomplished and what they need to do next. Upper-elementary and middle-school students enjoy longer working periods (90 minutes). In scheduling, however, remember that much valuable time is lost getting art materials out and putting them away again.]

The final products students are capable of creating are magnificent. Students will generate visual feasts in books, posters, masks, mobiles, dolls, and other art objects inspired by fairy tales. Books can be made in all sizes and shapes. A student book, for example, of "The Frog Prince" may be fashioned from pages shaped as water-lily pads.

The benefits of student-created works of art are enormous. The creativity of youth is challenged, enhanced, and honored. Diversity of talent is celebrated. Students who have always been the verbal "top guns" in the class are likely to develop an entirely new appreciation for the talents and skills of many of their artistically talented peers. Students also gain a better understanding of visual literacy through well-planned art experiences. They come to realize that words and pictures can be combined in nearly infinite variety to tell stories and to educate. They gain as well a new appreciation for the genius and craftsmanship of gifted storytellers, writers, and illustrators. Most of all, students are given the opportunity—and most will rise to the occasion—to be creative and to construct original works of art that become outstanding models of their originality and individuality.

"THE FROG PRINCE" RESOURCES

Traditional Stories

Berenzy, Alix. 1989. *A Frog Prince*. New York: Henry Holt.
> An elaborate adaptation of the story with gorgeous, romantic illustrations. When the frog is rebuffed by the spoiled and selfish princess, he goes off on a grand quest to find a princess who will see the good in him. The quest is filled with high adventure illustrated with darkly beautiful paintings.

Galdone, Paul. 1975. *The Frog Prince*. New York: McGraw-Hill.
> Galdone, a premier illustrator of fairy tales, used life models from a pond on his Vermont farm. He adapts and retells the tale from the Brothers Grimm. His colorful, stylized illustrations perfectly capture the magic of an imagined fairy tale setting. Galdone creates miracles with the expressions on the faces of the characters.

Grimm, Jacob, and Wilhelm Grimm. 1989. *The Frog Prince*. Trans. by Naomi Lewis. Illus. by Binette Schroeder. New York: North-South Books.
> Schroeder lends the book a dreamlike feel with her exquisite paintings. Her use of subtle colors and multipaneled scenes appears as royal, brocaded tapestries in this realization of an 1812 version of the familiar tale by the Brothers Grimm of the cursed prince and the willful princess.

Isadora, Rachael. 1989. *The Princess and the Frog*. New York: Greenwillow.
> Isadora faithfully re-creates the Brothers Grimm tale of the prince bewitched by an evil fairy, turned into a frog, and saved by a beautiful princess who becomes his queen. Her impressionistic watercolor paintings are beautiful and suggest an early twentieth-century setting and manner of dress.

Ormerod, Jan, and David Lloyd. 1990. *The Frog Prince*. Illus. by Jan Ormerod. New York: Lothrop, Lee & Shepard.
> In this retelling based upon the tales of the Brothers Grimm and England's Robert Chamberes, the evil spell is broken when the princess allows the frog to sleep in her bed for three nights. By the third night, she has come to love the frog, and her love is the transforming power. Ormerod's illustrations make superb use of color and motion. The frog, appropriately, makes grand leaps that all but vault him from the pages. The illustrator's use of borders is also striking as is her pastel and gray-green palette.

Tarcov, Edith H. 1974. *The Frog Prince*. Illus. by James Marshall. New York: Four Winds.
> Marshall brings his typical wit and grace to this retelling of the Brothers Grimm tale of a somewhat petulant princess who is reluctant to fulfill her pledge to the frog prince who retrieved her golden ball and exacted from her a promise.

"The Frog Prince" Variation

Scieszka, Jon. 1991. *The Frog Prince Continued*. Illus. by Steve Johnson. New York: Viking.
Did the petulant princess and the Frog Prince live happily ever after? Not exactly. Scieszka, well-known for his other fairy tale spoofs *The True Story of the Three Little Pigs By A. Wolf* (Viking, 1989) and *The Stinky Cheese Man* (Viking, 1992), fractures yet another fairy tale with his typical flair for wit and good humor.

Videocassettes

The Frog Prince. Shelley Duvall, producer; Eric Idle, director. Faerie Tale Theatre Series. Livonia, MI: Playhouse Video. 1982. 55 minutes. Videocassette.
Comic prince Robin Williams stars as the Frog Prince who retrieves the lost golden ball of the spoiled princess, played by Terri Garr in this Faerie Tale Theatre production. Rene Auberjonois is the king who forces his daughter to be true to her word. It is worth noting in this art-related chapter that the set decorations for the video are modeled on the work of American artist Maxfield Parrish.

The Frog Prince. Jackson Hunsicker, director. Los Angeles: Cannon Films. 1988. 86 minutes. Videocassette.
Zora is sure that her stepsister will be chosen as the new queen. Ribbit hops to her rescue, but she must also break the spell he is under.

FINELY ILLUSTRATED FAIRY TALE BOOKS

The fairy tale books listed and annotated here are beautiful, artistic interpretations of well-known fairy tales that are not featured in one of the chapters of this book. Yet they are books so splendid in their artistic realization that children should not miss them. They are listed here alphabetically by tale. With some advance planning they can be collected by library media specialists and arranged for viewing as a sort of fairy tale art gallery.

"East of the Sun and West of the Moon"

Dasent, George Webb. 1991. *East of the Sun and West O' the Moon*. Illus. by P. J. Lynch. Cambridge, MA: Candlewick Press.
The story of the great white bear and a heroic maiden is beautifully illustrated by Lynch and based on a translation of the Norse tale by Sir George Webb Dasent.

"Hansel and Gretel"

Grimm, Wilhelm, and Jacob Grimm. 1979. *Hansel and Gretel*. Trans. by Elizabeth Crawford. Illus. by Lisbeth Zwerger. New York: William Morrow.
  The Austrian illustrator Zwerger has distinguished herself as one of the world's foremost illustrators and visual interpreters of the classic fairy tales. She proves why in this lovely version of the sad tale of abandoned children.

———. 1980. *Hansel and Gretel*. Trans. by E. Lucas. Illus. by Susan Jeffers. New York: Dial.
  Jeffers's full-color artwork is, as always, very special and beautiful.

———. 1984. *Hansel and Gretel*. Retold by Rika Lesser. Illus. by Paul O. Zelinsky. New York: Dodd, Mead & Co.
  Zelinsky's oil paintings radiate an "old world" feeling that one suspects the Brothers Grimm would greatly appreciate. Lesser provides valuable endnotes about the authenticity of her retelling. Zelinsky received a Caldecott Honor citation for the book.

———. 1990. *Hansel and Gretel*. Retold and illus. by James Marshall. New York: Dial Books.
  As he did in so many works for children, Marshall finds warmth, charm, and good humor in this classic fairy tale. His witch is simultaneously appealing and appalling.

Ross, Tony. 1989. *Hansel and Gretel*. Woodstock, NY: Overlook Press.
  Ross's villains are appropriately ghastly and his heroes triumph with pluck. Ross finds a sense of humor in fairy tales that few others match.

"Puss in Boots"

Perrault, Charles. 1990. *Puss in Boots*. Trans. by Malcolm Arthur. Illus. by Fred Marcellino. New York: Farrar, Straus & Giroux.
  Marcellino's Puss is so bold and captivating, he does not even need words to draw readers to him. In a unique publishing move, all words were banished from the front cover of this picture book, relegating mention of the title, author and illustrator to the back cover. Wordless, the cover sits royally upon a library or bookstore shelf like a great, unframed portrait of a French noble of ages past. And so it is. The noble "Puss" is beautifully and richly rendered in masterful paintings that capture both French court life and pastoral peasant scenes. Marcellino returned to the world of fairy tales in 1992 with an equally beautiful interpretation of Hans Christian Andersen's *The Steadfast Tin Soldier* (New York: HarperCollins).

"Rapunzel"

Grimm, Jacob, and Wilhelm Grimm. 1982. *Rapunzel*. Retold by Barbara Rogasky.
Illus. by Trina Schart Hyman. New York: Holiday House.
There is an eerie, dark side to Hyman's paintings that brings out the evil of
the witch and Mother Gothel and make the efforts of the king's son to free
Rapunzel appear uncommonly valiant. (See profile of the illustrator in the
"Little Red Riding Hood" chapter.)

———. 1992. *Rapunzel*. Illus. by Carol Heyer. Nashville, TN: Ideal Children's
Books.
Heyer uses bold colors in her seemingly magical acrylic paintings. The colors
allow her to capture all of the sense of wonder found in this classic tale of a
princess imprisoned in a tower.

"Rumpelstiltskin"

Galdone, Paul. 1985. *Rumpelstiltskin*. New York: Clarion Books.
Galdone gloriously captures the thrill of fairy tale mystery and magic in his
vivid, bold illustrations of the fated story of the miller's daughter who must
spin straw into gold. Galdone's little man is a rather jolly evocation of the
Rumpelstiltskin character.

Sage, Alison. 1991. *Rumpelstiltskin*. Illus. by Gennady Spirin. New York: Dial
Books.
A highly regarded Russian illustrator creates a feeling of ages past with his
paintings for the Brothers Grimm retelling of the story of *Rumpelstilzchen*.

Stanley, Diane. 1997. *Rumpelstiltskin's Daughter*. New York: Morrow Junior Books.
Accomplished illustrator Diane Stanley changes and fast forwards the classic
story of the miller's daughter. Meredith (the miller's daughter) much prefers
Rumpelstiltskin to the vain and greedy king. They marry and have a lovely,
sunny daughter whom the king's guards eventually discover and seize in
order to force her to spin straw into gold. The bright and clever lass
completely outwits the king and, in doing so, brings peace and prosperity
back to the kingdom. Stanley's illustrations are as cheerful as her tale. Older
readers will particularly enjoy her sly visual allusions to Picasso and other
great painters throughout the pages of the book.

Zelinsky, Paul O. 1986. *Rumpelstiltskin*. New York: Dutton Books.
With its paintings that look as if they should be hanging on the walls of a great
European art museum, the book was awarded a Caldecott Honor. Zelinsky
perfectly captures the feel of Europe in an earlier age. A helpful note on
scholarship on the text of the Brothers Grimm version of the story is included.

"Sleeping Beauty"

Early, Margaret. 1993. *Sleeping Beauty*. New York: Harry N. Abrams.
Early, who lives in France, uses as her model the same chateau in the Loire Valley that is believed to have been Charles Perrault's inspiration and intended setting for the classic fairy tale of the princess who sleeps for 100 years. Early's vibrant oil paintings are highly detailed as are her ornamental borders, which are decorated with gold paint. Her afterword on historical accuracy serves as a model to students of the possible commitment to scholarship.

Minters, Frances. 1996. *Sleepless Beauty*. Illus. by G. Brian Karas. New York: Viking.
This hip "Sleeping Beauty" tale, set in the funky New York City of the present, is a return visit to fairy tales by this team. Their first attempt to bring fairy tales into modern urban environments was *Cinder-Elly* (Viking, 1994) wherein Prince Charming is a basketball star. Both are told in verse. Both *Sleepless Beauty* and *Snow White in New York* are set in New York City in the twentieth century, and, intriguingly, both heroines are rescued by pop musicians.

"Snow White and the Seven Dwarfs"

French, Fiona. 1986. *Snow White in New York*. New York: Oxford University Press.
French's *Snow White in New York* offers a dramatic contrast to Burkert's version and to the classic Walt Disney film animation, *Snow White and the Seven Dwarfs*. French's tale is set amid the splendor and sophistication of the jazz age in New York. Everything is sleek with straight, hard lines. Bold, riotous yellow and orange colors compete for dominance with bold, black lines (and headlines: Snow White Dead) and cool blues in this masterful retelling of an old, old tale.

Grimm, Jacob, and Wilhelm Grimm. 1972. *Snow White and the Seven Dwarfs*. Trans. by Randall Jarrell. Illus. by Nancy Ekholm Burkert. New York: Farrar, Straus, and Giroux.
Burkert sets the tale in the Middle Ages, and her clothing, furnishings, and other objects in her beautiful paintings reflect the artist's careful research and attention to accurate details. The illustrations earned her Caldecott Honor recognition.

Happily Ever Afters

Written and Illustrated By . . .

Students who have special talents in the art of book illustration may want to consider an outstanding competition for gifted young illustrators. "Written and Illustrated By . . ." is one national competition in which young writers and illustrators, ages 6 through 19, create their own books. For information on this fine program, contact Landmark Editions, Inc., P.O. Box 4469, Kansas City, MO 64127. Hardback copies are available for purchase of many of the books that have won awards since the program's 1986 inception. Popular illustrator Dav Pilkey was one of the early student winners in this program. The sample works provide students with models of the truly exceptional work achieved by gifted, task-committed young people.

REFERENCES

Ernst, Karen. 1994. *Picture Learning: Artists and Writers in the Classroom*. Portsmouth, NH: Heinemann.

Hubbard, Ruth Shagoury, and Karen Ernst. 1996. *New Entries: Learning and Writing and Drawing*. Portsmouth, NH: Heinemann.

Lipman, Jean. 1989. *Calder's Universe*. Philadelphia: Running Press. Alexander Calder cited on p. 261.

Scieszka, Jon. 1991. *The Frog Prince Continued*. Illus. by Steve Johnson. New York: Viking.

Chapter *8*

The Three Little Pigs: Building Houses and Bringing Home the Bacon

CHAPTER PREVIEW

In this chapter two superb teachers share exemplary projects to stimulate and challenge primary, upper-elementary, and middle-school students. Holly Hudson's "Bring Home the Bacon" backpack serves as a model of the valuable kinds of home-school connections teachers can facilitate both to develop literacy and extend creative learning beyond the classroom walls. Susan Valleroli Brock describes explorations her students make into the world of architecture based on encounters with "The Three Little Pigs" and other classic fairy tales. Outstanding media for the study of "The Three Little Pigs" are also recommended.

The popular British fairy tale "The Three Little Pigs," thanks to the adaptation of the story for young children by folklorist Joseph Jacobs (1854-1916), is one of the most popular stories in the world. Jacobs himself believed the tale must have had its roots in the German story of "The Wolf and the Seven Little Kids" told by the Brothers Grimm. His reasoning was that little pigs do not have hair on their chinny chin chins, but little goats do (Jacobs 1972). Of course, Walt Disney's marvelous animation version and its Silly Symphony film song "Who's Afraid of the Big Bad Wolf" contributed mightily to the continued popularity of this simple beast tale of three pigs who leave their mother to go off on their own for the first time and do battle with a wicked wolf. Outstanding print and video versions of the classic story along with creative activities for students to extend the story are listed at the end of the chapter. First, however, the folktale serves as the catalyst for examining two creative approaches to meet the needs of gifted, creative, and talented students through enrichment explorations and extensions. Although "The Three Little Pigs" content is central to both of

181

the exemplary projects shared here—student backpacks and architecture studies—the projects may also serve as models of creative teaching practices that can be applied to nearly any content.

Backpacks

Wise teachers encourage lifelong learning by helping their students extend learning beyond the classroom. They provide great alternatives to television's wasteland. One way they accomplish this miracle is by creating interactive fairy tale backpacks. What are backpacks? They are portable, miniature learning centers packaged in backpacks, book bags, or briefcases. Backpacks can be filled with fairy tale books and laminated reprints of articles about fairy tales, bears, pigs, and related fairy tale content. They also contain activity cards students complete themselves or with the help of older family members. Backpacks may contain hand puppets, felt pieces, and other manipulatives students can use to retell fairy tales to family and friends. Students check out the backpacks from the classroom or library media center and complete a desired number of activities over a weekend or throughout a school week. Laminated (for protection from heavy usage) activity cards may be directed reading assignments. For example, one of Hudson's "Three Little Pigs" activity cards invites students to read the two versions of the folktale found in the backpack and then compare them. Other backpack activities may relate to any other skills and talents teachers want to emphasize: critical and creative thinking, problem solving, visual communication, art skills, and so on. While some of the backpack activities can be individually completed, it is a good idea also to include other action-oriented paired or group tasks that allow the participating child to involve parents, siblings, and others in the exciting take-home adventure.

Backpacks permit all students—especially those who are gifted and talented—to extend their learning beyond the classroom. They also provide opportunities for families to experience some of the fun and excitement of the fairy tale unit going on at school. Indeed, it is a good idea to include in the backpack a bibliography of books and other media for continued study of fairy tales.

Backpacks can be about any topic or subject matter. This author describes an invention backpack in *Inventing, Inventions, and Inventors: A Teaching Resource Book* (Flack 1989). Or backpacks can be related to other literature genres, such as biography, science subjects, hobbies, and mathematics problem solving. The following backpack description highlights "The Three Little Pigs." It stands as a model for additional backpacks related to other fairy tales or other topics and themes.

BRING HOME THE BACON: A PRIMARY-GRADES BACKPACK

Holly Hudson is a first- and second-grade teacher at Penrose Elementary School in Colorado Springs, Colorado. Students and parents opening her "Bring Home the Bacon" backpack find the following contents:

Welcome letters to student users and the user's parents

Three books:

> *The Three Little Javelinas* by Susan Lowell (Northland, 1992)
>
> *The Three Little Pigs* by David McPhail (Scholastic, 1995)
>
> *The True Story of the Three Little Pigs* by Jon Scieszka (Viking, 1989)

Pig-shaped, laminated activity cards (see examples below)

One blank "Ears to You" work sheet

One small, plastic measuring cup

One plastic bag of popcorn kernels

One blank Venn diagram

Create-a-Pig Ziploc bag containing:

> Large and small balloons
>
> Paper clips
>
> Corks
>
> Rubber bands
>
> Twist ties in two sizes
>
> Safety pins
>
> Clothespins
>
> Bread-sack closers (clamps)

One "Pig-tionary" game

One "Pig-tionary Dictionary"

One "Pigliography" of classic and contemporary children's books with pig characters. (Representative authors: Beatrix Potter, Arnold Lobel, David McPhail, Jane Yolen, and Arthur Geisert)

One student evaluation form

One parent evaluation form

A student's experience with "Bring Home the Bacon" begins with a letter of welcome from the teacher. In her note to students, Hudson invites them to explore all the contents of the backpack and to choose those activities they think they will most enjoy. The message to students includes a special plea to be sure all materials are returned to the backpack. A similar letter to parents provides a brief explanation of the backpack as voluntary homework, notification that some activities will require parent participation or supervision, and notice that some of the activities are cumulative and depend upon completion of reading or other activities. She underscores the importance of the backpack being a fun and rewarding experience for each child. Finally, the teacher sincerely requests parent feedback through the completion of the enclosed parent evaluation form.

The parent evaluation form includes these questions: Were the activities appropriate for your child? Do you have any suggestions for improving this backpack? What is your overall impression of the concept of voluntary homework through backpacks?

Sample student questions for evaluation include: Which activity was your favorite and why? Which activity was your least favorite and why? What other topics would you like to find in classroom backpacks?

Figure 8.1 is a pig template that may be duplicated. Figure 8.2 lists the activity prompts and questions posed by Hudson for her students. Teachers can make multiple copies of the pig template on poster board or construction paper. The text for each activity card found in Figure 8.2 can be written directly onto the activity cards with markers, crayons, or pens or copied onto slips of paper that are then affixed to the pig activity cards, as shown in Figure 8.3. The activity cards may then be laminated and placed in a "Bring Home the Bacon" backpack.

Teachers or classroom volunteers should inventory each backpack when it is returned to ensure that all necessary items are enclosed. Student and parent evaluation forms are removed and reviewed by the teacher. New copies of the same student and parent evaluation forms and fresh copies of the Venn diagram and "Ears to You" work sheets are repacked in the backpack, and it is ready for the next subscribing student to use.

Another item Hudson places in her "Three Little Pigs" backpack for students is her own original game, "Pig-tionary." The game is based on the popular game "Pictionary" and requires a minimum of two players. Her "Pig-tionary" words include:

sow thistle　hogtie　pig-skin　hogwash　pig-in-a-blanket

pig pen　piggy bank　pig boat　pig sty　pigheaded　hedgehog

A small, spiral-bound notebook serves as a "Pig-tionary Dictionary" with definitions of all the words or phrases found on the "Pig-tionary" game cards. Players take turns being the artist or the guesser. The artist chooses a "Pig-tionary" card and has two minutes to draw the word so that the guesser can identify it correctly. If the guesser correctly identifies the word, the artist receives one point. If the guesser misses the word, the artist looks the word up in the "Pig-tionary" and reads it aloud to the guesser. After each turn, roles are exchanged.

Do backpacks work? Yes! Here is one experience Hudson relates.

> I have a very talented group of first graders who need challenges to keep their interest in reading high. I sent the backpack home with one student, and our agreement was that it would be returned within one week. A week came and went, and the backpack wasn't returned. I began to ask about it daily and was assured each day that it would be returned the next day. After this went on for a week, I asked this student, who was normally so responsible, if something had happened to the backpack. My young friend blushed to the very roots of her hair and replied that her dad wasn't done with all the activities yet! Sometimes one never knows where family involvement will lead! (Personal correspondence from Holly Hudson to Jerry Flack, December 6, 1996.)

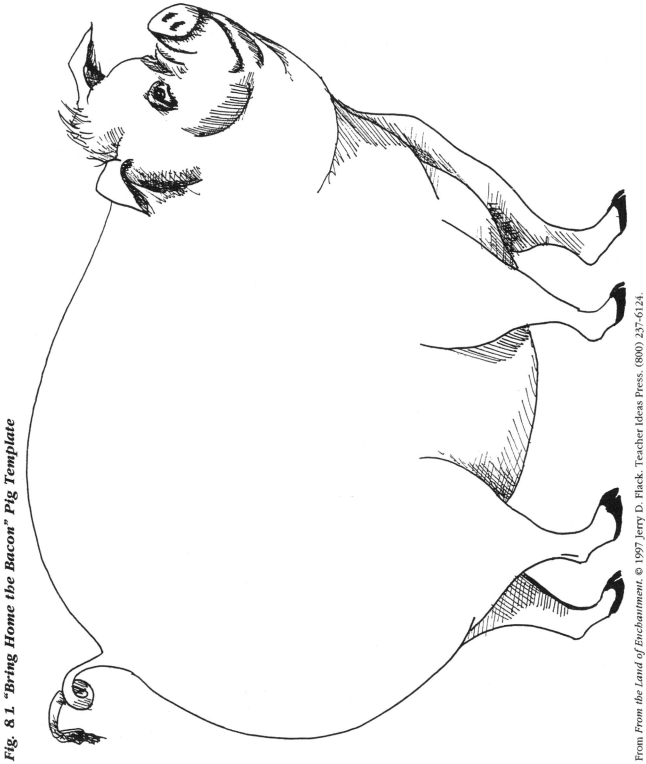

Fig. 8.1 "Bring Home the Bacon" Pig Template

Fig. 8.2 "Bring Home the Bacon" Activity Cards

1. You are a reporter for a newspaper for pigs, *The Pork Report*. After interviewing the wolf and the third little pig, you must write the real story of the wolf and the three little pigs. You may ask only six questions of each, and your questions must begin with *who, what, when, where, why,* or *how.* Write your questions so that you can get the most information possible.

2. Extra! Extra! Write a news story of the events in "The Three Little Pigs" based upon your interviews with the wolf and the third little pig. Include a clever headline and an illustration.

3. Wolf Proof. You are the second little pig. You ask yourself: How might I wolfproof my stick house? List as many ideas as you can, then write an advantage and a disadvantage list for your top five ideas.

4. Using two of the three books in the backpack, complete a Venn diagram comparing the two stories read. Try to find the most unusual similarities and differences you can. (*Note:* See "Little Red Riding Hood" chapter for a definition and example of a Venn diagram used as a comparison tool.)

   Dickory, dickory, dare,
   The pig flew up in the air;
   The man in brown soon brought him down,
   Dickory, dickory, dare.[1]

5. What If? What if pigs really could fly? Create a crossing sign for flying pigs! Use words, pictures, or both.

6. Design a pig catcher for flying pigs! Draw a picture or construct a model of a pig catcher.

7. Rhyme time. Make a list of as many words that rhyme with *pig* (e.g., *big*) as you can in three minutes. Ready! Set! Go!

8. Write and illustrate a pig-rhyming book using your list of rhyming words. A sample page might read: Pigs wearing wigs. Your illustration might be two pigs trying on wigs.

9. Find the Create-a-Pig Ziploc bag in the backpack. Create a pig using one of each item but not more than three. You may not add any materials other than those found in the backpack bag with the exception of crayons or markers for decorating your pig. Contents include:

Large and small balloons	Paper clips
Corks	Rubber bands
Twist ties in two sizes	Safety pins
Bread-sack closers (clamps)	Clothespins

   ---
   1. *Mother Goose's Nursery Rhymes.* Edited by Walter Jerrold. Illus. by John Hassall. (New York: Dodge, p. 83).

10. "No, not by the hair of my chinny chin chin!" How many other ways can you think of to tell the wolf he cannot come in? Work with a partner. Work by yourself. Race with a friend.

11. Ears to You! What do pigs like to eat? Why, corn, of course. Estimate how many kernels it will take to fill the cup (find plastic cup and plastic sack of popcorn kernels in the backpack). Enter your estimate on the "Ears to You" work sheet in the backpack. Now count. Enter the total on the work sheet. Find other items in your kitchen, and predict if it will take more or fewer to fill the cup, then estimate how many it will take, then count. What conclusion can you draw from your data? Note: The "Ears to You" work sheet contains these questions:

    How many corn kernals will fill the cup? estimate _____ count _____
    How many _____ will fill the cup? estimate _____ count _____
    (Repeat the _____ question two additional times so that students try such variants as rice, beans, and pasta to fill the cup.)

    What conclusions can you draw from the information you now have? Do you think this will work with other items? Why or why not?

12. Did you ever notice how many stories have three in them? Think of as many stories as you can that have three of anything. How about "Three Billy Goats Gruff" for a starter? If you run out of ideas, ask your mom or dad or a grandparent for some additional ideas.

13. You are a construction contractor who has been called by the Pig Family to rebuild the straw house. You see that it needs a frame to support it. Build the strongest frame you can from just six soda straws and ten straight pins. Make sure it is windy-wolf proof. Be careful with the straight pins too!

14. IGPAY ATINLAY. Take the first consonant off a word, put it at the end, and add *ay*, and you have Pig Latin! Rewrite your favorite rhyme in Pig Latin, and see if your family can guess what it is! Oodgay Ucklay!

15. A Pig Tale. Start with this simple sentence: I love pigs! Now drop one word from the sentence, and add two more words to make a new sentence that makes sense. Keep on building your pig sentence by dropping one word and adding two new words at each turn. Get your friends and family to join you in sentence building. Take turns. Go hog-wild! Build the longest sentence you can.

Fig. 8.1 "Bring Home the Bacon" Pig Template

You are a reporter for a newspaper for pigs, *The Pork Report*. After interviewing the wolf and the third little pig, you must write the real story of the wolf and the three little pigs. You may ask only six questions of each, and your questions must begin with *who, what, when, where, why,* or *how.* Write your questions so that you can get the most information possible.

MAGIC, MORTAR, AND BRICKS

Susan Valleroli Brock is a library media specialist at Broadmoor Elementary School in Colorado Springs, Colorado. Working with upper-elementary and middle-school students, she creates and facilitates challenging enrichment experiences with architecture based upon students' familiarity with "The Three Little Pigs." Susan Valleroli Brock shares her unit on architecture and "The Three Little Pigs" here.

ARCHITECTURE AND THE THREE LITTLE PIGS

Inquiry and Discovery

It is difficult, if not impossible, to separate literary experiences from literacy learning. As a teacher and media specialist working with gifted children since 1978, I have developed thematic units intended to foster literacy through literary experiences. The idea for an architecture focus originated in response to the expressed interests of students. Their input initiated as well as shaped the development of the unit, which, in turn, provided a context for relevant literary and literacy experiences.

Houses come in all shapes, sizes, and styles. Because of this interesting diversity and the wide array of traditional and modern fairy tales whose plots revolve around a piece of architecture, the built environment, which is architecture in its broadest sense, was chosen as the focus of this unit. The melding of fairy tales and architecture offers a kaleidoscope of possibilities for igniting the curiosity and creativity of children whose inquiring minds continue to seek answers to questions about the world and the forces that shape it.

The houses, schools, skyscrapers, bridges, parks, and barns we encounter daily provide the settings in which we work and play. In a sense the built environment frames our actions and helps shape the course of our lives. Because of the roles played by architecture, all of us from children to adults can benefit from learning more about it.

What better time to introduce children to the world of architecture than when they are already captivated by the subject, through exposure to such imaginative fictional scenes as the wolf huffing and puffing at the doors of the Three Little Pigs' houses or mesmerized by descriptions of the prince hacking his way through the thorny undergrowth covering the castle of Sleeping Beauty?

Observe the fascinated expressions of children as they listen to descriptions of the tiny cottage of the Seven Dwarfs. Recall your own delight with the scrumptious descriptions of the gingerbread house when "Hansel and Gretel" was first read to you. Wise teachers seize every opportunity to provide meaningful literary and literacy experiences for children. Certainly, the enchanting structures that they encounter in literature provide the basis for many meaningful learning experiences.

In my teaching I have found that children are still interested in fairy tales. Most are intrigued by the towering skyscrapers, imposing castles, colossal bridges, and gargantuan mansions that exist both in literature and in the real world. Children have an insatiable curiosity and seek answers to their many questions about imaginary and real architectural structures. In my language-arts teaching experiences, children inevitably question why the house of the third pig withstood the gale-force winds of the wolf, while the homes of his brothers were totally demolished. I have yet to meet a student who was not interested in the formidable prison fortress of Rapunzel or awed by the towering skyscrapers of the real world. As children take a closer look at these structures they can begin to make deeper connections with the physical world and develop an understanding and appreciation of the structures and forces that dominate, shape, and significantly impact the world and their own lives.

Architecture as a unit of study can provide a concreteness to the learning process. It is a perfect vehicle for introducing numerous abstract math concepts, particularly those relating to geometry and physics. Problem-solving skills and creativity can be developed through the intermingling of fairy tales and architecture. The melding of literature (fairy tales) and science (architecture) can produce unlimited literacy experiences that invite children to explore not only the world of books but the real world. This marriage of the mythical world of fairy tales and the factual world of architecture invites children to question, reflect, explore, and discover significant truths about human experience and the world. Architecture, or built-environment education, is not a new subject to be added to an already full curriculum. It is an approach to traditional areas of study that can easily be integrated into an existing curriculum.

The architecture-fairy tales unit has been tested in kindergarten through sixth-grade classrooms. The organization consists of the following components.

Group Sessions

Group sessions are times for students to share their ideas and general knowledge on the focus theme. This is the time for dialogue, information exchange, and the generation of questions for further inquiry. It is during the group sessions that several tales are read aloud and the focus theme is introduced. In the architecture focus unit, fairy tales in which architecture significantly affects plot are read and discussed. The success of the unit hinges upon a continuous exchange of information. The group sessions provide opportunities for important dialogue among students and teachers. These sessions are instrumental in determining the overall course the unit will take.

Independent Research and Writing Sessions

Once students have been introduced to several fairy tales in which architecture figures prominently, they are encouraged to explore related areas of interest individually, with a partner, or in small groups. Class time is allotted for this purpose. Students may work in the classroom or in the resource room. It is beneficial to have in the classroom or media center a wide variety of magazines such as *Architectural Digest, Better Homes and Gardens, Southern Living*, and *House Beautiful* as well as books about architecture and collections of picture books of classic and modern fairy tales. To facilitate research, it is advantageous

to make prior arrangements with the media specialist to have a selection of appropriate reference materials on reserve in the library. Also, scheduling blocks of time for students to work in the library in advance is most beneficial.

Journals

A journal for recording responses to fairy tale readings and for keeping track of relevant architecture terms, questions, and project ideas is vital to the unit. The journal serves as a communication tool that enables the teacher to carry on a continuous dialogue with each student. Most journal entries are about architecture, but some prompts can tease the creativity of students. For example, a prompt may ask students to assume the character of either the wolf or one of the three pigs and enter a series of diary entries on behalf of that character.

Architecture Project

The combination of architecture and fairy tales offers endless enrichment possibilities. Architecture easily lends itself to the creation of tangible products. Students are required to design a project, conduct research, and actually create a product relating to the architectural concepts examined in the unit. Students' journal entries generate many of the ideas for the individual and group projects. For example, several students translated architecture terms into a portrait gallery containing drawings of individuals whose features represented such architectural concepts as tension, compression, arch, balance, cantilever, corbel, and dome. The portrait of a rotund, potbellied gentleman that was used to demonstrate a cantilevered structure was my favorite. This gentleman was appropriately named Cantor Levy! Some students formed construction teams and designed and built models of fictional and real buildings, while other groups used drama to demonstrate architectural concepts. The most popular dramatization was the scene of the big, bad wolf huffing and puffing at the doors of the little pigs' houses! Our "wolf" possessed industrial-strength lungs; a commercial blower fan was used to simulate the strong winds produced by the hungry wolf. Needless to say, just like the houses of the first two pigs, our straw and twig constructions were demolished by the gale-force winds produced by the wolf. Thanks to the help of a mason, our brick "house" remained intact.

Bricks and Buildings

Humans have always crafted shelter. The first building materials were those offered by Mother Nature: stone, mud, grass, saplings, and wood. Architects still use these materials, but additional man-made materials are now available for construction.

The humble, unassuming brick was the first widely successful man-made building material and the true hero in the story "The Three Little Pigs." Brick is small, lightweight, basic in form, and cheap! This versatile material can satisfy the needs of unskilled laborers or the artistic demands of master designers and craftsmen. Bricks represent a unique concept in building materials because, unlike naturally occurring wood or stone, bricks are a transformed material. The raw materials that make up bricks have to be combined in a certain way, shaped, then fired. Archaeologists speculate that the concept of masonry had its origins in the creation of low walls from stone and mud. The precursor to mortar was wet mud packed into the cracks of stone walls. The use of brick as a building material first became popular during the Roman Empire. Brick remains a popular building material today.

Readers make sense of text by bringing prior knowledge to the text. Prereading dialogue is an important preparatory activity because it helps students and teachers become aware of what prior knowledge is available for comprehension and what knowledge is needed to anticipate and predict meanings. I use prestory dialogue to show students how they can use their knowledge to formulate questions about content and enhance comprehension.

Because brick, which is the first transformed building material, is the architectural star of "The Three Little Pigs," I begin the prereading dialogue by writing the words *transform*, *transformer*, and *transformation* on the chalkboard. I then ask students to respond and explain the meaning of any of those words.

Most children are familiar with the popular transformer toys, so they should have no problem relating to the second word. I have observed that lower-elementary students are able to extrapolate from their knowledge of the transformer toy and figure out the meanings of the other two words. After classes reach consensus that the three words have something to do with change, confirmation of their definitions are made by consulting a dictionary.

Additional group activities include brainstorming materials used to build houses, developing criteria for evaluation of identified construction material, and evaluating the suitability of materials based upon the criterion developed by the class. If possible, also invite a mason or bricklayer to come to school and demonstrate the process of brick construction to classes.

Once the principles of laying masonry have been presented, invite students to demonstrate their understanding by performing the task themselves. This is a rather messy activity, but students have a wonderful time showing their understanding, and usually they are quite proficient at laying the bricks. Certainly their problem-solving skills are strengthened as a result of this sticky, concrete activity. With proper planning and precautions such as using a painter's drop cloth or lots of newspaper spread on tables and the floor, the mess can easily be contained and damage averted.

The architecture-fairy tales unit has been developed from student-generated questions. These questions provided a framework for developing the unit and for transforming a literature experience into a practical literacy experience.

Many questions are formulated by my students following a walking tour of an old section of Colorado Springs that has many brick buildings. Students view brick houses in need of repair, new brick office buildings under construction, and a wide variety of styles of contemporary and older brick homes. They are amazed by some spectacular brick mansions that have rather gloriously weathered the test of time.

The following are typical questions generated after the walking field trip and a reading of the story "The Three Little Pigs."

How did brick come to be?

What is brick made of?

Bricks are set in many different patterns. Do different patterns of bricks mean different things?

How do bricks over doors and windows stay in place?

What are building codes?

What does it mean when a building has failed, and why does it happen?

What is an architect's professional responsibility?

What is sick building syndrome?

What are firmness, commodity, and delight?

Once students center on particular questions, they initiate research to find answers to questions they have posed.

Independent Research

As students pursue answers to their questions, their research reveals that many of the Three Little Pigs' problems could have been eliminated with proper building codes and restrictions and the services of professional architects.

Individual students share background information with other students during group-dialogue sessions. Background information relating to the architecture may be located in any number of fine media-center resources or from personal contacts with architects and builders. The following resources may prove useful to teachers who want to engage students in the study of architecture.

Architecture Book Resources

Adam, Robert. 1995. *Buildings: How They Work*. New York: Sterling.
  A fine resource about architecture for younger students. Includes brief chapters on building with bricks to create walls, castles, and palaces.

Architecture and Construction. 1996. Voyages of Discovery Series. New York: Scholastic.
  In this interactive Voyages of Discovery book, readers are treated to a fine survey of architecture, including a history lesson and some fascinating connections. The building of the pyramids of ancient Egypt is contrasted with the construction of I. M. Pei's glass pyramid in Paris for the Louvre Museum in 1985. The building of castles is also explored.

Munro, Roxie. 1986. *Architects Make Zigzags*. Washington, D.C.: National Trust for Historic Preservation Press.
An imaginatively designed and illustrated alphabet book about key architecture terms and features. Columns, eaves, facades, gables, and verandas are just a few of the stops on this creative building journey.

Thorne-Thomsen, Kathleen. 1994. *Frank Lloyd Wright for Kids: His Life and Ideas*. Chicago Review Press.
This wonderful book combines biography and engineering in delightful ways. Students learn about the life of a great architect and while doing so also learn design principles of architecture. Twenty-one highly imaginative activities are also included in the child-friendly book. If not used in the classroom, this book makes for great partnership reading by parents and children.

Tobin, Dan, ed. 1994. *From the Ground Up: Modeling, Measuring, and Constructing Houses*. Seeing and Thinking Mathematically in the Middle Grades Series. Portsmouth, NH: Heinemann.
In this spiral-bound unit book teachers find all the plans, black-line masters, and other resources they need to invite students to apply mathematics to solving a variety of design and construction problems associated with building a house. They base roof costs on finding the area of triangles, and they estimate floor and ceiling costs by finding the area of any polygon. Students act as architects in designing and constructing a model home.

Tritton, Roger, ed. 1992. *The Visual Dictionary of Buildings*. Eyewitness Visual Dictionary Series. New York: Dorling Kindersley.
This large-format visual dictionary strikingly reveals components of buildings, such as domes, ceilings, and arches and presents a history of architecture from ancient Egypt up to the present time.

Wood, Richard. 1995. *Architecture*. Legacies Series. New York: Thomson Learning.
Wood explores modern and ancient architecture around the world. The contributions from Egypt, Asia, the Middle East, and the Celts are considered. Excellent text is complemented by colorful drawings and photographs.

Architecture Projects

Most projects develop in response to questions students generate. Some students build models of the straw, twig, and brick houses of the Three Little Pigs and then devise and conduct tests to show the relative safety of each structure. Others research the composition of bricks and make their own bricks. Still others conduct a demonstration of bricklaying for their classmates. (One fifth-grade group taught this skill to second-graders.)

One especially popular project is the design and building of a playhouse to be used in the kindergarten or another place. This ambitious construction project is a great way to encourage cooperation among classes. It requires forethought

and detailed planning, but it is worth the effort. My gifted classes—kindergarten through sixth grades—worked out the details of fund-raising, collecting materials, and allocating specific construction jobs. We used building plans purchased from a local hardware and building-supply center. The decorator touches were designed by the students. With lots of adult supervision, even the youngest students had an opportunity to use the following building tools: hammer, crosscut saw, keyhole saw, level, square, brace and bit, and electric screwdriver. The finished product was a quaint country cottage located in a corner of the library. It was used as a reading nook for students.

It is a great idea to invite an architect or draftsman to work with classes to design sets of blueprints. This may be followed up with an invitation to a builder to work with your class to construct the class-designed class structure. Working at the United States Air Force Academy, I was fortunate to have access to cadets who were required to design and construct something as a public-service project. One group of cadets designed and built a wooden play set for our playground. All the time and materials were donated! There are lots of generous individuals who may be willing to contribute to special projects. Don't be afraid to ask!

After looking into "sick building syndrome," two students decided to investigate radon poisoning, another building horror. This is a common problem in Colorado and a concern in many housing areas of Colorado Springs. Some students brought in a radon-testing kit and demonstrated its use by testing the radon content of our classroom. Fortunately, our classroom levels of radon were in the acceptable range. Asbestos was another problem students investigated. During one entire summer their school was torn apart to remove asbestos, which had been used in the construction process a quarter of a century earlier.

Architecture-Fairy Tales Unit Extensions

Walls and their relationship to "The Three Little Pigs" is not the only architectural connection that can be made with fairy tales. Doors are as old as humankind. Even prehistoric man knew the need to close off the entrance to his cave or tent against predators, enemies, or inclement weather.

If we look at windows as the eyes of a house, then a door is its mouth. Doors, like mouths, are active! When we pass through a doorway, we encounter and most likely become involved in what lies beyond. Closed doors tell us of the desire for privacy or of another's rejection. They can engulf and imprison us or welcome us to a haven from the outside world when it becomes too hectic or demanding. Doors frame our reunions and farewells and enclose us in warm, familiar surroundings. They guard us from unwanted visitors and unpleasant weather. Yet doors admit surprises, like an unexpected package from the mail carrier or a surprise visit from a friend.

Doors mark our crossings between inside and outside, between public and private, between personal and social. Through doors we pass from one contact point to the next—arriving, departing and returning. In the story "Little Red Riding Hood," the fate of the grandmother, the wolf, Little Red Riding Hood, and the woodcutter hinge on their passage through the door of the grandmother's house. As each passes through this doorway, his or her life takes an unexpected turn!

Students may contemplate and research walls, doors, windows, or other structural components found in architecture. Regardless, the connection between architecture and fairy tales is a wonderful relationship well worth pursing with eager students.

"THE THREE LITTLE PIGS" RESOURCES

Teachers and media specialists who use "The Three Little Pigs" for backpacks, architecture units, and additional creative projects found in the Happily Ever Afters component of this chapter may take advantage of several wonderful versions of the classic English tale in both print and video formats.

Traditional Stories

Bishop, Gavin. 1989. *The Three Little Pigs*. New York: Scholastic.
   A New Zealand author-illustrator colorfully recalls the classic tale of the third little pig's cunning ability to outsmart the voracious wolf.

Claverie, Jean. 1989. *The Three Little Pigs*. New York: North-South Books.
   Claverie's simple line drawings, both colored and black and white, are so well done that they seem to come alive on the pages of the book. Highly original perspectives and sly touches of humor add zest to the telling. The wolf appears in a suit and tie, but as the effort of blowing down the houses becomes increasingly challenging, he takes off his coat, rolls up his sleeves, and really goes to work!

Disney, Walt [prod.]. 1987. *Walt Disney's Three Little Pigs*. New York: Simon & Schuster.
   Stills from the classic Disney 1933 "Silly Symphony" animated version of the English tale of three brothers, their houses, and the big bad wolf. An especially useful and informational afterword is provided by Allen Eyles about the creation of the original cartoon and its later propaganda value and use during the Second World War.

Galdone, Paul. 1970. *The Three Little Pigs*. New York: Clarion.
   Sprightly, cheerfully colored drawings lend charm and wit to this retelling of the cautionary tale of the first two unvigilant pigs who become breakfast and lunch for a big, bad wolf. Galdone's wolf is appropriately vile.

Marshall, James. 1989. *The Three Little Pigs*. New York: Dial.
   Marshall bestows charm and good humor upon all his characters, even the nasty wolf. The wolf gobbles up the first two little pigs, but he is no match for the industry and cleverness of the third little pig, who builds a most sturdy Victorian cottage of bricks and outwits the wolf at every turn. Marshall's versions of fairy tales, including the story of "The Three Little Pigs," will no doubt delight children for generations to come.

McPhail, David. 1995. *The Three Little Pigs*. Favorite Tales Series. New York: Scholastic.
McPhail does wonders with pigs—one of his favorite subjects—so he is naturally at the top of his form in presenting the wolf and the three little pigs with good humor and charm. In McPhail's version, the third little pig, through her industry, saves her two brothers.

Rounds, Glen. 1992. *Three Little Pigs and the Big Bad Wolf*. New York: Holiday House.
The wolf in Rounds's words and pictures is lean and very, very mean. There are not many survivors in this version. There is, however, in this traditional picture book, a starkness and economy of both word and line.

Zemach, Margot. 1988. *The Three Little Pigs*. New York: Farrar, Straus & Giroux.
Zemach provides superb illustrations to complement her traditional telling of the tale. The first two pigs are eaten, but the third little pig had "wolf soup for supper. Yumm-yum!"

Ziefert, Harriet. 1995. *The Three Little Pigs*. Illus. by Laura Rader. New York: Puffin Books.
The simple narrative and repetitive dialogue of the wolf and the three pigs is easily read in the large print provided. Humorously, it is the nerdlike third little pig who wears glasses and works tirelessly building a brick house who survives to enjoy a full stomach and a hot cup of tea.

Variations and Other Treatments

Anno, Mitsumasa, and Tuyosi Mori. 1986. *Socrates and The Three Little Pigs*. New York: Pilomel.
The Japanese illustrator and author use the story "The Three Little Pigs" to introduce probability to students. The book is wonderfully clever. Alas, it is currently out of print, but copies should be available in most public libraries given the author-illustrator's popularity and publishing history.

Celsi, Teresa. 1992. *The Fourth Little Pig*. Austin, TX: Steck-Vaughn.
The fourth pig is the sister of her paranoid, porcine brothers. She blows their house down and gets them back out in the fresh air of life. This charming adaptation provides this story with a whole new moral.

Hooks, William H. 1989. *The Three Little Pigs and the Fox*. Illus. by S. D. Schindler. New York: Macmillan.
A tale of "The Three Little Pigs" from the Great Smoky Mountains. In this Appalachian version, highlighted by delightful illustrations, the little sister pig, Hamlet, proves to be the wisest, craftiest, and most courageous pig of all.

Laird, Donivee Martin. 1992. *The Three Little Hawaiian Pigs and the Magic Shark*. Illus. by Carol Jossem. Honolulu: Barnaby Books.
Two good parents send their three children out into the world when it is time for them to be on their own. The story follows familiar lines except for the replacement of the evil wolf by a cunning and malevolent shark who magically is able to come onto shore. The building material of the first little pig is pili grass, the second makes use of driftwood, and the third little pig builds a sturdy domicile of lava rocks. The unlucky shark ends up in the dump. A glossary of Hawaiian words is included.

Lowell, Susan. 1992. *The Three Little Javelinas*. Illus. by Jim Harris. Flagstaff, AZ: Northland.
Lowell charmingly retells the classic story in a Southwest setting where a coyote and three javelinas (wild, piglike animals that inhabit the deserts of the American Southwest and northern Mexico) are the replacement characters. The first two young javelinas foolishly use tumbleweeds and saguaro-cactus ribs as building materials. Jim Harris's vibrant paintings are filled with the same charm and humor as Lowell's words. An excellent "Tools for Teachers" study guide for this book may be obtained from the publisher: Northland Publishing, P.O. Box 1389, Flagstaff, AZ 86002-1389.

Scieszka, Jon. 1989. *The True Story of the Three Little Pigs*. Illus. by Lane Smith. New York: Viking.
This wildly popular variant gives the wolf the stage so that he might tell his own side of the story. He only went to the first little pig's house of straw to borrow a cup of sugar. Could he help it if his sneezing destroyed the little pig's house? Smith's illustrations perfectly capture the humor found in Scieszka's resourceful retelling. This scurrilous account by A. Wolf will not be taken lightly by members of the Pig family. They may want to see it become a banned book.

Vozar, David. 1993. *Yo, Hungry Wolf!* Illus. by Betsy Lewin. New York: Dell.
"The Three Little Pigs" is given a rap treatment in this collection of rap verses about the famous or infamous wolf as portrayed in three famous stories. The other accounts celebrate the wolf's famous encounters with Little Red Riding Hood and The Boy Who Cried Wolf.

Videocassettes

The Three Little Pigs. Walt Disney, producer; Bert Gillett, director. 1933. Burbank, CA: Buena Vista Home Video. 10 minutes. Videocassette.
"Who's Afraid of the Big Bad Wolf" became a rallying song in the Great Depression when this classic animated film first appeared in 1933. It not only cheered the nation, it won an Academy Award as Best Short Animated Film and remains one of the great classic movie cartoons.

The Three Little Pigs. Shelley Duvall, producer; Howard Storm, director. Faerie Tale Theatre Series. Livonia, MI: Playhouse Video. 1984. 51 minutes. Videocassette. In this delightful live-action version of the famous tale of children going out into the big world alone for the first time, Jeff Goldblum portrays the evil wolf. His problems include a continuously complaining wife who demands he find pork to serve when they entertain a couple, the Coyotes. Billy Crystal plays the part of the wiser third brother. The actors are bolstered and the script enhanced by much good humor and colorful sets and costumes—plus a jazz-music score by Stephen Barber.

Happily Ever Afters

There are myriad extensions of "The Three Little Pigs" that teachers and media specialists can use to provoke student creativity. The following prompts and challenges are written directly to students so that they may be easily and immediately implemented.

CNN Reports

Select a dramatic moment in "The Three Little Pigs" where at least two of the characters are involved in a face-off. One example might be the point at which the wolf demands that the second little pig let him into the house made of sticks. Stop the action, and call in CNN reporters and cameras. Write a script, or improvise the scene for CNN wherein one or more reporters interview the two characters, solicit their views on the crisis situation, and size up the situation for the news-starved public. Use videotaping equipment to capture the grand moment for your peers.

Lazy Pigs

The basic moral or lesson of "The Three Little Pigs" is: Don't be lazy. But everyone is lazy sometimes. Can you draw a picture of yourself at leisure? Write a story about your favorite time to be lazy or about a time when you were like the first and second little pigs and should not have been lazy. (This idea was shared with the author by preschool teacher Kathy Dutke.)

Marshmallow Houses

Use toothpicks and marshmallows to build your own "little pig" house. Can you build it so that the wolf cannot blow it down? When your house is complete, create your own new version of "The Three Little Pigs," incorporating the details and consequences of your new marshmallow house. Write and illustrate your story, or practice it and tell it to your friends.

Interior Decorating

Most versions of "The Three Little Pigs" accentuate the house structures and pay scant attention to interior decoration. Examine such magazines as *Architectural Digest* and other home-decoration magazines that feature interior design. Use your own drawing skills or pictures cut from magazines to present an attractive portfolio revealing the interior setting of one of the little pigs' homes.

When Pigs Fly!

If the three little pigs could only have flown, they could have easily escaped the harassment and villainy of the big bad wolf. They could have built tree houses. But how do you make pigs fly? Your task is to redesign the pig to make it fly. One super tool used by inventors, designers, and other problem solvers is called morphological forced connections. It is easier to use than it is to say! First, take any object, and analyze it according to its basic attributes or component parts. Attributes are the components that make up an object. The components of a desk, for example, may be legs, writing surface, and drawers. Next, consider all possible values of each of the separate attributes. Values are the possibilities for each attribute. Desk tops or writing surfaces can be made of glass, wood, metal, and other substances. Once all the possible values of each attribute are listed, new product configurations are suggested by making random connections among them.

Morphological forced connections are most easily made when a grid such as figure 8.4 is constructed and used. Across the top horizontal axis, list the attributes or various body parts of the pig: snout, ears, legs, tail, and so on. Next, brainstorm all kinds of possible values or variations for each part, and place these responses in the vertical boxes. Finally, select from among the many options to arrive at a new configuration of parts needed to make the pig fly. Examples are shown in figures 8.4 and 8.5. In figure 8.5, the pig's tail functions as a rotary blade and lifts the pig helicopter fashion. But this is only one possible way to redesign the pig. Can you come up with some other ways to create an aerodynamic pig?

By the way, once you have genetically reengineered the pig, here is another challenge for you. As a result of the wealth gained from Pigs Airlines, the Pigs have become one of America's wealthiest families. However, they have been largely unsuccessful in their attempts to break into Newport society. How might the great psychologist Pigmund Freud help the Pigs overcome the stigma of their family name and history?

Fig. 8.4 When Pigs Fly!

Attribute				
Snout	Ears	Legs	Tail	Body
pointed, stiff	floppy	muscular	rotary	inflatable
	large, floppy		propeller	sleek
	drooping	winglike		

Values

From *From the Land of Enchantment.* © 1997 Jerry D. Flack. Teacher Ideas Press. (800) 237-6124.

Fig. 8.5. The All-New Helicopter Pig.

Use your creativity to imagine how the Pig family might take advantage of their new wealth to employ some of the following experts. How might society writer Porcina von Slop of the *Animal Farm Gazette* write an account of the wedding of Priscilla Pig to Porker "Razorback" Swiney? What sort of grand mansion might the famous architect Frankfurter Lloyd Wright design for the Pigs? The great artist Pigcasso is going to create a giant mural for the entryway to the new Pig Mansion featuring the family crest of the Pig family. Help Pigcasso design the Pig family crest. Pretend to be the famed poet Swineburn. Create an ode to celebrate the Pigs' newfound fame and glory. The Pigs are having a grand ball to honor notable swine. What notable names can students add to this preliminary list of honored guests?

The Pig Hall of Fame

    Kevin Bacon

    Sir Francis Bacon

    Albert Einswine

Frankenswine

Pigmund Freud

George and Ira Gershswine

Hamlet, Prince of Danish Hams

Miss Piggy

John Philip Sowsa

Gertrude Swine

Wilbur

Frankfurter Lloyd Wright

No Chimney for the Wolf?

Ever since Clement Moore penned "The Night Before Christmas" children all around the world worry about whether Santa Claus will visit them if their house or apartment does not have a chimney or fireplace. Kind writers and parents have assured them that the absence of a chimney or fireplace does not deter Santa from making his appointed rounds. But what would happen if the third little pig had no chimney for the wolf to climb down? Suppose his (or her) home is heated by rooftop solar panels. The old pot-of-boiling-water solution won't work without a fireplace. What might the third little pig do to get rid of the pestiferous wolf lurking outside the door? Describe and illustrate a possible solution.

REFERENCES

Flack, Jerry. 1989. *Inventing, Inventions, and Inventors: A Teaching Resource Book.* Englewood, CO: Teacher Ideas Press.

Jacobs, Joseph. 1972. *English Folk and Fairy Tales.* 3d ed. New York: G. P. Putnam's Sons. Notes on p. 250.

Chapter *9*

Celebrating "Beauty and the Beast" with a Classroom Museum

CHAPTER PREVIEW

In this culminating chapter, teachers and students will draw upon the processes and skills learned in previous chapters, using them to conceive, research, plan, construct, and operate their own museums.

No one flunks museum!

—Frank Oppenheimer,
    founder of San Francisco's Exploratorium

Museums are society's cultural memory banks.

—David Dean

WHAT ARE MUSEUMS, AND WHERE DID THEY COME FROM?

The Museums Association defines a museum as "an institution which collects, documents, preserves, exhibits, and interprets material evidence and associated information for the public benefit" (Pearce 1993, 2). The broad purpose of museums is to acquire, conserve, and exhibit natural phenomena and human artifacts of the planet. The word *museum* is derived from the Greek word *muse* and its reference to Greek mythology. The Muses were the nine daughters of Zeus and Mnemosyne who became the patron goddesses of all the arts. The Muses included Calliope, goddess of epic poetry; Terpsichore, goddess of dance and choral song; and Clio, goddess of history. It is not difficult to perceive how places designed to house collections drawn from the arts became "museums." The first museums

205

may have been created by Alexander the Great, who collected natural objects and human artifacts from the wide world he conquered. Modern museums evolved in the great cities of Renaissance Italy in the fifteenth century, when princes and other wealthy individuals began to build fabulous private collections in Florence and elsewhere. For several centuries, museums were exclusively private collections. The first museum built for public use was the British Museum, established in 1753.

There are many different kinds of museums. Some of the most familiar to students are museums of art, history, natural history, and science. Students may also be familiar with special-interest museums such as music and sports halls of fame. The newest kind of museum from a historical standpoint is the children's museum. They began to appear in the United States in the first quarter of this century as the "learning by doing" theories of Maria Montessori and John Dewey gained popularity. Brooklyn, Boston, and Indianapolis were American cities with early children's museums. Whereas traditional museums espoused a hands-off posture, the new children's museums expected and even invited children to touch the objects and to interact with the displays. The author of *Doing Children's Museums* characterizes them as follows: "Essentially, children's museums are learning playgrounds, full of choices that encourage visitors to pursue their own interests as far as they can" (Cleaver 1992, 5).

The unique and positive climate of museums in general, and especially children's museums, has not been lost on educators and researchers. The guaranteed success factor is brilliantly articulated by Frank Oppenheimer, founder of San Francisco's world-famous children's museum, the Exploratorium, in the quotation at the outset of the chapter: "No one flunks museum!" (Gardner 1993, 199). In *The Creative Spirit* science writer Daniel Goleman states, "A children's museum is defined not only by its target audience, but by the artful combination of entertainment with education" (Goleman 1992, 91). Howard Gardner, whose brilliant work on multiple intelligences is described in chapter 1 of this book, comments on the positive benefits of these institutions: "Children's museums have retained the potential to engage students, to teach them, to stimulate their understanding and most important, to help them assume responsibility for their own future learning" (Gardner 1993, 199).

There is a good reason for the placement of a chapter on the creation of student-made museums as the final chapter in this book. The creation of a student-designed and operated children's museum is a splendid culminating activity in any study of fairy tales and allows—indeed, begs for—the use of all the processes and skills learned and developed by students in all the preceding chapters. Classes can use creative problem-solving (CPS) steps to determine the big idea or theme of a fairy tale museum. Teams within classes can use CPS as well as SCAMPER and other tools described in the "In the Kingdom of Ideas" chapter to drive their creative thinking in designing and planning exhibits for the museum for which they will be personally responsible.

One example: Real obstacles students may face are issues of size, scale, and space. Students may have observed dioramas in natural history exhibitions that are enormous. Real specimens in an Arctic diorama may include polar bears, seals, arctic foxes, and even beluga whales placed in a replica of their vast Arctic habitat. A single natural history museum diorama can be as large as several schoolrooms. Today, many schools are bursting at the seams, and space is at a premium. Securing a vacant classroom for a single display, not to mention an entire exhibition, is an impossibility. Such constraints, however, need not be defeating. Students can apply attribute listing and SCAMPER techniques in planning their displays. First, they consider the attributes of good natural history dioramas. These attributes include animal or plant specimens or representations, habitats, and captions. Next, students apply the SCAMPER tool to their "problem." How might they use such concepts as "minify" and "alter" to their advantage? Where a natural history diorama may be enormous in scope, the student-created diorama can present the same basic attributes in a miniature environment that may be as small as a shoe box or even a matchbox. The resulting product demonstrates how a potential problem is converted into a positive opportunity to create a first-rate museum display.

Bloom's Taxonomy (see figure 2.1 on p. 33 in the "Jack and the Beanstalk" chapter) will be especially useful to students when they decide the level of thinking they want museum visitors to use. Just as teachers use this list of action verbs to design questions and activities in instructional planning, students can activate the list to determine the level or complexity of thinking they desire visitors to their museums to exhibit. Of course, museum-exhibition designers are always mindful of the multiple intelligences all people have along with varying learning styles. Thus, students can draw from the list of multiple-intelligence descriptive behaviors (see figure 1.2 on p. 7) in the "Cinderella" chapter to build exhibits that are multisensory and appeal to and make use of many kinds of intelligences. The art design and illustration processes and projects described in "The Frog Prince" chapter will similarly prove useful to students as they create both two- and three-dimensional artwork for museum exhibitions.

Museum researchers (Dean 1994; Serrell 1996) emphasize the importance of labeling strategies, which provoke positive social interaction among visitors. One group of students may recall the needs as articulated by Abraham Maslow and discussed in this book in relationship to the behavior of Jack in "Jack and the Beanstalk." When designing the text for their exhibit about "Jack and the Beanstalk" or another interactive fairy tale exhibit, these students may create questions that ask visitors to analyze specific behaviors of characters based on Maslow's theories about needs and motivation.

Teachers can emphasize the point that labels at an exhibit need not be just declarative sentences. Provocative exhibits may involve questions to stimulate discussion among visitors. Striking labels for a "Beauty and the Beast" museum exhibit may present critical-thinking questions about the fairy tale that will promote lively discussions among visitors. A display or interest-area exhibit featuring *Beauty and the Beast* movie posters, large student drawings of characters and scenes from the fairy tale, and a variety of book versions of the tale may serve as the backdrop for thoughtful questions designed for interactive engagement. How might fairy tale-museum visitors respond to the challenge to use their critical-thinking skills to answer the following sort of questions boldly labeled and illustrated in a "Beauty and the Beast" gallery poster?

Can you flex your thinking muscles?
Answer these questions about "Beauty and the Beast."

What might have happened had the roles been reversed at the end of the story? Would Beast have loved an "ugly" Beauty?

How do you think Beast felt when people saw him?

Is it right to judge people by their appearance?

Is it right that so many fairy tales associate good with physical beauty and evil with anatomical deformity or the absence of common perceptions of physical attractiveness?

What would the world be like if everyone were "ugly"?

How might people be judged if no one could see?

Can you think of any other creatures who are or were part animal or beast and part human?

What do you think English poet John Keats (1795-1821) meant when he wrote:

> "Beauty is truth, truth beauty
> —that is all
> Ye know on earth, and all ye
> need to know"?

Posters noting Maslow's hierarchy of needs or Kohlberg's levels of moral reasoning may also be included in a display that invites visitors to classify the behaviors exhibited by the characters Beauty, Beast, Beauty's father, Beauty's sisters (in the Madame LePrince de Beaumont book and video versions), or Gaston (in the Disney film version). Highly interactive exhibits that invite touching, provoke discussions, and tease the imagination greatly enhance learning opportunities for visitors of all ages.

Interactive museums, children's or otherwise, serve to prick the slumbering curiosity and creative potential of students. Museum curators, whether teachers or students, use a cornucopia of vital skills and talents when they create museum environments that are positive and accepting, inviting, and curiosity provoking. Museum exhibits should be dynamic and participatory. Activities should also be varied enough to encourage the development and use of a variety of talents: artistic, poetic, mechanical, physical, and intellectual. Creativity definitely reveals itself in the production of learning materials and interactive exhibits. Student experiences in designing and constructing museum exhibits provide opportunities to develop and showcase students' talents. Further, imaginative museum exhibits tempt all participants to explore creative thinking and stimulate the creation of imaginative products. Importantly, designing museum exhibits should not be the exclusive province of teachers or other adults. Teachers may initially create and introduce museum exhibits, but students should be encouraged to develop and produce their own materials that add to or change existing exhibits and to create brand-new exhibitions.

The author has worked with several teachers in the creation of classroom or schoolwide museums designed and operated wholly or at least in part by students. The praise for such projects from participating teachers is unanimous. Motivation soars. Excitement is catching when creating really terrific products that are going to have a genuine audience. Importantly, most of the motivation is intrinsic. Children's pride in their museum creations eclipses considerations of letter grades, and classroom museum experiences build bridges to the future and lifelong learning. Museum visitation is essentially an intrinsically motivated activity. No one offers external rewards to people for appreciating culture. The museum-building experience expands appreciation for museums in general and all they have to offer.

The application of a wide array of valuable skills is observable to the teacher, administrators, parents, and the community. Cooperation among students is heightened. Students enjoy collaborating to build displays and exhibits that are larger, grander, and more intricate and involved than any they could individually achieve. Students develop real respect for the intelligences and talents of others. Yes, Jimmy has read more about beasts and dragons than anyone else in the class, but he develops a fresh appreciation for Sandy's drawing skills when his storehouse of knowledge about beasts is magically transformed into great statements for a classroom exhibit about creatures found in fairy tale literature. Teachers who facilitate student-produced classroom museums report enormous pride and pleasure in the end results of their students' efforts.

A "Beauty and the Beast" Museum?

Students can literally create a "Beauty and the Beast" museum with several exhibits devoted to that tale alone. Classes can also design a "Beauty and the Beast" museum featuring different tales of beauties and beasts from cultures all around the world. In this case, *Beauties and Beasts* (Hearne 1995) will be enormously helpful. Expanding further on this idea, students can create fairy tale museums. Each team chooses a particular fairy tale, such as "Cinderella" or "Jack and the Beanstalk," and builds an exhibit around it. One group of students may build an exhibit demonstrating the worldwide appeal of "Cinderella" stories, while another group creates an exhibit focusing upon the Brothers Grimm, their best-known tales, and German life and culture during their lifetimes. Students can move still farther afield and create a beast museum. A bestiary museum might be the culmination of a unit on fairy tales, mythology, or fantasy. Teams focus on beasts such as the lion in *The Lion, the Witch, and the Wardrobe* (Lewis 1994), or the Minotaur from Greek mythology.

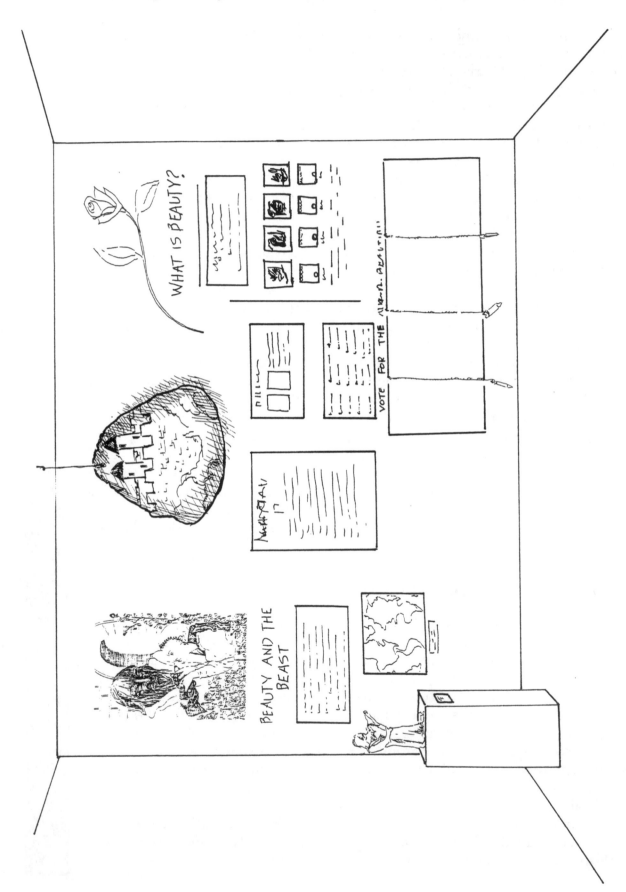

Students may also build on works such as Graeme Base's *The Discovery of Dragons* (Base 1996), in which the popular Australian illustrator (writing as scientist Rowland W. Greasebeam) provides the "natural history" of such dragons as the Great Snow Dragon of Greenland and the St. George's Dragon of English fame. The students can provide answers to such questions as: Why have people believed in dragons through the ages? How are dragons of Chinese culture different from the dragon slain by St. George of England? Of course, student-created museums need not be limited to fairy tale or fantasy content. The point of the entire book has been to demonstrate how broad processing skills such as critical thinking and creative problem solving may be generalized and transferred to any situation students encounter and any content area teachers share.

CHILDREN'S MUSEUM RESOURCES

Teacher Resources

There are many first-rate books for teachers and students that may serve as guides to first-time museum builders. The resources listed here are divided into professional resources for adult supervisors or older students and resources that will be especially useful to children.

Because of their technical nature and limited audiences, some of the resources described here will not be found on the shelves of local libraries but can be found in college and large metropolitan-library collections. Teachers do not need to access all the titles, since much basic museum exhibition-development information is standard to several texts. Even so, texts such as Beverly Serrell's *Exhibit Labels: An Interpretive Approach* merit the effort taken to obtain them through interlibrary loan.

Brown, Vinson. 1954. *How to Make a Home Nature Museum.* Illus. by Don Greame Kelley. Boston: Little, Brown.
> Although this guide is more than 40 years old, it contains excellent suggestions and tips for setting up displays that are not bound by time. See also Vinson Brown, *Building Your Own Nature Museum* (New York: ARCO, 1984).

Cleaver, Joanne. 1992. *Doing Children's Museums: A Guide to 265 Hands-On Museums.* Charlotte, VT: Williamson Publishing.
> Following a discussion of the history and merits of hands-on, exploratory, children's museums, the author profiles 265 children's museums, providing descriptions of each along with vital data such as addresses, phone numbers, hours of operation, admission costs, and accessibility for wheelchairs. A must resource for families that enjoy travel.

Dean, David. 1994. *Museum Exhibits: Theory and Practice.* New York: Routledge Kegan Paul.
> Although Dean's text is intended for an audience of professional museum curators and design personnel, the discussions are neither arcane nor overly technical. The author provides fresh perspectives on motivations visitors bring to museum exhibits, plus he offers a great many practical tips on fashioning

exhibitions that appeal and instruct. Two features are especially useful to educators: a comprehensive glossary, with the essential vocabulary and definitions; and the plentiful use of photographs and drawings that illustrate good museum-exhibit design and production.

Gardner, Howard. 1993. *Multiple Intelligences: The Theory in Practice.* New York: Basic Books.
Gardner accentuates the children's museum as an instructional model teachers should attempt to emulate. He examines why children's museums work, educationally speaking, while many schoolhouse models do not.

Goleman, Daniel, Paul Kaufman, and Michael Ray. 1992. *The Creative Spirit.* New York: E. P. Dutton.
The authors provide a short but interesting portrait of the Capital Children's Museum in Washington, D.C.

MacDonald, George F., and Stephen Alsford. 1989. *Museum for the Global Village.* Hull, Canada: Canadian Museum of Civilization.
Museums around the world and across time are described as they were studied in preparation for building the Canadian Museum of Civilization. A fine discussion is provided of great children's museums, such as the Indianapolis Children's Museum and the Exploratorium in San Francisco.

Marx, Pamela. 1992. *Classroom Museums: Touchable Tables for Kids.* Illus. by Rebecca Hirsch. Glenview, IL: Goodyear Books.
Marx's first-rate resource is filled with great ideas for the construction of classroom museums on such topics as backyard nature, the history of flags, Native Americans, sugar and chocolate, fiber and fabrics, and winter festivals. Excellent graphics enhance the reading experience and provide valuable displaying tips.

Pearce, Susan M. 1993. *Museums, Objects, and Collections: A Cultural Study.* Washington, D.C.: Smithsonian Institution Press.
Pearce provides an excellent history of museums in the modern era. She examines the philosophy of collecting and how museums make and structure meaning for society. Because the scholarly text was first published in England, most of the examples cited are drawn from British museums.

Serrell, Beverly. 1996. *Exhibit Labels: An Interpretive Approach.* Walnut Creek, CA: Altamir Press.
Most people would assume a book focused on writing labels for museum exhibits would be extremely technical and geared to a limited, intended audience. Happily, this book is filled with both wisdom and great practical ideas teachers can use in many learning experiences or environments to make their museums (classrooms) extremely inviting and meaningful to their visitors (students). Serrell ranges far and wide in examining learning theories, the psychology of observing and interacting with the environment, and other fascinating topics. The glossary of basic museum terminology will be especially useful to teachers and students who want to share a common vocabulary while building classroom museums.

Videocassette

Partnerships That Work: The Museum, the Zoo, the Community, and Kids. Bebe Nixon, writer-producer; Bernie Zubrowski, director. Boston: WGBH Educational Foundation. 1995. 49 minutes. Videocassette.

Student Resources

Belloli, Adrea P. A., and Keith Godard. 1994. *Make Your Own Museum.* New York: Ticknor & Fields.
This resource kit includes a book describing museums and collections. Seventy-plus works of art are represented in the form of stickers and punch-out figures that children can use to decorate the fold-out walls and rooms provided. The book is based on the J. Paul Getty Museum in California.

Booth, William, Paul Briten, and Fenella Scott. 1987. *Themes Familiar: Research and Display in the Primary School Using Everyday Objects.* Illus. by Lyn Gray. Twickenham, England: Belair Publications, Ltd.
This book can be used by teachers and students. It is especially useful because of the color photographs of exhibits built around the 15 themes or topics that form the body of the book. Themes include balloons, bicycles, boxes, clocks, hats and headgear, ladders, letters, mirrors, newspapers, and telephones. The color photographs show students how to use tiers and varying levels within displays to make classroom-museum exhibits compact, attractive, stimulating, and interactive. Each of the themes or topics is complete with suggested literature to accompany the subject and encourage thematic, integrated, and interdisciplinary learning. Language, science, mathematics, technology, computer programs, arts and crafts, music, and physical-education connections are suggested in each theme unit. One caution: The book is published in England, and some of the resources suggested may not be available in the United States or Canada.

Brown, Laurene Krasny, and Marc Brown. 1986. *Visiting the Art Museum.* New York: E. P. Dutton.
This lovely picture book portrays a family's visit to an art museum. Real artworks from great American museums are reproduced within the full-color book illustrations. The book is entertaining in its own right, but it is also quite useful to students as a visual guide to first-class ways to display objects.

Freeman, Sara. 1996. *Kids as Curators: Museum Explorations.* Step-by-Step Series. Grand Rapids, MI: Instructional Fair. ·
An inexpensive, straightforward guide to museums with sound advice on how to enjoy public museums and how to create minimuseums at home and at school. Good, basic definitions of art, science, natural history, history, and children's museums. Museum jobs are also defined. Simple, yet effective line drawings as illustrations. Includes a fine bibliography.

Gerstenfeld, Sheldon L. 1994. *The Aquarium Take-Along Book.* Illus. by Paul Harvey. New York: Puffin Books.

Gerstenfeld, a veterinarian, takes readers behind the scenes to learn about aquatic animals as they are enjoying an aquarium visit. The material is explained so well and the book is so enjoyable that readers profit from it even if they stay at home. Cheerful pen-and-ink illustrations move the text along nicely as do the author's "Behind the Scene" features. The book introduces jellyfish, octopuses, water turtles, sharks, puffins, sea otters, and a host of other sea creatures. All the excellent, insightful entries can serve as first-rate models for students who want to explain objects and experiences in their own museums.

Gibbons, Maurice. 1991. *How to Become an Expert: Discover, Research, and Build a Project in Your Chosen Field.* Tucson, AZ: Zephyr Press.

The use of simplistic cartoons in this book may turn off older students. Even so, the author provides some fine rubrics and guides for students in selecting areas of interest and building expertise, which is a first step in eventually creating museums.

Papajani, Janet. 1983. *Museums: A New True Book.* Chicago: Children's Press.

Papajani provides a basic introduction to museums, how they began, and different types of museum specialization, such as art, natural history, science, and special interests (Baseball Hall of Fame). A beginner's glossary is also provided along with large-type print and colorful photographs for illustrations. Indexed.

Richardson, Joy. 1993. *Inside the Museum: A Children's Guide to the Metropolitan Museum of Art.* New York: Harry N. Abrams.

This fascinating and fun book provides an informative perspective about how museums function, who does what work, and how museums (the Metropolitan, in particular) have evolved over time. One does not have to actually travel to New York City to enjoy and profit from this marvelous text. "Fascinating Facts," "Eye Spy," and "Your Turn" activities make the book a journey of interactive fun for youthful readers.

Zack, Linda R. 1995. *Building Self-Esteem Through the Museum of I: 25 Original Projects That Explore and Celebrate the Self.* Minneapolis, MN: Free Spirit.

The primary intent of Zack's book is enhancement of self-esteem, an admirable goal. However, students and teachers can adapt many of the artifacts and projects she recommends to the specific content of their museums. For example, the directions for creating a "Self-Quilt" may easily be adapted to the fashioning of a "Beauty and the Beast Quilt."

STUDENTS CREATING MUSEUMS: TWO TIME LINES

There is no "right" way to approach the museum-building method to learning. Strategies vary according to time constraints, the age and maturity of students, and other factors. Ideally, when circumstances allow, preliminary activities involve class field trips to museums and presentations to classes by museum personnel. Field trips can take on special meaning when teachers prompt students to note promising museum-display practices as well as the content of particular exhibitions. What presentations do they enjoy? What factors make them inviting? How do museums use space both within exhibits and throughout the entire facility? How does the museum handle traffic flow? Note all the different ways artifacts may be displayed (e.g., suspended from the ceiling; placed on a pedestal). Are labels positioned at a variety of eye levels? What sizes and styles of print fonts make it easier and more enjoyable for visitors to read museum placards? How important is color in museum exhibits? Are some particular colors used more often than others? If so, which colors? Are the colors and textures of walls and other backgrounds important factors in museum presentations? If entire classes cannot visit area museums, ask student volunteers to visit museums with their families, noting particularly effective exhibition techniques and reporting their findings back to the class.

Museum personnel or docents (volunteers) familiar with the acquisition, preservation, and exhibition of museum collections can be invited to the school to share specimens and artifacts as well as professional "secrets" about exhibitions with classes. Their expertise and familiarity with exhibitions can be most significant in alerting students to ways of fashioning exciting interactive museum experiences for their prospective audiences.

Another preliminary activity involves the preparation of a glossary of museum terminology. With only minimal planning, teachers can select core terms they want students to know. Assign one or more terms from the glossary to gifted or highly motivated students for research. In the weeks before the museum-building experience begins, these students should locate definitions and share them orally with classmates and possibly enter them into the "Museum Glossary" file in the word processing program of the classroom computer. Twenty different students can each enter a single word plus its definition. The terms can then be alphabetized and subsequently printed as a glossary for all students. Standard museum terminology may include words such as *artifact, caption, catalog* (verb), *children's museum, collection, conservation, conservator, curator, diorama, display, exhibit* (noun), *exhibit* (verb), *exhibit catalog* (noun), *exhibition, gallery, label, model, museum(s), props,* and *registrar*.

Teachers who want to use a simulation to build excitement about museums may find Interact's *Museum* to be appealing. This creative simulation is designed for students in grades four through eight. A wealthy art patron, Mona Pizarro, bequeaths ten million dollars for the establishment of a community art museum. There are plenty of stipulations attached to the gift, however, that send students scurrying for information about art and museum display. Order from Interact, 1825 Gillespie Way #101, El Cajon, CA 92020-1095. Phone: 1-800-359-0961.

Teachers who do not have the luxury of time or opportunities for museum field trips may need to dispense with these preliminary activities and move immediately to the business of encouraging students to design, develop, and operate classroom museums.

Dean (1994) outlines four phases of the museum exhibition development process that suggest stages students can also follow. They are *conceptual phase*, *development phase*, *functional phase*, and *assessment phase*.

In the first phase, curators, educators, and others gather ideas, determine exhibition scope, and consider schedules. The developmental phase is divided into two stages: planning and production. Planning involves setting goals, researching, estimating costs, appropriating tasks, and creating educational and promotional plans. Production entails preparing and mounting the exhibition and opening it to the public. The functional phase addresses the operation and maintenance of the exhibition, preventing deterioration of displays, providing security, and having plans for dismounting the exhibition. The assessment phase may involve writing a report about the success of the exhibition as well as noting improvements to be made in future museum exhibitions.

These four phases of museum-exhibition development can serve students well in the planning and execution of their own museum exhibitions. Indeed, one of the goals of museum creation for students should be students' parallel development of time-management skills and responsibility. When working with students, guiding questions for each phase may help students remain focused on their multiple tasks.

Conceptual Phase: What is the big idea (see below) of your exhibition? What do you want your museum exhibition to mean to people? What pleasures do you want your parents to derive from their visit to your museum?

Development Phase: What kind of exhibits will you have? Is there a budget? Who is responsible for what display materials, labels, invitations, and so on? How much time is available for construction of exhibits and their subsequent setup? What resources are needed for the creation of exhibits?

Functional Phase: When will the museum open? Who will conduct tours? Will there be live demonstrations as a feature of the exhibition? If so, what classes will need to be missed? What permissions need to be secured in advance? What maintenance and preservation efforts are needed (e.g., care of animals such as gerbils)? Who will help dismantle the exhibition when it is completed? Who will be responsible for returning borrowed items? Are there special people (e.g., school custodian) who should receive thank-you notes?

Assessment Phase: How will the success of the classroom-museum exhibition be judged? What, if any, data will be collected? Is a formal evaluation report required? If so, who writes it, and when is it due? What has been learned from the museum-exhibition experience?

BIG IDEAS

Serrell (1996) states that all exhibits and labels within them are doomed to failure if there is not a big idea to serve as the driving force and purpose of the exhibit. The big idea supplies an exhibition with its meaningfulness. Big ideas also provide focus to all people involved in the exhibition. The big idea becomes the tool that provides all the team with a common focus and goal. Big ideas need not be declarative statements. Good interactive labels and captions provoke thinking often with big ideas introduced as questions. For example, the big idea for a "Beauty and the Beast" museum might be: What is beauty? Each team can then determine how it wants to structure a display that will help visitors answer the question. One team, for example, may note the visual beauty found in illustrator Jan Brett's *Beauty and the Beast* (1989). This team can build a display about Brett and her works. Brett has fashioned other fairy tales such as "Goldilocks and the Three Bears" (see annotation in that chapter), plus she has featured other beasts such as trolls in many of her works.

A big idea or big question for a school or classroom museum focused upon many different fairy tales might be posed more broadly: Why do fairy tales last? A team using "Cinderella" as content may help visitors answer the question by accentuating the popularity of rags-to-riches stories, both real and fanciful. Another team may illustrate the universal desire of parents to secure the safety of their children through a sharing of global, multicultural versions of "Little Red Riding Hood."

Of course, museums and the big ideas that drive their exhibitions need not be oriented solely to fairy tales. First-graders in one Iowa classroom build a Grandparents Museum with this big idea: Grandparents are great! Students bring pictures and three-dimensional objects to school that celebrate their grandparents. They also paint pictures of their grandparents. All the artifacts make up the unique museum, which is celebrated with a grand opening on the occasion of a Grandparents' Day Tea.

Two Colorado sixth-grade teachers coordinate a student-produced museum exhibition about oceans. The big idea is the oceans and man. Teams of four to six students interpret the big idea in many different ways. One team approaches the big idea or theme from the perspective of how humans pollute and endanger the oceans. Their museum display provides a diverse display of information about man-made ocean disasters. Visitors can perform a quick, interactive science experiment, floating cooking oil on water and cleaning up the "spill" with paper towels. Another team approaches the big idea from a completely different perspective, highlighting ways humans have been inspired by the sea. One of their exhibits displays posters and book copies of Hans Christian Andersen's "The Little Mermaid." In one corner of their exhibit a VCR continuously plays the Walt Disney animated film of Andersen's tale. A third team focuses on ship disasters, including the presentation of models, books, and informative posters about the sinking of the *Titanic*. Because these students attend a parochial school, a fourth team built an exhibit around references to how the Bible speaks to the seas.

Once students have selected the big idea that drives their museum efforts, they can conduct research and plan the displays to be featured in their museum. In museum planning, students need to understand that museums are people places foremost. Good exhibitions help people achieve a sense of belonging. They are also multisensory, with critical visual elements such as bright colors and bold graphics capturing and holding people's attention. Sounds, tactile opportunities, and even smells also help bond people with exhibitions. Labels and captions

should tell stories and conjure up lasting images for visitors. Often, contexts and frameworks for objects help visitors best learn about them. But note that a story line helps in unifying an exhibition.

Good exhibits are visitor friendly. Beverly Serrell writes: "Most visitors are eager to learn, but they do not want to spend much time or effort in trying to figure things out. Good labels can attract, communicate, inspire, and help visitors get what they are seeking" (Serrell 1996, 47).

Students should recall the exciting, interactive nature of first-class exploratory museums. The challenge is to find ways to make their own displays interactive. Are there things visitors can touch, taste, or smell? Are there simple experiments visitors can perform quickly? Are there important questions to provoke critical or creative thinking? Can visitors make a quick product to take away with them?

Although teachers may not like the idea of evaluating students' museums, accountability is a reality for both students and teachers. Figure 9.1 is one teacher's attempt to share standards for museum exhibits and displays with her students.[1] The project is a school Wilderness Museum, and it is described thoroughly in Happily Ever Afters at the end of this chapter. This rubric is presented to students at the front-end of the museum project. There is never any doubt as to what they must do to succeed. The rubric may be used to evaluate both individual and group work. Letter grades can be assigned as teacher need and discretion dictate.

Before the teacher ever uses the rubric to judge student projects, she or he should encourage students to engage in self-checks, such as answering questions about their museum products prior to final submissions. A checklist is found in figure 9.2.

---

1. The rubric was created by Caren Kutch, Resource Teacher, Pine Valley Elementary School, Air Academy School District, Colorado Springs, Colorado, to guide students in their creation of materials for the schoolwide Wilderness Museum. Used with permission.

Fig. 9.1. Museum Exhibit Rubric

	A	B IN PROGRESS	C BASIC	D PROFICIENT	E ADVANCED	F WORLD-CLASS	G
1							
2	TITLE	Too general, not specific or interesting (e.g., "Deserts")	Generally accurate but lacks interest (e.g., "California Deserts at Night")	Appropriate title for display (e.g., "Night Life of California Deserts")	Arouses interest and curiosity (e.g., "Secrets of the Desert Night")	"Also See..." Suggests an extension to the topic.	
3	VISUAL AIDS	Pictures, drawings, or graphs have little or no connection to topic.	Pictures, drawings, and graphs relate to topic.	Pictures, photographs, and graphs add to the understanding of the story.	Photographs and pictures enable the eye and mind to easily and logically follow the story.	Viewers want to know more. Display is unique and original.	
4	LABELING	Key information for labels is incorrect or missing. Wording is not written neatly.	Not all information is included on labels. Labels can be read. Limited eye appeal.	Labels are neat and easily read.	Label gives both generic and scientific name of object. Date and location are included. Colorful and eye appealing.	Labeling reflects theme in color choice, design, texture, and shape.	
5	OVERALL DISPLAY	Haphazard arrangement of display. Difficult to understand. Unclear as to purpose of display.	Information is included but not organized in a logical or sequential fashion.	All components are included. The display is neatly done.	The display has balance and is arranged in a natural and logical way for the telling of the story.	An overview accompanies display explaining the student's thinking behind the display.	
6	RESEARCH	Uses one source from the following: encyclopedia, scientific books, atlas, almanac, magazine, media.	Uses a minimum of two data sources, including at least one of the following: encyclopedia, scientific book, atlas, almanac, magazine, media.	Uses a minimum of three data sources, including at least three of the following: encyclopedia, scientific book, atlas, almanac, magazines, media, and interview.	Uses a minimum of four sources, including encyclopedia, scientific books, atlas, almanac, magazines, media, as well as interview with an expert.	A minimum of five resources were used in the production of the display. There is clear evidence that these sources guided the project as well as providing ideas for extensions.	
7	PROCESS LOG	Not consistently kept. Facts are listed but no evidence of metacognition.	Process Log is consistently kept. Two-sentence explanations of mental processes involved.	Four-sentence explanations showing thoughts on paper as project evolves.	Writing is engaging. Talking on paper as well as sharing frustrations and celebrations of experiences as project evolves by responding personally to experience.	More than four sentences expressing thoughts. The writing is interesting and engaging and shows evidence of future goals relating to project and adjustments to be made for future projects.	
8	SHARING INFORMATION	There is little, if any, evidence of preparation, organization, or practice for the presentation.	There is some evidence of preparation and organization. The delivery is understandable.	The information is presented in an interesting manner. There is evidence of interest in the topic.	There is evidence of strong preparation, organization, and interest in topic.	The delivery is excellent. Questions are answered with specific and correct information and elaborated details.	

Fig. 9.2 Museum Exhibit Self-Check List

Give yourself one, two, or three points per item, with three being advanced or world-class.

_____ Did you include a title that conveys the theme of your product?

_____ Did you include illustrations, photographs, pictures, or drawings to add interest?

_____ Are your labels neatly, clearly, and accurately written?

_____ Does your project reflect time, energy, and pride?

_____ Does your display tell the beginning, middle, and end of a story?

_____ Did you include your process log, and does it show a minimum of four entries to guide you in the completion of the project?

_____ Did you present information in an interesting manner showing evidence of interest in the topic?

_____ Research: Include two points for each reference you used in gathering background information.

_____ Did you finish on time?

Bonus Points

_____ Did you do more than what was required (10 points)? Note: This is your opportunity to pat yourself on the back!

Please explain why you feel you earned these bonus points.

_____

_____

_____

_____

_____

_____

_____

Name_____

ABC BRAINSTORMING

Brainstorming as introduced in the chapter "In the Kingdom of Ideas" can take many different forms as individuals, pairs, and teams work to generate ideas and solutions. One approach is called ABC brainstorming. Participants use the old friend, the ABCs, to prompt and direct creative thinking. Using at least 26 lines, the letters of the alphabet are written vertically down the side of a piece of paper or on the chalkboard. For each letter of the alphabet, participants think of ideas for the problem or project under consideration. In this case, a class is generating possible products for their "Beauty and the Beast" museum. The generic list of outcomes is a good beginning point for teachers and students planning any kind of museum. With few exceptions, such as a kaleidoscope and commercial-product tie-ins generated by the Disney movie *Beauty and the Beast*, the objects will be student made.

Once the enormous range of possible products is suggested, students then put their creative spirits to work in choosing products to elaborate. A student who previously had no idea what to do for the "Beauty and the Beast" museum is attracted to the idea of making a collage. How can she tie that product into the big idea of the museum? Sally decides to create a "Beauty and the Beast" collage of the perceptions people have worldwide of the concepts of "beauty" and "beasts." She explores libraries, the Internet, and other resource sites to locate photographs, paintings, and even verbal descriptions including verse in her pursuit to determine how people understand and communicate the two concepts, "beauty" and "beasts."

The purpose of ABC brainstorming is to generate many ideas, not to find a set number of responses for each letter of the alphabet. It is both acceptable and understood that ideas and objects will not necessarily be generated for every letter of the alphabet. After an initial session of ABC brainstorming, students will likely go back to their lists and add to them, often finding ideas and products for letters not filled in during the original session. Figure 9.3 represents a possible ABC brainstorming list students might generate.

"BEAUTY AND THE BEAST" RESOURCES

Teachers who desire to have students read a variety of storybook versions of the classic "Beauty and the Beast" fairy tale will find the following annotated bibliography helpful. The titles prove especially useful to teachers and students who wish to create their "Beauty and the Beast" Museums.

Traditional Stories

Apy, Deborah. 1983. *Beauty and the Beast*. Illus. by Michael Hague. New York: Holt, Rinehart & Winston.
    The French roots of the classic story are apparent in both Apy's faithful retelling and in the architecture and costumes found in Hague's magical paintings. After Beauty and the prince are transported to his dominions, all that remains in the garden where the beast resided is a magical unicorn.

Fig. 9.3. ABC Brainstorming List for "Beauty and the Beast" Museum

A. Audiotapes, annotated bibliographies, action research
B. Brochures (student-made), bar graphs, biographical portraits
C. Collections, cartoons, collages, charts
D. Dioramas, drawings
E. Experiment reports, easel-board displays
F. Film posters (e.g., Walt Disney's *Beauty and the Beast*), fact sheets
G. Graphs
H. Histograms, HyperStudio presentations
I. Interviews (videotaped), inventions, interactive exhibits
J. Journals
K. Kaleidoscopes (with rose patterns)
L. Lectures and demonstrations
M. Museum visitors' guide, maps, mobiles, murals, music
N. Newspapers
O. Observation records
P. Poetry (student), posters, portfolios
Q. Questions (and answers)
R. Research findings, relief maps
S. Storyboards, slide shows, scrapbooks, soft sculptures, songs, storytelling
T. Test results (surveys, and so on), travelogues
U. Utensils and other hands-on equipment
V. Videocassettes (student-made videos or commercial products)
W. Watercolor art products
X. X-rays, eXperts (student)
Y. Yearbooks of student accomplishments
Z. Zodiac signs for Beauty and Beast, zillions more ideas

Brett, Jan. 1989. *Beauty and the Beast*. New York: Clarion Books.
> Brett based the text on a 1910 English version of the tale by Sir Arthur Quiller-Couch. Her paintings are enchanting. She brings to this story's illustrations the same grace, style, and elaborate detail that characterize all her work and make her a top favorite of children.

Hautzig, Deborah. 1995. *Beauty and the Beast*. Illus. by Kathy Mitchell. Step into Reading Series. New York: Random House.
> Hautzig provides an easy-to-read interpretation of the tale of a beautiful, young woman who chooses goodness over beauty and transforms the beast into a handsome prince. The colorful illustrations evoke the fantasy inherent in the story and provide strong visual clues for early readers.

LePrince de Beaumont, Madame Jeanne-Marie. 1990. *Beauty and the Beast*. Trans. by Richard Howard. Illus. by Hilary Knight. Afterword by Jean Cocteau. New York: Simon & Schuster.

This magnificent oversize picture book is a literal translation of the original tale told by Madame LePrince de Beaumont (1711-80). Cocteau, creator of the French cinema masterpiece *Beauty and the Beast*, notes that the author lived in England and is believed to have fashioned her original fairy tale after stories she had heard of British and Scottish nobility hidden away in secret places because of birthmarks or deformities. Knight's glorious illustrations have great theatricality that is suggestive of sets and scenes from grand opera. Cocteau provides a fascinating commentary on the story and his own film version of it.

Mayer, Marianna. 1978. *Beauty and the Beast*. Illus. by Mercer Mayer. New York: Four Winds Press.

Mayer's telling of the story of Beauty, the brave and selfless youngest daughter of the unlucky merchant, is faithful to the original tale, and Mayer's richly textured full-color paintings and black-and-white borders summon forth a world the reader can truly believe is filled with enchantment, brave deeds, and a handsome prince.

Singer, A. L. 1991. *Beauty and the Beast*. Illus. by Ron Dias. New York: Disney Press.

This is a full-length book version of the 1991 Disney animated film featuring full-color replications of the cartoon settings and characters highlighted with red rose borders.

Willard, Nancy. 1992. *Beauty and the Beast*. Illus. by Barry Moser. San Diego, CA: Harcourt Brace Jovanovich.

Two giants in children's literature combine their talents in this unusual rendering geared for older readers. The tale opens in a splendid New York City townhouse in the early 1900s. When a family's fortunes change, they must move to a rural area of New York state. Beast's castle is modeled on a real home, Wilderstein, in the Hudson River Valley. Moser's dramatic woodcut engravings significantly contribute to the mood and mystery of the tale. See also *East of the Sun and West of the Moon* by the same collaborators (Harcourt Brace Jovanovich, 1989). Willard adapts the Scandinavian tale into a drama that is excellent for readers' theatre. Moser's illustrations are executed in watercolors.

Variations and Other Treatments

Hearne, Betsy. 1993. *Beauties and Beasts*. Illus. by Joanne Caroselli. The Oryx Multicultural Folktale Series. Phoenix, AZ: Oryx Press.

Hearn's anthology provides a world view of stories featuring beauties and beasts. She begins with the most famous story, told by the French aristocrat Madame LePrince de Beaumont, but she includes stories as old as the Greco-Roman myth of "Cupid and Psyche." In all, Hearne shares 27 stories from North America, Japan, Jamaica, Russia, Turkey, and Africa. Hearne's collection is an

indispensable resource for students who wish to create a cultural museum based upon "Beauty and the Beast" stories and legends.

Hooks, William H. 1994. *Snowbear Whittington: An Appalachian Beauty and the Beast*. Illus. by Victoria Lisi. New York: Macmillan.
European settlers to North America brought their favorite stories of the Old World to the new. Over time the particulars of these stories first told in Europe were changed to allow them to fit better into the new landscapes of their telling. Yet such eternal truths as the healing power of true love remained constant. Nell, the Appalachian Beauty, possesses courage, and she loves Snowbear Whittington as both man and white bear, hence freeing him from the evil spell. The characters and the settings are beautifully rendered by Lisi in both black-and-white drawings and full-color paintings.

Videocassettes

Beauty and the Beast. Jean Cocteau, director. In French with English subtitles. Chicago, IL: Public Media Home Visions. 1946. 93 minutes. Videocassette.
Secondary students and teachers may enjoy viewing the 1946 classic cinema version, widely hailed as one of the great French films. Jean Marais and Josette Day star in Cocteau's great film testament to the power of love. The sets are magical, and the music is majestic.

Beauty and the Beast. Shelley Duvall, producer; Roger Vadim, director. Faerie Tale Theatre Series. Livonia, MI: Playhouse Video. 1983. 50 minutes. Videocassette.
The Faerie Tale Theatre production of *Beauty and the Beast* features Susan Sarandon as Beauty and Klaus Kinski as Beast. In creating the mysterious, atmospheric gardens and palace of Beast, director Vadim takes many cues from the great French cinema version created by Jean Cocteau.

Beauty and the Beast. Mordicai Gerstein, director. Hi-Tops Video Series. Los Angeles, CA: Heron Communications. 1988. 27 minutes. Videocassette.
Mia Farrrow narrates this lovely animation treatment of "Beauty and the Beast" featuring the art of Daniel Tesser and music by Ernest Troost. Beautiful pastel drawings illuminate the story of the young woman whose loving heart breaks the spell under which Beast is imprisoned.

Beauty and the Beast. Kirk Wise and Gary Trousdale, directors. Burbank, CA: Walt Disney. 1991. 84 minutes. Videocassette.
Contemporary students will be most familiar with this Disney musical animation version of Madame LePrince de Beaumont's tale. Disney's *Beauty and the Beast* was the first animated film to receive an Academy Award nomination for Best Picture. The film won the Best Picture Golden Globe Award and features the vocal talents of Robby Benson, Paige O'Hara, and Angela Lansbury. One of the highlights of the film is the Academy Award-winning music of Alan Menken and Howard Ashman. The film also achieved the unique distinction of being revived as a Broadway musical.

Happily Ever Afters

A Model Museum for and by Students

Most student-created museums found in classrooms or school build-ings are temporary exhibitions. At Pine Valley Elementary School on the grounds of the United States Air Force Academy in Colorado, resource teacher Caren Kutch has fashioned, with much student input, a Wilder-ness Museum that is entering its fourth year of existence. When the school's principal asked teachers to salvage any stored materials they needed from the school's "junk room" a few years ago, Kutch asked and received permission to turn the newly vacant classroom into a school museum centered upon two big ideas: (1) introducing all children to wilderness concepts and experiences; and (2) structuring all the activi-ties and experiences in the museum on Howard Gardner's multiple intelligences theory. Teachers, parents, community members (espe-cially senior-citizen volunteers), *and* students contribute to the exhibits and displays in the interactive museum. Volunteers built a tree house, teachers constructed a butterfly tree, and students created myriad products for the museum.

One class of second-grade students worked much of a year on a sustained science, reading, and art project that led finally to shoe-box and grocery-box dioramas, each featuring a wild animal in its natural habitat. Early in the school year the second-graders were immersed in a literature study of animals in the wild. Each picked an animal he or she wished to research and come to know thoroughly during the school year. As the students learned more about their animals of choice, they made sketches of the animals and their environments. Then they fashioned colorful paintings of their animals. Next they molded clay models of their animals, which were painted and subsequently fired in the school's kiln. Using the ceramic animals as models, the students finally created larger papier mâché replicas of wild animals. Using construction paper, pipe cleaners, and other art supplies, the students finally completed cardboard-box "environments" of such places as prairies, the Arctic, and the Everglades. When the students were satisfied with the look of their shoe-box wild environments, the wild-animal papier-mâché "specimens" they created were placed within the dioramas, and the completed dioramas were placed in the school's Wilderness Museum for all the other students and community members to enjoy. Everyone who visits the museum is mightily impressed by what the second-graders were able to create in this sustained, yearlong activity.

The second-grade nature dioramas are but one of the student offerings found in the school museum. Older students choreograph and present interpretive dances about trees or write and perform plays about protecting the environment. A particularly clever dramatic presentation involved an Academy Awards-like television presentation for nature, staged and presented on several occasions. The best film of the year in the students' live museum performance was "Forest Stump." A tall "tree" who received the best actress award appropriately thanked the sun and the rain for helping her "grow into my part." Fittingly, the trophies that winners received in the dramatization were seedling pine trees planted in decorated coffee cans. Students rightfully take enormous pride in their contributions to the school's museum whether those contributions be environmental dioramas, posters, or wilderness games they invent.

Again, the projects students complete at Pine Valley can serve as models. Just as Pine Valley students created wild-animal dioramas, other students may create fairy tale dioramas. Children select favorite characters from fairy tale literature and favorite scenes in which they appear. Using the processes described above, they will end up with shoe-box dioramas that feature their characters in appropriate settings.

Additional Museum Products

The following student prompts suggest types of activities and products than may be tailored to particular fairy tales or to other museum topics or "big ideas." For example, a grocery-bag puppet may take the appearance of the fairy tale character Snow White or Hansel, but such puppets can also be created as props and artifacts in student museums devoted to the study of wild animals or dinosaurs. A grocery-bag puppet might take the form of a coyote who explains, in a live performance for visitors, its life in the wild and its contacts with humans. A similar dinosaur puppet could share facts of its existence on Earth long, long ago.

Create a grocery-bag puppet of your favorite fairy tale character or create a newly imagined fairy tale character. Use the puppet to tell other classmates the classic or new fairy tale.

Produce a safety poster for younger children. For example, create a poster based on "Little Red Riding Hood" that advises against talking to strangers when alone.

Invent an interactive mathematics exhibit based on numbers found in fairy tales. Search fairy tales, fantasies, and nursery rhymes for significant numbers (e.g., 1001 Nights, 3 Bears, 7 Dwarfs, and 4 and 20 Blackbirds). Create original math games or puzzles based on fairy tale numbers that will challenge visitors to the fairy tale museum. Example: If the Three Bears and the Three Little Pigs happened to visit Beast's castle for supper and each could eat half a pie, how many pies should

Beast's baker prepare for dessert? Be sure to provide pencils and scratch paper in the exhibit if necessary.

Imagine that you're the beast's premier chef, and you've been asked to cater the wedding feast of Beauty and the beast. Design a commemorative scroll listing all the feast-banquet entrées. Make one of the entrées, and serve it to visitors to the "Beauty and the Beast" Museum.

Produce a "Beauty and the Beast" Museum Exhibition Catalog. Describe and illustrate various items to be viewed in the museum, and provide the appropriate text to explain all displays. Highlight the magical and wonderful things to be seen and enjoyed in the museum. If possible, take photographs of exhibitions or objects and pictures within displays, scan them, and include them in an exhibition catalog that is made available to museum visitors.

Write and illustrate a new version of "Beauty and the Beast." Two Texas elementary-school girls produced a modernized version of the tale titled "Barbie and the Ken." In the story, a wicked witch casts a spell that turns a handsome prince into a "Ken" doll. A contemporary beauty goes to a huge mall toy store to select a Barbie Doll and meets the bewitched "Ken." Through the power of her love, Beauty breaks the evil spell, and "Ken" once again becomes a living, breathing prince, and all live happily ever after. Can you think of an imaginative, new way to tell the story of "Beauty and the Beast"? Fashion huge storyboards to highlight the essential events in the new tale, and display them as a story to be read by visitors to the "Beauty and the Beast" Museum.

Design a mobile or large, soft sculpture that may be suspended from the ceiling of the "Beauty and the Beast" Museum. Subject matter may be portraits of the characters or symbols such as the rose that Beauty's father picks for her. (See "The Frog Prince" chapter for tips on creating mobiles.)

Be an architect or builder. (See a complete description of architecture and fairy tales in "The Three Little Pigs" chapter.) Draw the floor plans for the beast's castle. Then be a builder or engineer. Based on your blueprints, construct a model of a castle that can be displayed in the "Beauty and the Beast" Museum.

Outstanding museum exhibitions often feature live performances of music, storytelling, and drama. Prepare a dramatic presentation, complete with costumes, of a critical scene from the story of "Beauty and the Beast." A prepared script may be followed, or the scene can unfold as an improvisation. Plan one or more presentations of the three- to five-minute scene during the grand opening of the "Beauty and the Beast" Museum.

REFERENCES

Base, Graeme. 1996. *The Discovery of Dragons*. New York: Harry N. Abrams.

Cleaver, Joanne. 1992. *Doing Children's Museums: A Guide to 265 Hands-On Museums*. Charlotte, VT: Williamson.

Dean, David. 1994. *Museum Exhibits: Theory and Practice*. New York: Routledge Kegan Paul.

Gardner, Howard. 1993. *Multiple Intelligences: The Theory in Practice*. New York: Basic Books.

Goleman, Daniel. 1992. *The Creative Spirit*. New York: E. P. Dutton.

Hearne, Betsy. 1995. *Beauties and Beasts*. The Oryx Multicultural Folktale Series. Phoenix, AZ: Oryx Press.

Lewis, C. S. 1994. *The Lion, the Witch, and the Wardrobe*. New York: Harper.

Pearce, Susan M. 1993. *Museums, Objects and Collections: A Cultural Study*. Washington, D.C.: Smithsonian Institution Press.

Serrell, Beverly. 1996. *Exhibit Labels: An Interpretive Approach*. Walnut Creek, CA: Altamir Press.

Index

About the Author

Dr. Jerry Flack is a President's Teaching Scholar at the University of Colorado. Prior to his appointment to the School of Education at the University of Colorado (CU) at Colorado Springs in 1983, he was a classroom teacher in Michigan and Indiana for seventeen years. At CU he directs the Super Saturday Program for gifted children and a master's degree program in the education of gifted and talented children. He is the editor of the Gifted Treasury series for Teacher Ideas Press and the author of five books in the series, *Inventing, Inventions, and Inventors*; *Mystery and Detection*; *Lives of Promise*; *TalentEd*; and *From the Land of Enchantment*. He is a former member of the Board of Directors of the National Association for Gifted Children and the Advisory Board for Inventure Place, the home of the National Inventors Hall of Fame. He serves on the Editorial Advisory Panels of *THINK* and *Writing Teacher* magazines. In addition to receiving the lifetime title of President's Teaching Scholar from the University of Colorado, Dr. Flack has been named the National Future Problem Solving Program Teacher of the Year (1980); the University of Colorado at Colorado Springs Outstanding Teacher (1987); and the National Association for Gifted Children Early Leader (1988).

From **Teacher Ideas Press**

THE BEANSTALK AND BEYOND: Developing Critical Thinking Through Fairy Tales
Joan M. Wolf

Turn fairy tales and fairy-tale characters into a springboard for learning with this enchanting book! A multitude of activities challenge students to move beyond the simplistic study of fairy tales to develop problem-solving, critical-thinking, and creative-writing skills. **Grades 4–8**.
xiii, 133p. 8½x11 paper ISBN 1-56308-482-1

CRITICAL SQUARES: Games of Critical Thinking and Understanding
Shari Tishman and Albert Andrade

Developed through Project Zero at the Harvard School of Education, these simple but powerful games are designed to develop students' critical-thinking skills and deepen their understanding of topics they are already studying. **Grades 3–12**.
xv, 123p. 8½x11 paper ISBN 1-56308-490-2

TalentEd: Strategies for Developing the Talent in Every Learner
Jerry D. Flack

"The best little resource for classroom teachers!" according to *Teaching K–8*, this book shows how all children can learn well and achieve excellence if provided with opportunity and challenge. Activities promote literacy, integrated learning, diversity, and academic excellence. **Grades K–12**.
Gifted Treasury Series; Jerry D. Flack, Ed.
xiii, 249p. 8½x11 paper ISBN 1-56308-127-X

MYSTERY AND DETECTION: Thinking and Problem Solving with the Sleuths
Jerry D. Flack

Turn your classroom into a real Scotland Yard! This unique resource ties in dozens of problem-solving and enrichment activities with mystery and sleuthing. It is divided into topical chapters on language arts, art, social studies, future studies, and crime and punishment. **Grades 5–9**. *(Adaptable to other grades.)*
Gifted Treasury Series; Jerry D. Flack, Ed.
xx, 246p. 8½x11 paper ISBN 0-87287-815-5

INVENTING, INVENTIONS, AND INVENTORS
Jerry D. Flack

Flack's exciting, mind-stretching activities illuminate a rich, interdisciplinary field of study. Investigating inventions of the past and the present, funny inventions, and inventions we may see in the future provides a natural springboard to creative thinking. **Grades 7–9**. *(Adaptable for many grades.)*
xi, 148p. 8½x11 paper ISBN 0-87287-747-7

CREATIVE TEACHING: Ideas to Boost Student Interest
James P. Downing

Learn how to tap into your hidden creativity, engage students in the learning process, and foster creative thinking and expression with 75 activities, sample lessons, and numerous tips to get you started. **Grades K–12**.
xiii, 225p. 8½x11 paper ISBN 1-56308-476-7

For a FREE catalog or to place an order, please contact:

Teacher Ideas Press
Dept. B55 · P.O. Box 6633 · Englewood, CO 80155-6633
1-800-237-6124, ext. 1 · Fax: 303-220-8843 · E-mail: lu-books@lu.com

Check out the TIP Web site!
www.lu.com/tip